Romeo & Juliet Plainspoken

by

Greta Barclay Lipson, Ed.D.
The University of Michigan-Dearborn

and

Susan Solomon Lipson, M.A.T.

illustrated by Susan Kropa

Cover by Susan Kropa

ISBN No. 0-86653-283-8

Printing No. 1615

Good Apple, Inc.
23740 Hawthorne Blvd.
Torrance, CA 90505

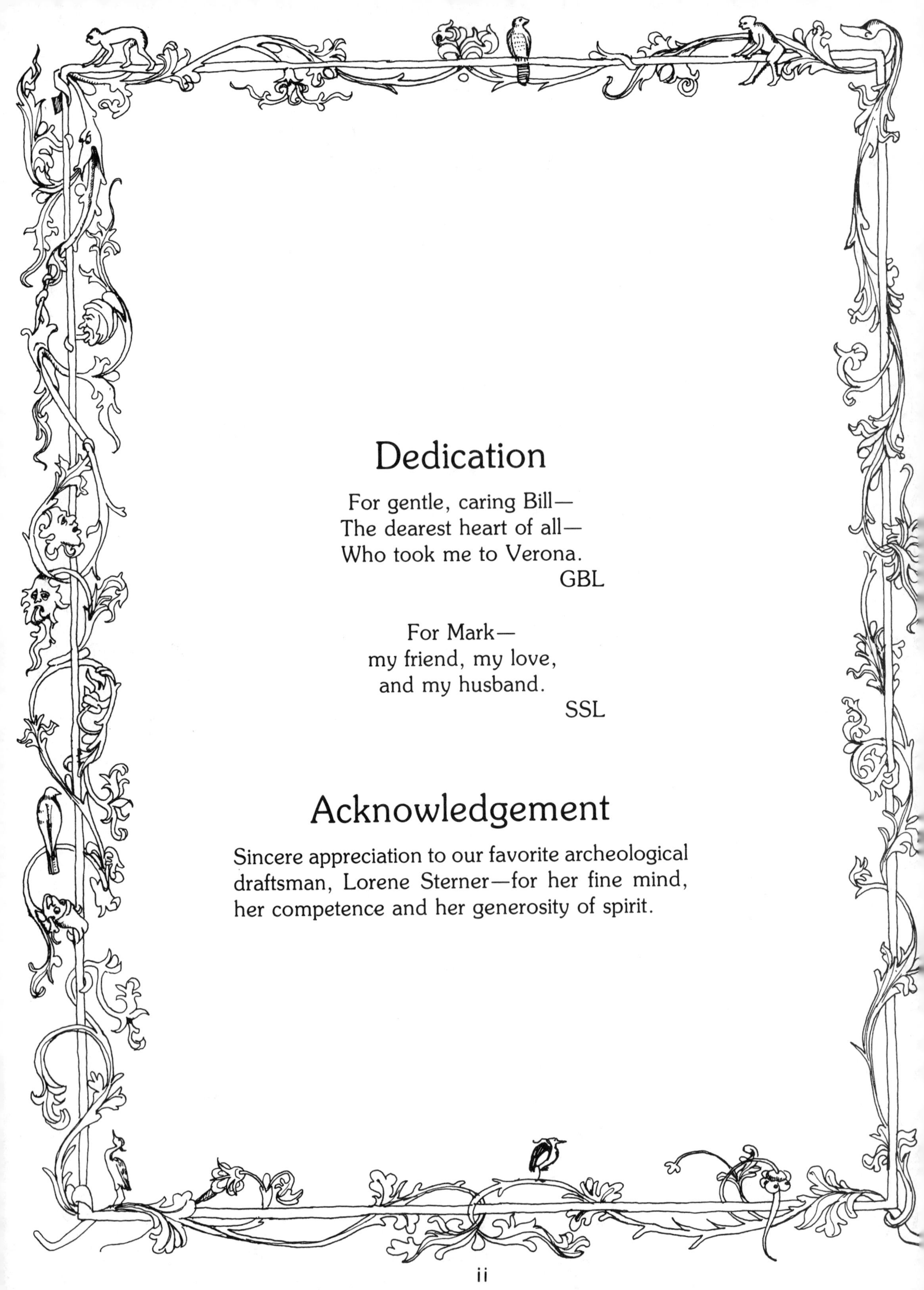

Dedication

For gentle, caring Bill—
The dearest heart of all—
Who took me to Verona.
GBL

For Mark—
my friend, my love,
and my husband.
SSL

Acknowledgement

Sincere appreciation to our favorite archeological draftsman, Lorene Sterner—for her fine mind, her competence and her generosity of spirit.

ROMEO & JULIET: PLAINSPOKEN

A Speech-by-Speech Modern Translation

Table of Contents

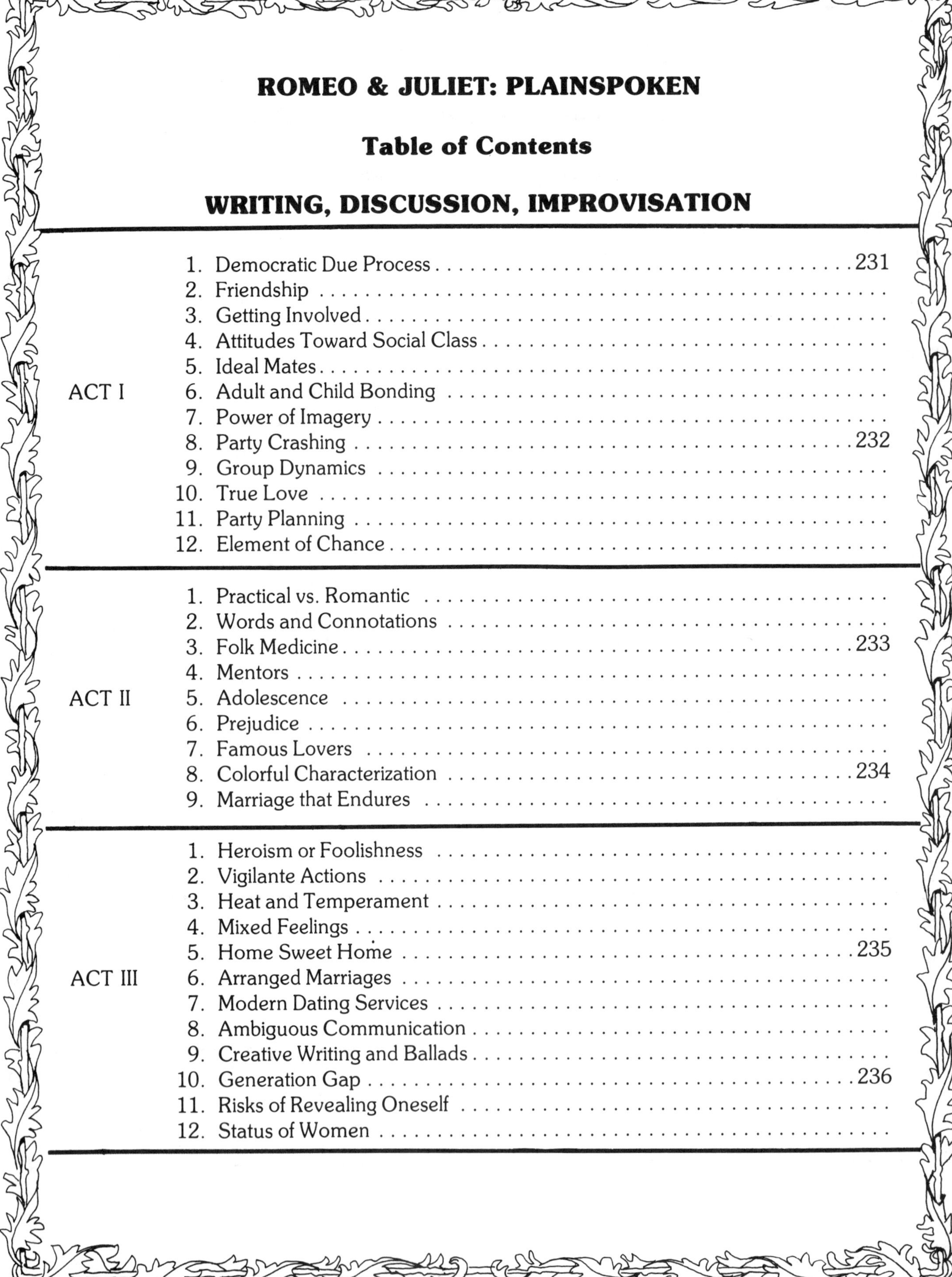

ROMEO & JULIET: PLAINSPOKEN

Table of Contents

WRITING, DISCUSSION, IMPROVISATION

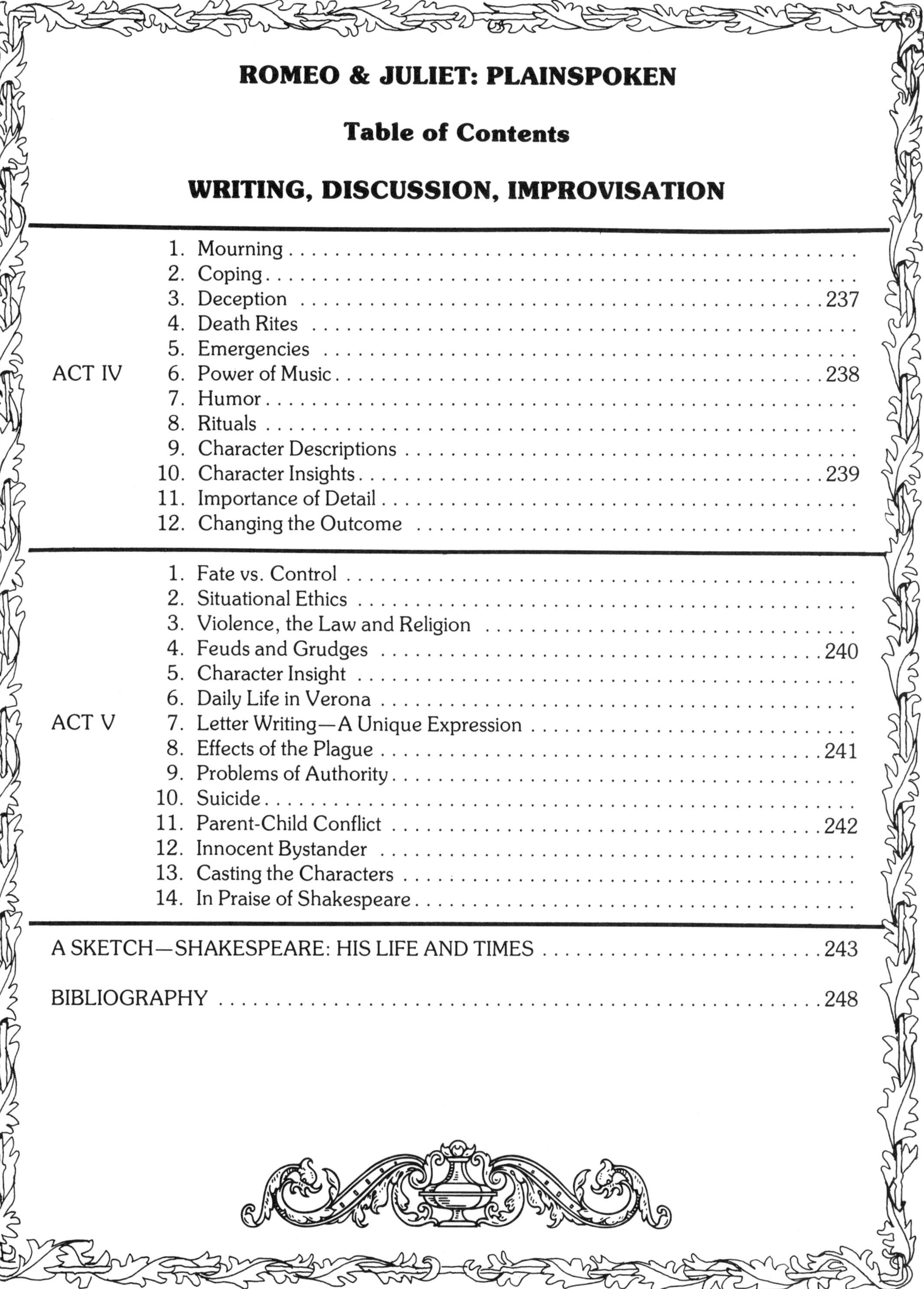

ROMEO & JULIET: PLAINSPOKEN

Table of Contents

WRITING, DISCUSSION, IMPROVISATION

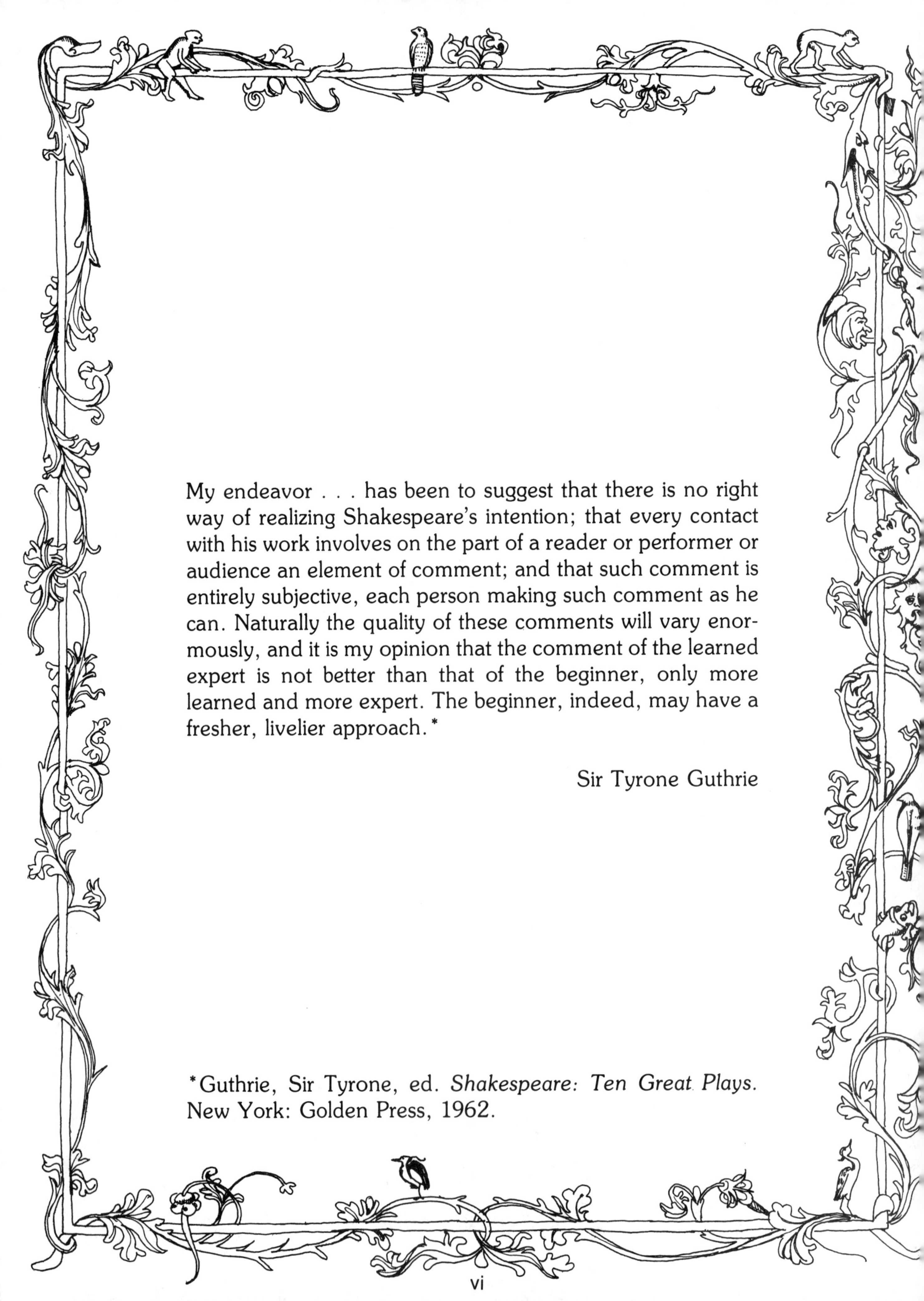

My endeavor . . . has been to suggest that there is no right way of realizing Shakespeare's intention; that every contact with his work involves on the part of a reader or performer or audience an element of comment; and that such comment is entirely subjective, each person making such comment as he can. Naturally the quality of these comments will vary enormously, and it is my opinion that the comment of the learned expert is not better than that of the beginner, only more learned and more expert. The beginner, indeed, may have a fresher, livelier approach.*

Sir Tyrone Guthrie

*Guthrie, Sir Tyrone, ed. *Shakespeare: Ten Great Plays.* New York: Golden Press, 1962.

Introduction

Because the English language has changed so markedly over the centuries, it was our objective, in this book, to make *Romeo and Juliet* more understandable and less forbidding to today's students. We have written a speech-by-speech modern translation which parallels the Shakespearean text. Our text begins and ends on the page precisely where Shakespeare's actors begin and end in the traditional play. It has been our experience in the classroom that when the language of the story has meaning in modern terms, it enhances the students' comprehension and enables them to penetrate the drama and pathos of the human condition as it unfolds in this tragedy.

We approached this project immensely respectful of the task and mindful of the Shakespearean scholar, Alfred L. Rowse, the eighty-year-old Oxford University Professor emeritus, who has written distinguished revisions of Shakespeare's plays. Rowse has expressed the strong opinion that periodically the plays must be revised to be more in keeping with modern rhetoric. He likens the job to "putting your head in a hornet's nest." Further, he asserts that "Quite a lot of Elizabethan grammar is very bad grammar today with its double comparatives and double negatives . . . Some words never existed as printed. Instead they were the mistakes of countless printers, actors, prompters and publishers."[1]

Of the thirty-seven plays written by William Shakespeare, *Romeo and Juliet* is the play that appeals most strongly to young people. Although it was written in the language of another century, the conflicts in this play are timeless. Both the consuming urgency of Romeo and Juliet's love and the ill-fated couple's defiance of their parents evoke a strong sense of identification from today's teenager.

When the play was first presented in 1595, we must remember that the life expectancy was strikingly shorter than today. In those days the chronology of one's life was compressed quickly from childhood to adulthood. Students are intrigued to learn that Romeo Montague was only sixteen years old and Juliet Capulet an innocent thirteen and that the course of their love and death takes place in the breathtaking progression of only four short days. Indeed, events move so swiftly that with each reading we wish that the grace of a little more time will stay our grief and avert the tragedy. Little wonder that in later productions during the Restoration in the seventeenth century, the play was produced with a happy ending on alternate evenings to ease the tender-hearted who knew the story.

This play, like Shakespeare's other works, is a tribute to his discernment of the human soul. For as long as young people fall in love precipitously, as long as their parents tremble for their well-being, and as long as the passion of youth collides with the tempered experience of age, this drama will be reenacted eternally, both on stage and in real life.

To the Student: Remember that the even-numbered pages are the original Shakespeare; the odd-numbered pages are the modern version.

[1] NBC *Today Show,* Gene Shalit Interview with A.L. Rowse and Richard Burton. April 27, 1984.

The Four-Day Story

Day 1: Sunday

The story begins in beautiful Verona, a city in Northern Italy. There is a blood feud between the Montagues and the Capulets, two of the city's distinguished families. So bitter is the animus between the two houses that even the servants of each household, like their noble masters, engage in street brawls. The play opens with yet another episode of wanton fighting started by Sampson and Gregory, two of Capulet's servants.

Prince Escalus, ruler of Verona, is sick to death of the senseless and dangerous street fighting of these two families and threatens that one more offense of violence in his city will constitute civil disobedience and will be punishable by death! There is evidence that the aging noble lords are ready to yield to the wisdom of this edict.

The Montagues have other concerns as well. Romeo's worried mother has asked her kindly nephew, Benvolio, to find the cause of her son's recent depression. Since the young cousins share a strong and loving bond, the reason for Romeo's mood is not difficult to discern. Romeo is hopelessly in love with Rosaline, a cool young woman who clearly does not return his love and emphatically rejects him. Solicitous about Romeo's well-being, Benvolio urges him to look seriously at other young beauties. He implores Romeo to stop his whining and sighing, for Romeo has become tiresome with his unremitting, lovesick posture which is often foolish and affected.

The two young men then chance upon an illiterate servant of the Capulets who solicits their help with a guest list he cannot read. In this way they learn that a masked ball is to be given that very evening by Lord Capulet. Romeo's interest is piqued because he sees Rosaline's name on the list of the invited guests. An enthusiastic Benvolio regards this opportunity to compare Rosaline to other eligible women at the party as a welcome solution to Romeo's lovesickness. Benvolio is certain that Romeo will then see that Rosaline is not the only prize in Verona. To go to the party uninvited as enemies of the hostile Capulet household is dangerous, to be sure; but the young men are daring enough to enjoy the challenge.

Before the party, Lord Capulet, father of Juliet, speaks to Count Paris, an attractive young relative of Prince Escalus. Paris is most eager to win the heart of Juliet. Though the handsome nobleman is a worthy suitor, Lord Capulet makes no commitments to give Juliet's hand in marriage. Hoping that a gentle courtship may begin, however, Lord Capulet encourages Paris to approach Juliet during the festivities. Lord Capulet feels some fatherly reluctance because Juliet, the child of his affection, is only thirteen years old.

Lady Capulet hears of the marriage proposal and goes directly to speak with her daughter about Paris. She enters Juliet's room and bids the Nurse to call the girl. As the young woman enters, she hears the two women discussing her. The Nurse warms to the conversation, for she has cared for Juliet since she was an infant. In Lady Capulet's conversation with the Nurse, we discover the coarse and earthy quality of this old peasant woman when Shakespeare introduces comedic meanderings and street humor into her dialogue. Lady Capulet talks of marriage and recalls that she was of a similar age when she was betrothed to

Juliet's father. The mother is much in favor of such a splendid union between Paris and her daughter. The young Juliet, all the while, listens to her mother's conversation politely. She agrees to look kindly upon Paris and his interest in marriage.

The hour of the party arrives, and among the guests are the masked and uninvited threesome—Romeo, Benvolio, and another close friend, Mercutio, a witty and dashing charmer. The dancing and festivities begin and Lord Capulet is a cordial and solicitous host who reflects on the joys of his youthful past. At this time Romeo searches for Rosaline's fair face but instead, through the crowd, sees Juliet for the first time. Her beauty is luminous and her radiance instantly captures his heart. As he makes his way through the crowd he forgets that there ever was a Rosaline, for now Romeo is intrigued with Juliet and is determined to know more about her. He asks a servant the name of this lovely girl but the servant is uninformed. Unknown to Romeo he is overheard by the vicious Tybalt, another member of the enemy Capulet family. Tybalt recognizes Romeo's voice, and his blood rages with the compulsion to do violence to Romeo at that very moment. It is only the firm and reasonable hand of Lord Capulet which forces Tybalt to contain himself. Lord Capulet restrains his belligerent nephew and reminds him that he has heard only praise for Romeo's decent and admirable character. Capulet is determined that above all, his party shall not be ruined by rancor. Tybalt, however, vows his own revenge.

None of this is known to Romeo as he moves quickly across the hall to meet the enchanting maiden whose name is still unknown to him. Romeo and Juliet speak to each other and after some flirtatious teasing, Juliet lets Romeo kiss her cheek. As the party ends, both young people are drawn deeply to one another and have fallen hopelessly in love. Driven by fate, the two discover separately from the Nurse that each of them is a child of Verona's feuding families; but this awareness does not deter them. Consumed with thoughts of his new love, Romeo leaves the party but yearns for the nearness of Juliet. He escapes from his friends Benvolio and Mercutio, who look for him persistently. The young Montague scales a wall enclosing the Capulet house and finds himself in the orchard beneath Juliet's window. Almost in answer to a prayer, he sees her through her window as she walks to the balcony. It is there, in the moonlight—she on her balcony and he below—that they exchange vows of love which elevate their souls beyond the power of containment. Separated physically though they are, they speak words of devotion and pledge their lives to one another in one of the most memorable, romantic scenes of passionate young love ever written in Western literature. Unwilling to postpone their destiny, Romeo and Juliet talk about marrying on the following day. Juliet promises to send a messenger at nine, the very next morning, to learn Romeo's plan for the time and place of their secret wedding ceremony.

Day 2: Monday

Romeo searches out his friend and confessor, the kindly Friar Laurence. He finds the priest gathering herbs in the awakening morning. Romeo shares his bittersweet news and asks for his mentor's guidance. The Friar hears Romeo's declaration of love for Juliet, the daughter of his father's enemy, and perceives in the young man a sincerity so earnest that it cannot be ignored. The Friar hopes that the unlikely union of these two children will heal the troublesome wound between the families. Despite the perils of this match, he agrees to perform the ceremony in his cell that afternoon.

A street scene ensues in which Benvolio and Mercutio discuss the strange disappearance of Romeo the night before. Having visited the Montague home earlier, they react to the arrival of a letter from Tybalt which formally challenged Romeo to a duel. Mercutio cannot endure Tybalt and he indulges in a litany of insults against the arrogant Capulet nephew. Even so, he acknowledges Tybalt's highly schooled fencing skills and ferocity. The young Romeo appears and his friends find him in much better spirits than he had shown the night before. They are pleased that the Capulet festivities did indeed lift Romeo's depression. Romeo now appears to be rational again. He is no longer the lovesick, spiritless target of ridicule. With Romeo no longer a likely victim for his barbs, Mercutio turns his devilish wit on Juliet's Nurse. The old woman has just arrived, seeking the promised information from Romeo. There is a verbal roustabout between Mercutio and the Nurse which is tasteless and bawdy. The earthy old woman is all at once an adversary, a foil, and a willing participant throughout the vulgar exchange of foul language. Romeo, however, manages to give his precious message to the Nurse who quickly returns to Juliet. Having arrived back home it takes the old woman a maddening length of time to reveal the information—preferring instead to complain about the aches and pains of her ancient bones. Juliet, almost hysterical, is barely civil enough to wait for the Nurse to reveal the time and place of the secret wedding. Later that afternoon in the priest's cell, amid doubt and haste, the two are wed according to the fateful plan.

Hours pass, and back on the street, Benvolio, the peacemaker, tries to prevail upon the mischievous Mercutio to come out of the summer heat. He urges him to stay out of trouble's way. Benvolio feels a vague disquiet about the Capulets. His anxiety is justified, for just then the villainous Tybalt appears on the scene looking for Romeo and clearly lusting for his blood. Romeo comes to join his friends and once Tybalt sights his victim, he ignores the others and taunts Romeo with churlish insults, desperate to provoke a fight. Romeo, unlike the others, realizes that Tybalt is a first cousin to his wife, Juliet, and tries to mollify his new kinsman with kind words, steadfastly refusing to be insulted by his new relative. Romeo's reserved behavior in the face of Tybalt's goading remarks bewilders Mercutio. He smarts with anger at Tybalt's reprehensible verbal assault and the humiliation of it all is too much for him. Unrestrained, he lashes out at Tybalt and does the manly thing: he fights Romeo's battle for him. Romeo impulsively tries to stand between them as the two fiercely engage in a slashing encounter. Ironically, it is Romeo's well-meaning intervention which makes it possible for Tybalt to drive his murderous sword under Romeo's arm and take the life of the brave and brilliant Mercutio. Romeo, driven almost mad with the realization that he inadvertently caused the tragic murder of his true and constant friend, redeems himself by killing Tybalt moments later.

Benvolio rushes the shocked Romeo away from the ghastly scene as he reels from the oppressive consequences of his act. For now Romeo has murdered Juliet's cousin, an act of violence which may mean his death as well. After Romeo flees, Benvolio prevails upon the Prince to set aside the penalty of death and spare Romeo's life because of cruel circumstance. The Prince yields to Benvolio and alters his decree. Romeo is no longer a spectator to the feud: he is now inextricably a participant. The Prince banishes Romeo from Verona forever!

Romeo must leave the city of his birth, his precious wife, and his loving parents, to be separated forever from all that he has known and held dear in his lifetime. Romeo runs and hides in Friar Laurence's cell, afraid of Juliet's reaction to his deed and in fear of his life. At the Capulet home the Nurse breaks the painful news to Juliet: Romeo has killed Tybalt and has been banished for his crime. Juliet, torn by her affection for her cousin, but overcome by her intense longing for her husband, sends her Nurse to reassure Romeo. She asks that he hasten to her chambers for their first night together as husband and wife. Romeo joins Juliet and they spend a passionate, tender night of love marred only by the anguish of their imminent separation.

Day 3: Tuesday

The light and birdsongs of morning filter through the yielding cover of night, and the two lovers must say goodbye. It is a parting full of pain and fraught with new grief because they do not know when they will ever see each other again. Romeo valiantly tries to assuage Juliet's sorrow with the promise that soon they will be together in Mantua where he has been banished.

Romeo leaves Juliet's chambers and at once Lady Capulet enters. She brings the shocking news to Juliet that her father has arranged her marriage to Count Paris to be held in two days. Juliet cannot contain her displeasure. Her outspoken resistance to the wedding plans baffles her parents. Juliet, always the obedient daughter, now rages against the news. She has no one to turn to for sympathy, because by this time her parents are furious. Even her loving Nurse presses for this exemplary union with Lord Paris. The Nurse, if nothing else, is a practical woman and she regards Romeo, the banished husband, as no husband at all. She praises Paris's superiority.

In desperation, Juliet seeks the help of Friar Laurence, who remains the only constant friend of the two young lovers. The priest, in his effort to help, conceives of a daring, though frightening plan, which he proposes to the desolate young bride: he will give her a potion with hypnotic powers. Juliet is to return home and drink it on the eve of her wedding day. The potion will instantly create a death-like state for forty-two hours, and she will appear to be a convincing corpse to the most discerning eye. Friar Laurence is aware that the seemingly dead Juliet will be placed in the family tomb and, according to custom, will not be buried. Most importantly, he assures her that he will send Romeo a letter apprising him of this somber plan. Romeo then is to arrive at the tomb to be reunited with Juliet upon her awakening—finally at liberty to flee to Mantua and safety.

Juliet, taking her leave of Friar Laurence, returns home to her parents and pleases them with conciliatory behavior. Her parents believe that the priest's good counsel has set her straight and that he has persuaded her to be sensible and accept their plans for her future. Overjoyed with his daughter's change of heart, Lord Capulet hastily changes the wedding day to Wednesday. Juliet dissembles as she goes through the motions of a bride-to-be, knowing full well the wedding will never take place. Lord and Lady Capulet are genuinely convinced she has seen the wisdom of the nuptial arrangements. When Juliet is left alone for the night, she is tortured with fear of the powerful potion in her possession and is racked with grief. She imagines the coldness of the tomb where she must lie. She trembles at the thought of lying next to her dead ancestors during her chilling interment in the burial vault. At last, in her unsettled state of mind, she hallucinates. She sees her dead cousin Tybalt in nightmarish pursuit of Romeo. Exhausted, in anguish, she drinks the powerful liquid and sinks into a coma.

Day 4: Wednesday

The next morning the hapless old Nurse discovers that her precious Juliet, intended to be a bride that joyous day, is lying in the cold embrace of death. The sweet promise of a wedding party has become, instead, a time of mourning for the bereaved parents of Juliet. The stricken household prepares the funeral procession to carry the girl to the family vault.

Romeo, now in Mantua, waits expectantly for news from home, but is unprepared for what follows. His servant, Balthasar, gently delivers to him the shocking news of Juliet's death. Consumed by grief and determined to be with her, even in death, Romeo hastens to a poor apothecary who is willing to sell him a deadly poison without asking questions. Although fate decreed that the lovers could not be together in life, Romeo resolves that he will suffer no more separations and will join Juliet in unassailable death. Alas, the crucial message informing Romeo of the intricate plan could not be delivered. Although Friar Laurence had dutifully given the letter to Friar John, it never reached Mantua. The authorities quarantined the priest in Verona for there was a threat of plague in the city. The letter, the potion, and Juliet's false death would have given them the ultimate gift of life together, had the plan worked—but the plan did not work. Destiny decreed otherwise. To avoid further disaster, Friar Laurence, now deeply concerned, rushes to the Capulet tomb. He dare not let Juliet waken alone!

As might be expected, another mourner comes to the churchyard to say his last good-bye. It is Count Paris who carries bridal flowers as a burial tribute to the young woman he was to marry. As he goes about his task lovingly, he is warned by his page, standing outside the vault, that an interloper is approaching. Paris sees Romeo approach with a crowbar in hand. He concludes that Romeo intends to despoil the tomb and recognizes him as the villain who killed Tybalt, Juliet's cousin. Count Paris believes that this wretched murder was the reason for Juliet's melancholia and death. The incensed Paris immediately challenges Romeo, who begs Paris to leave him alone. They clash, and Paris becomes another casualty in this family tragedy. As Paris lies wounded, he asks Romeo to carry him into the vault and let him die near Juliet. Romeo, numb with grief, complies. It is there in the tomb, at last with Juliet, that he cries his final words of eternal devotion over her lifeless form. Embracing her fragile body, Romeo drinks the deadly poison, kisses her sweet lips and dies by her side.

Old Friar Laurence, breathless and frightened, arrives at the Capulet tomb to find a nightmare of blood and swords outside the vault. Inside he is horrified to find the bodies of both Paris and Romeo. Just then Juliet awakens, sees Friar Laurence and asks him for her beloved husband. Forced to break the news quickly, he beseeches Juliet to come with him, for he is alarmed as he hears the watchmen approaching; but she is intransigent and will not leave her dead Romeo. Having taken in the tableau of death, she reaches for the bottle of poison clutched in Romeo's hand but finds it empty. With powerful resolution she seizes his dagger and plunges it into her tormented heart as she crumbles next to his body.

The alerted watchmen enter the tomb with the Prince, the Capulets, and the apprehended Friar. As Lord Montague enters and sees his young son's corpse he reveals the depth of his unspeakable loss. His wife has also died, so profound was her grief over her son's banishment. The tomb is sealed and the skeins of the tragedy are unraveled by the well-meaning

Friar Laurence and substantiated by Paris's page and Balthasar. The Prince then censures Lord Montague and Lord Capulet. He reproaches them for perpetuating the poisonous feud between the two families and the hatred that robbed them of the innocent lives of their only children. The bereaved men, Montague and Capulet, chastised in their guilt, clasp hands and resolve to forget their strife. As a final gesture, each father vows to build a golden statue in memory of the other's child. Here the tragedy comes to a close as the Prince laments:

A glooming peace this morning with it brings.
The sun for sorrow will not show his head.
Go hence, to have more talk of these sad things;
Some shall be pardoned, and some punished;
For never was a story of more woe
Than this of Juliet and her Romeo.

CAST OF CHARACTERS

MONTAGUE FAMILY AND FRIENDS

ROMEO MONTAGUE: a bright and well-bred young man in love with love, until he meets Juliet and becomes an authentic and earnest lover who makes a commitment of eternal devotion

LORD MONTAGUE: Romeo's father, whose blood feud with the head of the Capulet household becomes a threat to the peace of Verona

LADY MONTAGUE: Lord Montague's wife and Romeo's mother, who dies from grief over her son's banishment

MERCUTIO: a true friend to Romeo, a cousin of Prince Escalus; a young man of brilliance and wit

BENVOLIO: a cousin and loyal friend to Romeo; a gentle young man whose good sense casts him in the role of peacemaker

BALTHASAR: a loyal servant to Romeo

ABRAM: a servant to Lord Montague

FRIAR LAURENCE: a kindly Catholic priest; Romeo's confessor and mentor; he alone tries to help the two lovers in their cruel dilemma

FRIAR JOHN: a Franciscan monk; an associate of Friar Laurence

CAPULET FAMILY AND FRIENDS

JULIET CAPULET: a young girl of noble breeding whose innocence and goodness flowers into the deep passion of a woman who would die for love

LORD CAPULET: Juliet's father; an adversary in the feud; a sometimes cordial but undisputed hardheaded master of the household

LADY CAPULET: Lord Capulet's wife and Juliet's mother; she is eager for a marriage of status and security for her daughter

THE NURSE: Juliet's Nurse; a colorful, bawdy, peasant woman who is practical and outspoken

PETER: the Nurse's servant

SAMPSON and GREGORY: servants to Lord Capulet

TYBALT: a cousin to Juliet, a nephew to Lady Capulet; a bad-tempered young man and expert swordsman

PARIS: a cousin to the Prince; a young count who wants Juliet to be his wife

PRINCE ESCALUS: prince and ruler of Verona

PAGE TO PARIS

MINOR CHARACTERS

A DRUGGIST

THREE MUSICIANS

AN OFFICER

CHORUS

CITIZENS OF VERONA

GENTLEMEN AND GENTLEWOMEN OF BOTH HOUSES

PEOPLE IN MASKS

TORCHBEARERS

PAGES

GUARDS

WATCHMEN

SERVANTS

ATTENDANTS

SYNOPSIS BY SCENE

ACT I, Scene 1

Two Capulet servants provoke a fight with a servant from the house of Montague. Benvolio, Romeo's cousin, tries to stop the scuffle and asks Tybalt, a nephew of the Capulets, for help. Tybalt, however, antagonizes the situation until it is an all-out brawl. Prince Escalus, ruler of Verona, appears and threatens the life of anyone involved in any future Montague-Capulet fights.

Romeo's parents encounter Benvolio and ask if he has seen Romeo. Benvolio discusses Romeo's melancholy behavior, since the Montague's son has been sick with unrequited love for the fair Rosaline. Romeo appears and asks Benvolio for help, but his cousin advises him, instead, to consider the beauty of other girls. Romeo is resistant to the suggestion and does not want to forget Rosaline.

ACT I, Scene 2

Count Paris, a cousin to the Prince, asks Lord Capulet for Juliet's hand. Capulet is evasive and thinks his daughter too young for marriage. He also feels that Juliet herself must approve of Paris. To arrange a meeting between the two, Capulet invites Paris to a masquerade ball to be held at his home that same night where both young people will meet and appraise each other.

An illiterate servant from the Capulet household is sent to deliver party invitations for the Capulet ball. He cannot read and when he meets Benvolio and Romeo on the street, he asks them to please help him read the guest list. They discover Rosaline's name among the guests. Benvolio encourages Romeo to "crash" the party with him so that Romeo may find another beautiful girl to love. Romeo agrees but only because he expects to see Rosaline.

ACT I, Scene 3

Lady Capulet talks to Juliet of Paris's proposal. Juliet is not interested in marriage but is graciously willing to meet and speak with the young man. Her faithful Nurse, upon hearing that the distinguished Count Paris is the prospective groom, agrees with Juliet's mother and approves the union.

ACT I, Scene 4

Romeo, Benvolio, and Mercutio make their way to the Capulet party wearing masks and costumes. Mercutio is in very high spirits and entertains his friends as he delivers his witty Queen Mab speech which affirms the superficiality of love and other human foolishness. Romeo is not amused. Instead, he feels a grave foreboding as a result of their boldness in attending the party.

ACT I, Scene 5

Lord Capulet, the genial host, welcomes his guests. Romeo sees Juliet and falls hopelessly in love. Asking a servant the name of the young beauty, he is overheard by her cousin Tybalt, who recognizes his voice as an enemy Montague. Tybalt informs Lord Capulet that he is prepared to fight Romeo at that very moment, but Capulet defends Romeo as a "virtuous youth" and restrains Tybalt harshly.

Romeo and Juliet, though still strangers, speak, and each responds to the other with sudden, overwhelming passion. Later, when they part, they learn the devastating news that they are the children of the feuding families.

ACT II, Scene 1

Romeo eludes his friends after the party. He is upset with the implications of this new romance and wants to be alone. Reluctant to leave the grounds, he scales the wall into the Capulet garden. Mercutio and Benvolio continue to look for him while making foul jokes which they hope will provoke him to answer back, but Romeo does not respond.

ACT II, Scene 2

Juliet appears on her balcony and despairs aloud that her newly found love is a Montague. Her passionate declarations are overheard by Romeo who shares all that she feels. He announces his presence and they exchange vows of undying, profound love for each other. Romeo promises to find someone who will unite them in marriage on the following day. Juliet plans to send a messenger the next morning to learn of these wedding arrangements. Their love and their sense of urgency will not allow them to wait.

ACT II, Scene 3

Romeo goes to the cell of his priest, Friar Laurence, to tell him of his love for Juliet and his desire to marry her immediately. The Friar has some misgivings about Romeo's sincerity since Romeo was desperately in love with Rosaline only the day before. The Friar is convinced by Romeo's earnest entreaties, however, and agrees to perform the hasty ceremony in the hope that the marriage will heal the wounds between the two families.

ACT II, Scene 4

Mercutio and Benvolio joke about Tybalt's letter of challenge to Romeo, delivered to the Montague house earlier that day. They encounter Romeo in the street and are pleased that his mood is so changed and lighthearted. Soon after, Juliet's Nurse finds Romeo. He tells her happily of the wedding plans which are to take place in Friar Laurence's cell that afternoon. According to Romeo's plan, Juliet will inform her parents that she is going to confession. In truth, however, the visit to Friar Laurence's will be the occasion of her marriage. Meanwhile, Romeo's servant is to meet the Nurse behind the abbey wall to deliver a rope ladder for Romeo's use later that night. At that time, he will climb to Juliet's balcony when he visits her joyously as her new husband.

ACT II, Scene 5

Juliet waits patiently for her Nurse's return and the confirmation of her wedding plans. Once having arrived, the Nurse perversely prefers to talk about her aches and pains in search of sympathy. Juliet can barely contain her impatience and cajoles and beseeches the old woman to tell her the news which she longs to hear. The Nurse explains the plan and Juliet is ready to join Romeo in the Friar's cell for the wedding ceremony.

ACT II, Scene 6

The wedding arrangements proceed according to the plan. That afternoon in the Friar's cell, Romeo and Juliet are joined in marriage. Friar Laurence speaks to them of the enduring qualities of true love. At the same time he has doubts about the two young lovers marrying in such haste.

ACT III, Scene 1

Benvolio and Mercutio meet on a hot afternoon in the public square. Tybalt appears, still smarting with rage from the Capulet party. He is searching for Romeo with whom he wants to duel. When Romeo enters the scene, Tybalt proceeds to insult him in an attempt to goad him into fighting. However, Romeo exercises self-control, for he realizes Tybalt is Juliet's first cousin and he must not fight him. He attempts to pacify the fiery Tybalt but to no avail. Mercutio is inflamed by this bewildering scene and takes up Romeo's defense. Mercutio draws his sword and engages Tybalt. Romeo intercedes and tries to separate the two, but in so doing makes it possible for Tybalt to wound Mercutio fatally. Romeo, filled with remorse, kills Tybalt and is rushed away by Benvolio who later explains the tragedy to Prince Escalus. The ruler listens and defers the death sentence: Romeo is banished forever to Mantua.

ACT III, Scene 2

As Juliet prepares for her first and only night with Romeo, the Nurse comes with the news that her cousin Tybalt is dead and Romeo has been banished for the crime. Juliet is torn with grief over her cousin's death and her husband's cruel fate. Consoled by the knowledge that Tybalt was determined to kill Romeo, her devotion to her husband prevails. Juliet is disconsolate, but her Nurse knows that Romeo is hiding in Friar Laurence's cell and promises Juliet to bring him back as planned.

ACT III, Scene 3

Friar Laurence tries to comfort a suicidal, hysterical Romeo who is hiding from the authorities in the priest's cell. He informs Romeo that the Prince has set aside the death sentence and has ordered his banishment to Mantua instead. Romeo is inconsolable at the thought of separation from Juliet. The Nurse arrives, bringing a ring from Juliet as a gesture of her love. The old woman assures Romeo of his bride's loyalty and urges that he hurry, for time is short. Friar Laurence, too, encourages him to spend this last remaining evening with his bride and enjoins Romeo to protect his safety and leave for Mantua at dawn. The Friar expresses hope that Romeo will be pardoned in the future and will eventually be able to return home. He assures the young man that he will keep him informed of all news from home.

ACT III, Scene 4

Lord Capulet meets again with Paris to discuss the possibility of the young man's marriage to his daughter. Juliet's grief over her cousin Tybalt seems excessive and is a source of worry to her father. Convinced that he knows what is best for her, he is no longer prepared to wait for her acceptance of Paris who has been most understanding through these sad circumstances. Although there has been no time for a courtship, Lord Capulet makes the impulsive decision that the wedding will take place in three days.

ACT III, Scene 5

Romeo bids Juliet good-bye in a sorrowful parting after their sweet night together. Quickly following his departure, Lady Capulet enters her daughter's room announcing Juliet's forthcoming marriage to Paris on Thursday. Juliet is horrified and disbelieving as she pleads with her parents for a delay. In response, her father is enraged and in a burst of temper threatens to disown her if she refuses to accept his decision. Juliet feels abandoned, for even her faithful Nurse advises her to turn her back on Romeo, her legal husband, and marry Paris, who is a more sensible choice. Disillusioned, she resolves never to reveal her secrets to her Nurse again and decides to seek help from the Friar as her last resort.

SYNOPSIS BY SCENE

ACT IV, Scene 1

Paris is discussing the wedding arrangements with Friar Laurence in the priest's cell when Juliet arrives unexpectedly. Paris leaves and the weeping Juliet pours out her grief and desperation to the priest. He proposes that she falsely consent to marry Paris and then initiate his dangerous plan to prevent the marriage. The Friar gives her a powerful potion to be taken the night before the wedding. The drug will give her the cold and lifeless mask of death for forty-two hours—long enough for the bereaved family to make funeral arrangements and inter her body in the Capulet vault. In the meantime, Friar Laurence will write Romeo about the daring plan so that he can be with her when she awakens in the vault and take her back to Mantua to live with him.

ACT IV, Scene 2

Juliet returns home from Friar Laurence's cell and tells her parents that he has persuaded her to obey her father's wishes. Obediently, she expresses her willingness to marry Paris and submit to her father's judgment. She shows no sign of duplicity as she goes through the motions of participating fully in the wedding preparations. In no way does she betray her unwavering resolution that this wedding will never take place. Overjoyed at his daughter's change of heart, Lord Capulet decides that the nuptials will take place earlier than planned; the young couple will be wed on Wednesday.

ACT IV, Scene 3

Juliet feels a great urgency to say her prayers for the many sins she is about to commit. The Nurse is fully aware that Juliet's marriage to Paris is sinful. When Juliet dismisses her for the night, the Nurse leaves, understanding implicitly that Juliet must ask for forgiveness. What is not revealed to the Nurse is Juliet's guilt over the covert plan she is about to execute. Left alone, Juliet is victimized by her own fears and terrified of the potion. When she contemplates the vault where she will be placed, Juliet is unnerved at the thought of waking alone in that chilling place of death. Overcome with uncertainty, exhausted and at the limits of her sanity, she drinks the potion and falls on her bed unconscious.

ACT IV, Scene 4

The wedding morning has arrived and the entire happy household is bustling in preparation for the joyous event. Lord and Lady Capulet are lighthearted, though sleepless, since they have been up all night directing the activities. The bridegroom, Paris, arrives with the musicians and Lord Capulet sends the Nurse to help Juliet dress in her bridal gown.

ACT IV, Scene 5

The excited Nurse bustles about in Juliet's bedroom with great good cheer. She teases Juliet lovingly and tries to awaken the young bride. When she draws back the bed-curtains, she is shocked to find Juliet in a death-like coma. Hysterical, the Nurse summons the entire household. Responding to her cries, they share her devastating discovery. Grief descends upon the Capulets as they convert all the joyous preparations for the wedding into the mournful rituals of a funeral.

ACT V, Scene 1

Balthasar, Romeo's servant, travels to Mantua with the ghastly news of Juliet's untimely death. Gently, he tells Romeo of her burial in the family tomb. As Romeo listens, tortured with grief, he devises a plan. He buys a powerful poison from a druggist and then sets out for Verona to join his beloved Juliet in the serenity of death.

ACT V, Scene 2

As promised, Friar Laurence sends Friar John with a message for Romeo. In this important letter he outlines his elaborate plan with Juliet and explains the need to prevent Juliet's forced marriage to Paris. Further, he describes the use of the hypnotic potion as a desperate measure to avoid the ceremony. Details of the potion's powerful effect and the time of Juliet's awakening are carefully articulated. The letter emphasizes that Romeo must be present when she opens her eyes in the vault. Unfortunately, Friar John detained by a quarantine in the city, returns two days later and gives the undelivered letter to Friar Laurence, who realizes the plan is ruined. Well aware that Juliet will awaken in three hours all alone in the tomb, Friar Laurence rushes anxiously to the churchyard to be with her.

ACT V, Scene 3

The churchyard is in darkness as Romeo encounters Paris who is mourning at the tomb of Juliet. Paris, outraged at this final blasphemy by the criminal Romeo, threatens to arrest him. In contrast, Romeo begs Paris to leave, but the young count resists his pleas. A fight ensues and a desperate Romeo kills Paris. Romeo then enters the tomb. He sees his beloved Juliet and drinks the deadly poison. Moments later, Friar Laurence arrives as Juliet awakens and discovers her young husband dead. The Friar begs her to come with him to safety, but Juliet steadfastly refuses. He departs quickly, for he hears the watchmen approaching. Juliet, determined to end her life, seizes Romeo's dagger and plunges it into her breast. The city is alerted by the watchmen who assemble all the people implicated in the tragedy. They gather in the vault where they witness the pathetic sight of three young people lying dead. The Prince and both families listen to Friar Laurence as the details of the story are recounted. Montague and Capulet, chastised for the destruction they have wrought, join hands and finally put their pernicious feud to rest.

[THE PROLOGUE]

[Enter *Chorus.*]

Chor. Two households, both alike in dignity,
In fair Verona, where we lay our scene,
From ancient grudge break to new mutiny,
Where civil blood makes civil hands unclean.
From forth the fatal loins of these two foes
A pair of star-crossed lovers take their life,
Whose misadventured piteous overthrows
Doth with their death bury their parents' strife.
The fearful passage of their death-marked love,
And the continuance of their parents' rage,
Which, but their children's end, naught could remove,
Is now the two hours' traffic of our stage,
The which if you with patient ears attend,
What here shall miss, our toil shall strive to mend.

[*Exit.*]

[ACT I]

[Scene I. A street in Verona.]
Enter *Sampson and Gregory* (with swords and bucklers) of the house of *Capulet.*

Samp. Gregory, on my word, we'll not carry coals.
Greg. No, for then we should be colliers.
Samp. I mean, an we be in choler, we'll draw.

ACT I, Scene 1

THE PROLOGUE

(Enter CHORUS.)

CHORUS: Once there were two families of equal station and prestige who lived in the city of Verona, Italy, where this story takes place. In Verona another bout of fighting has broken out in a long-standing and bitter feud between the Montagues and the Capulets. Each family has both perpetuated and endured the physical and bloody assault. From each of these adversarial households come the young lovers of this story. Romeo, the young man, is the son of Lord and Lady Montague while Juliet is Lord and Lady Capulet's daughter. The two meet and fall in love, aware that their union will bring sorrow to their parents. The death of these two young people becomes the source of such profound grief for the parents that the tragedy finally ends the feud and brings peace to both bereaved families.

(CHORUS leaves.)

ACT I

(Scene 1: A street in the city of Verona.)

(Enter SAMPSON and GREGORY with swords and shields of the house of CAPULET.)

SAM: Gregory, I promise you, I won't be insulted.

GREG: Absolutely, for then we'd be no better than coal-workers.

SAM: I mean that if we're provoked, we'll fight.

Greg. Ay, while you live, draw your neck out of collar.

Samp. I strike quickly, being moved.

Greg. But thou art not quickly moved to strike.

Samp. A dog of the house of Montague moves me.

Greg. To move is to stir, and to be valiant is to stand. Therefore, if thou art moved, thou runnest away.

Samp. A dog of that house shall move me to stand. I will take the wall of any man or maid of Montague's.

Greg. That shows thee a weak slave, for the weakest goes to the wall.

Samp. 'Tis true; and therefore women, being the weaker vessels, are ever thrust to the wall. Therefore I will push Montague's men from the wall and thrust his maids to the wall.

Greg. The quarrel is between our masters and us their men.

Samp. 'Tis all one. I will show myself a tyrant. When I have fought with the men, I will be cruel with the maids: I will cut off their heads.

Greg. The heads of the maids?

Samp. Ay, the heads of the maids, or their maidenheads. Take it in what sense thou wilt.

Greg. They must take it in sense that feel it.

Samp. Me they shall feel while I am able to stand; and 'tis known I am a pretty piece of flesh.

Greg. 'Tis well thou art not fish; if thou hadst, thou hadst been poor-John. Draw thy tool! Here comes two of the house of Montagues.

Enter two other *Servingmen* [*Abram* and *Balthasar*].

Samp. My naked weapon is out. Quarrel! I will back thee.

GREG: Yes, and while you live, keep yourself out of the hangman's noose.

SAM: I will act quickly if someone provokes me.

GREG: But no one is antagonizing you here.

SAM: Even a dog from the Montague household could make me angry.

GREG: To move means to run, and to be valiant means to hold your ground. Therefore, if you are moved, you will run away.

SAM: Any dog from the Montague house shall move me to be valiant and thereby hold my ground. I am superior to any man or woman of the Montague's and shall therefore be allowed to walk closest to the houses on the street.

GREG: But you will be considered weak instead since it will be easy to push you into the walls of the houses.

SAM: That is true; and that is why women, being the weaker sex, often find themselves in that very same predicament. Therefore, I will push Montague's men away from the wall and throw his women to the wall where I may take my pleasure.

GREG: The quarrel is between our masters and us, their servants.

SAM: There's no difference. I will act like a tyrant. After I have defeated the men, I will be cruel to their women. I will cut off their heads.

GREG: The heads of the maids?

SAM: Yes, the heads of the maids, or their maidenheads. You may take my remarks any way you like.

GREG: People will take it in the way that they feel it.

SAM: They will have to feel me while I am able to stand, and everyone knows what a handsome piece of flesh I am.

GREG: It is a good thing you are not a fish. If you were, you would have been a piece of salted fish. Draw your sword. Here come two men from the house of Montague.

(Enter two other servants—ABRAM and BALTHASAR.)

SAM: My sword is ready. Start a fight. I will support you.

Greg. How? turn thy back and run?
Samp. Fear me not.
Greg. No, marry. I fear thee!
Samp. Let us take the law of our sides; let them begin.
Greg. I will frown as I pass by, and let them take it as they list.
Samp. Nay, as they dare. I will bite my thumb at them; which is disgrace to them, if they bear it.
Abr. Do you bite your thumb at us, sir?
Samp. I do bite my thumb, sir.
Abr. Do you bite your thumb at us, sir?
Samp. [*Aside to Gregory*] Is the law of our side if I say ay?
Greg. [*Aside to Sampson*] No.
Samp. No, sir, I do not bite my thumb at you, sir; but I bite my thumb, sir.
Greg. Do you quarrel, sir?
Abr. Quarrel, sir? No, sir.
Samp. But if you do, sir, I am for you. I serve as good a man as you.
Abr. No better.
Samp. Well, sir.

Enter *Benvolio.*

Greg. [*Aside to Sampson*] Say "better." Here comes one of my master's kinsmen.
Samp. Yes, better, sir.
Abr. You lie.
Samp. Draw, if you be men. Gregory, remember thy swashing blow. *They fight.*
Ben. Part, fools! [*Beats down their swords.*]
Put up your swords. You know not what you do.

GREG: How will you do it? Are you going to turn your back and run away?

SAM: Don't be afraid of me.

GREG: In truth, I am afraid of your promise.

SAM: Let's stay on the right side of the law. Let them start the trouble.

GREG: I will make a face as I pass them—then let them do with it as they please.

SAM: You mean, as they dare. I will make an insulting gesture to them and see if they can stand it.

ABR: Are you making an insulting gesture to me, sir?

SAM: Well, I was making an insulting gesture.

ABR: You mean you were doing it to us?

SAM: (Aside to Gregory) Gregory, if I say yes, is it legal?

GREG: (Aside to Sampson) No, it is not legal, Sampson.

SAM: No, I didn't make the gesture to you, Abram. I just simply made a gesture.

GREG: Are you looking for an argument, Abram?

ABR: I am not looking for an argument! No sir!

SAM: Well, if you are, you've found the right person. The man I work for is just as good as the man you work for.

ABR: Don't you mean that the man you work for is really better than the man I work for?

SAM: Well, sir. (Enter BENVOLIO.)

GREG: (Aside to Sampson) Go ahead, Sampson. Say Lord Capulet is better than Lord Montague because here comes one of Lord Capulet's relatives now.

SAM: Yes, Abram, he is better!

ABR: You're lying!

SAM: If you are men, then draw your swords! Gregory, remember your crushing blow!

(They fight.)

BEN: You big fools, you don't know what you're doing. (Beats down their swords.) Put your swords away.

Enter *Tybalt.*

Tyb. What, art thou drawn among these heartless hinds?
Turn thee, Benvolio! look upon thy death.
Ben. I do but keep the peace. Put up thy sword,
Or manage it to part these men with me.
Tyb. What, drawn, and talk of peace? I hate the word
As I hate hell, all Montagues, and thee.
Have at thee, coward! [*They*] *fight.*

Enter three or four *Citizens* with clubs or partisans [and an *Officer*].

Officer. Clubs, bills, and partisans! Strike! beat them down!
Citizens. Down with the Capulets! Down with the Montagues!

Enter *Old Capulet* in his gown, and his *Wife.*

Cap. What noise is this? Give me my long sword, ho!
Wife. A crutch, a crutch! Why call you for a sword?
Cap. My sword, I say! Old Montague is come
And flourishes his blade in spite of me.

Enter *Old Montague* and his *Wife.*

Mon. Thou villain Capulet!—Hold me not, let me go.
M. Wife. Thou shalt not stir one foot to seek a foe.

Enter *Prince Escalus,* with his *Train.*

Prince. Rebellious subjects, enemies to peace,
Profaners of this neighbor-stained steel—

ACT I, Scene 1

(Enter TYBALT.)

TYBALT: What are you doing—fighting with these servants? Turn around and face your death.

BEN: All I was doing was trying to keep the peace. Either help me settle these men down or draw your sword against me.

TYBALT: You're a bit of a hypocrite, Benvolio! You are talking about peace and you already have your sword drawn. I hate the word *peace* as much as I hate hell and the Montagues and you. Let's go, coward!

(They fight.)

(Enter 3 or 4 CITIZENS with clubs and an OFFICER.)

OFFICER: Use your clubs and blades. Strike them! Beat them down!

CITIZENS: Down with the Capulets! Down with the Montagues!

(Enter LORD CAP. in his gown and LADY CAP.)

LORD CAP: What's going on? I'll join in this fray. Wife, get me my long sword.

LADY CAP: Oh, come now. A crutch would be more your style. Why do you ask for a sword?

LORD CAP: I *said* I want my sword. Old man Montague is coming and has his sword out to defy me.

LORD MONT: Capulet, you villain. Wife, don't hold me back. Let me at him.

LADY MONT: You will not move one inch from here to go after an enemy.

(Enter PRINCE with his men.)

PRINCE: Rebellious subjects, hear me! You are enemies of the peace for staining your swords with your neighbors' blood. Why don't you listen to what I am saying?

Will they not hear? What, ho! you men, you beasts,
That quench the fire of your pernicious rage
With purple fountains issuing from your veins!
On pain of torture, from those bloody hands
Throw your mistempered weapons to the ground
And hear the sentence of your moved prince.
Three civil brawls, bred of an airy word
By thee, old Capulet, and Montague,
Have thrice disturbed the quiet of our streets
And made Verona's ancient citizens
Cast by their grave beseeming ornaments
To wield old partisans, in hands as old,
Cankered with peace, to part your cankered hate.
If ever you disturb our streets again,
Your lives shall pay the forfeit of the peace.
For this time all the rest depart away.
You, Capulet, shall go along with me;
And, Montague, come you this afternoon,
To know our farther pleasure in this case,
To old Freetown, our common judgment place.
Once more, on pain of death, all men depart.

Exeunt [*all but Montague, his Wife, and Benvolio*].

Mon. Who set this ancient quarrel new abroach?
Speak, nephew, were you by when it began?

Ben. Here were the servants of your adversary
And yours, close fighting ere I did approach.
I drew to part them. In the instant came
The fiery Tybalt, with his sword prepared;
Which, as he breathed defiance to my ears,
He swung about his head and cut the winds,
Who, nothing hurt withal, hissed him in scorn.
While we were interchanging thrusts and blows,
Came more and more, and fought on part and part,
Till the Prince came, who parted either part.

ACT I, Scene 1

You men are not men but beasts that satisfy your anger with your own blood. You will be tortured if you do not throw your weapons down and hear what I have to say. Three bloody street fights started over a trifling word, from you, old Capulet, and Montague. You have disturbed our quiet streets three times. Even our best citizens have become involved. Their weapons, just like these citizens, have grown rusty during times of peace, and now are used to perpetuate your intense hatred. If you ever disturb the peace of this city again, you will not live to tell about it. For the time being, Capulet, come with me; Montague, I'll see you this afternoon so we can discuss this matter further in Freetown. Once again to the rest of this mob, on pain of death, get out of here!

(They all leave except LORD MONTAGUE, LADY MONTAGUE, and BENVOLIO.)

LORD MONT: Who started this argument again? Were you here when it began, Benvolio?

BEN: When I came up here, Capulet's servants were starting a fight with your men, Uncle. I drew my sword to stop it when Capulet's nephew, Tybalt, drew his sword and goaded me into a duel but no harm came to us. We fought and the servants fought until Prince Escalus came and stopped all the action.

M. Wife. O, where is Romeo? Saw you him today?
Right glad I am he was not at this fray.
Ben. Madam, an hour before the worshiped sun
Peered forth the golden window of the East,
A troubled mind drave me to walk abroad,
Where, underneath the grove of sycamore
That westward rooteth from the city's side,
So early walking did I see your son.
Towards him I made, but he was ware of me
And stole into the covert of the wood.
I—measuring his affections by my own,
Which then most sought where most might not be found,
Being one too many by my weary self—
Pursued my humor, not pursuing his,
And gladly shunned who gladly fled from me.
Mon. Many a morning hath he there been seen,
With tears augmenting the fresh morning's dew,
Adding to clouds more clouds with his deep sighs;
But all so soon as the all-cheering sun
Should in the farthest East begin to draw
The shady curtains from Aurora's bed,
Away from light steals home my heavy son
And private in his chamber pens himself,
Shuts up his windows, locks fair daylight out,
And makes himself an artificial night.
Black and portentous must this humor prove
Unless good counsel may the cause remove.
Ben. My noble uncle, do you know the cause?
Mon. I neither know it nor can learn of him.
Ben. Have you importuned him by any means?
Mon. Both by myself and many other friends;
But he, his own affections' counselor,
Is to himself—I will not say how true—
But to himself so secret and so close,

ACT I, Scene 1

LADY MONT: Benvolio, have you seen my son Romeo today? I'm certainly glad he wasn't in this fight.

BEN: I saw Romeo an hour before sunrise. I had some things on my mind and took a long walk. While walking in a grove of sycamore trees on the west side of town, I saw your son. He saw me too, but he avoided me by going into the woods. However, since we respect each other, I decided to give him his privacy and not pursue him.

LORD MONT: I've seen him sighing and weeping at dawn quite often lately. As the sun rises each day Romeo secludes himself in his bedroom and shuts out all light. He'd better get some help with this depression or else he'll be in a lot of trouble.

BEN: Uncle, do you know what is causing Romeo's depression?

LORD MONT: No, I don't know and he won't tell me.

BEN: Have you tried more than once to find out what the trouble is?

LORD MONT: Yes, I have tried repeatedly and so have many other friends, but Romeo keeps the cause a secret and will not reveal the reason for his mood.

So far from sounding and discovery,
As is the bud bit with an envious worm
Ere he can spread his sweet leaves to the air
Or dedicate his beauty to the sun.
Could we but learn from whence his sorrows grow,
We would as willingly give cure as know.

Enter *Romeo.*

Ben. See, where he comes. So please you step aside,
I'll know his grievance, or be much denied.
Mon. I would thou wert so happy by thy stay
To hear true shrift. Come, madam, let's away.
Exeunt [*Montague and Wife*].
Ben. Good morrow, cousin.
Rom. Is the day so young?
Ben. But new struck nine.
Rom. Ay me! sad hours seem long.
Was that my father that went hence so fast?
Ben. It was. What sadness lengthens Romeo's hours?
Rom. Not having that which having makes them short.
Ben. In love?
Rom. Out—
Ben. Of love?
Rom. Out of her favor where I am in love.
Ben. Alas that love, so gentle in his view,
Should be so tyrannous and rough in proof!
Rom. Alas that love, whose view is muffled still,
Should without eyes see pathways to his will!
Where shall we dine?—O me! What fray was here?—
Yet tell me not, for I have heard it all.
Here's much to do with hate, but more with love.
Why then, O brawling love! O loving hate!
O anything, of nothing first create!

Romeo is like a bud eaten by a malicious worm before the flower can spread its sweet leaves to the air and reveal its beauty to the sun. If we knew the cause of his sorrow, we would willingly help him. (Enter ROMEO.)

BEN: Here comes Romeo now. Let me handle this. I'll find out what the problem is; and if I don't it won't be because I haven't tried.

LORD MONT: I hope you'll be lucky enough to hear Romeo's secret. Come, Wife, let's go home. (LORD and LADY MONTAGUE leave.)

BEN: Good morning, cousin.

ROMEO: Is it only morning?

BEN: Of course, the clock just struck nine.

ROMEO: Oh my, time drags and minutes seem like hours when you're unhappy. Was that my father who left so quickly?

BEN: Yes, it was. But to change the subject, what is making you so miserable?

ROMEO: I am miserable because I do not have that thing which would make my time go by so very quickly.

BEN: Does that mean you are in love?

ROMEO: No, out—

BEN: You're "out of love"?

ROMEO: No, I am in love, but I am out of favor with the one I love.

BEN: It's too bad that gentle love has to be so rough with you.

ROMEO: It's too bad that love is blind and yet it still, despite this handicap, has its way. Say, where would you like to eat?—Oh, my word! (ROMEO looks around.) Was there a fight here? Don't tell me—I have heard it all before: I see there was a great commotion here having much to do with hating one's enemy; but even more it has to do with love and loyalty for one's family. So in the name of absurdities—brawling love and loving hate—something bad has been created out of nothing.

O heavy lightness! serious vanity!
Misshapen chaos of well-seeming forms!
Feather of lead, bright smoke, cold fire, sick health!
Still-waking sleep, that is not what it is!
This love feel I, that feel no love in this.
Dost thou not laugh?
Ben. No, coz, I rather weep.
Rom. Good heart, at what?
Ben. At thy good heart's oppression.
Rom. Why, such is love's transgression.
Griefs of mine own lie heavy in my breast,
Which thou wilt propagate, to have it prest
With more of thine. This love that thou hast shown
Doth add more grief to too much of mine own.
Love is a smoke raised with the fume of sighs;
Being purged, a fire sparkling in lovers' eyes;
Being vexed, a sea nourished with lovers' tears.
What is it else? A madness most discreet,
A choking gall, and a preserving sweet.
Farewell, my coz.
Ben. Soft! I will go along.
An if you leave me so, you do me wrong.
Rom. Tut! I have lost myself; I am not here:
This is not Romeo, he's some other where.
Ben. Tell me in sadness, who is that you love?
Rom. What, shall I groan and tell thee?
Ben. Groan? Why, no;
But sadly tell me who.
Rom. Bid a sick man in sadness make his will.
Ah, word ill urged to one that is so ill!
In sadness, cousin, I do love a woman.
Ben. I aimed so near when I supposed you loved.
Rom. A right good markman! And she's fair I love.
Ben. A right fair mark, fair coz, is soonest hit.

It is just as ridiculous as heavy lightness and serious foolishness. It is like shapeless chaos of well-shaped forms, or feathers of lead, or bright smoke, or cold fire, or sick health, or ever-wakeful sleep. These things cannot exist side by side. This love I feel for my family is not one I take any pleasure in. Don't you think it's funny?

BEN: No, Cousin, I weep instead.

ROMEO: What makes you cry?

BEN: I weep over your troubles.

ROMEO: This the way of love. It causes me great pain, but your concern and tears increase my grief. Love is full of fire and passion and sighs. When love is good it sparkles in lovers' eyes. But when love is bad the tears of lovers may fill an ocean. What else is it? It is madness, and choking gall, and bittersweet all at the same time. Farewell, my cousin.

BEN: Wait a moment and let me go with you. If you leave me when you feel this way, you are shutting me out.

ROMEO: Forgive me for I am not myself. I am very confused. I don't know what is going on.

BEN: Tell me truthfully and seriously—whom do you love?

ROMEO: What do you expect me to say in my sadness?

BEN: I don't want to make you sad. Just tell me whom you love, seriously.

ROMEO: Don't make me suffer even more when I feel this way. Don't add to my grief. Seriously, cousin, I love a woman.

BEN: I was right, then, to think your sadness was over the love of a woman.

ROMEO: You were right on the mark. And the one I love is beautiful.

BEN: It was easy for me to guess about this. Such a fair target would easily be hit by Cupid.

Rom. Well, in that hit you miss. She'll not be hit
With Cupid's arrow. She hath Dian's wit,
And, in strong proof of chastity well armed,
From Love's weak childish bow she lives unharmed.
She will not stay the siege of loving terms,
Nor bide the encounter of assailing eyes,
Nor ope her lap to saint-seducing gold.
O, she is rich in beauty; only poor
That, when she dies, with beauty dies her store.
Ben. Then she hath sworn that she will still live chaste?
Rom. She hath, and in that sparing makes huge waste;
For beauty, starved with her severity,
Cuts beauty off from all posterity.
She is too fair, too wise, wisely too fair,
To merit bliss by making me despair.
She hath forsworn to love, and in that vow
Do I live dead that live to tell it now.
Ben. Be ruled by me: forget to think of her.
Rom. O, teach me how I should forget to think!
Ben. By giving liberty unto thine eyes:
Examine other beauties.
Rom. 'Tis the way
To call hers (exquisite) in question more.
These happy masks that kiss fair ladies' brows,
Being black, puts us in mind they hide the fair.
He that is strucken blind cannot forget
The precious treasure of his eyesight lost.
Show me a mistress that is passing fair,
What doth her beauty serve but as a note
Where I may read who passed that passing fair?
Farewell. Thou canst not teach me to forget.
Ben. I'll pay that doctrine, or else die in debt.

Exeunt.

ROMEO: But there you miss the mark! For she will not be hit with Cupid's arrow for, like Diana, she prefers a life of chastity. She will not yield to love nor money. It is sad that when she dies, the richness of her unspent beauty will not have been passed on to the children she should have had.

BEN: Has she really sworn herself to virginity?

ROMEO: Yes, she has; and what a waste, what a pity! She will not be responsible for any future generations. She is wise in thinking about the rewards of chastity, but she has renounced love, and because of her vows, I feel like a dead man. She is so beautiful that her decision causes me despair because my love is unfulfilled.

BEN: Listen to me, Romeo. Forget her!

ROMEO: Show me, please, how to forget her!

BEN: Just give yourself the liberty to look at other women.

ROMEO: If I look at others, she will seem even more beautiful. The masks that women wear to protect their faces from the sun only serve to remind us of the fair faces underneath. When we have lost a treasure we still remember it. The beauty of any woman only reminds me of the beauty of my beloved. Farewell. You cannot teach me to forget.

BEN: I will convince you that you are wrong, or else die trying.

(They leave.)

[Scene II. A street near the Capulet house.]

Enter *Capulet, County Paris,* and [*Servant*]—the *Clown.*

Cap. But Montague is bound as well as I,
In penalty alike; and 'tis not hard, I think,
For men so old as we to keep the peace.
Par. Of honorable reckoning are you both,
And pity 'tis you lived at odds so long.
But now, my lord, what say you to my suit?
Cap. But saying o'er what I have said before:
My child is yet a stranger in the world,
She hath not seen the change of fourteen years;
Let two more summers wither in their pride
Ere we may think her ripe to be a bride.
Par. Younger than she are happy mothers made.
Cap. And too soon marred are those so early made.
The earth hath swallowed all my hopes but she;
She is the hopeful lady of my earth.
But woo her, gentle Paris, get her heart;
My will to her consent is but a part.
An she agree, within her scope of choice
Lies my consent and fair according voice.
This night I hold an old accustomed feast,
Whereto I have invited many a guest,
Such as I love, and you among the store,
One more, most welcome, makes my number more.
At my poor house look to behold this night
Earth-treading stars that make dark heaven light.
Such comfort as do lusty young men feel
When well-appareled April on the heel
Of limping Winter treads, even such delight
Among fresh female buds shall you this night

ACT I

(Scene 2: A street near the CAPULET home.)

(Enter LORD CAPULET, PARIS, and a foolish SERVANT.)

LORD CAP: Both Montague and I are responsible for keeping the peace and that is not difficult for old men. We would both have to pay a penalty for breaking the peace.

PARIS: You are both honorable men and it is a pity that you have both been enemies for so long. But now, my lord, what about my request to marry your daughter, Juliet? Do you have an answer?

LORD CAP: Only to repeat what I said before. Juliet is still only a child of thirteen—let's give her two more years to be of marriageable age.

PARIS: There are happy mothers today who are even younger than Juliet.

LORD CAP: Young brides often suffer physically for marrying so soon. She's my only living child and she is my hope. Be patient, gentle Paris, try to win her heart; but remember, my consent depends upon her consent to marry you. Tonight I'm having a party with many guests and you are also invited as a special guest. So come to my humble home tonight when the stars make the dark heavens light. My young guests will celebrate the coming of spring along with the pretty young girls who will also be there.

Inherit at my house. Hear all, all see,
And like her most whose merit most shall be;
Which, on more view of many, mine, being one,
May stand in number, though in reck'ning none.
Come, go with me. [*To Servant, giving him a paper*] Go,
sirrah, trudge about
Through fair Verona; find those persons out
Whose names are written there, and to them say,
My house and welcome on their pleasure stay.
Exeunt [*Capulet and Paris*].

Serv. Find them out whose names are written here! It is written that the shoemaker should meddle with his yard and the tailor with his last, the fisher with his pencil and the painter with his nets; but I am sent to find those persons whose names are here writ, and can never find what names the writing person hath here writ. I must to the learned. In good time!

Enter *Benvolio and Romeo.*

Ben. Tut, man, one fire burns out another's burning;
One pain is lessened by another's anguish;
Turn giddy, and be holp by backward turning;
One desperate grief cures with another's languish.
Take thou some new infection to thy eye,
And the rank poison of the old will die.
Rom. Your plantain leaf is excellent for that.
Ben. For what, I pray thee?
Rom. For your broken shin.
Ben. Why, Romeo, art thou mad?
Rom. Not mad, but bound more than a madman is;
Shup up in prison, kept without my food,
Whipped and tormented and—God-den, good fellow.
Serv. God gi' go-den. I pray, sir, can you read?

There will be many beauties there to be seen and Juliet, though she may not be the prettiest, is incomparable in her worth. Come along with me. (To SERVANT, giving him a paper.) Find these people on my invitation list in the city of Verona and extend a welcome to my party tonight.

(LORD CAPULET and PARIS leave.)

SERVANT: I'm supposed to find all these people whose names are written here. I can do my job as well as a shoemaker who works with a yardstick or a tailor working on the sole of a shoe or a fisherman with a pencil or a painter with a fishnet. How can I do it when I can't read the names on the list? I must find someone who can read immediately. (Seeing Romeo and Benvolio.) What luck! Here come two gentlemen who can help me.

(Enter BENVOLIO and ROMEO.)

BEN: Romeo, here's more advice. One fire will put out another. One pain will lessen another pain; dizziness will be helped by turning around and around. One desperate grief is cured by another kind of suffering. If you want to get rid of one eye infection, expose yourself to a new one.

ROMEO: Your plantain leaf salve is an excellent remedy for an infection or injury.

BEN: What are you talking about?

ROMEO: About your bruised shinbone.

BEN: Romeo, have you gone crazy?

ROMEO: No, but I'm more bound up than a lunatic is. I am like a madman who suffers confinement and torment in prison. My prison is the torment of a love denied. (To SERVANT) Good afternoon, good fellow.

SERVANT: Good afternoon, sir. I hope you can help me—can you read?

Rom. Ay, mine own fortune in my misery.

Serv. Perhaps you have learned it without book. But I pray, can you read anything you see?

Rom. Ay, if I know the letters and the language.

Serv. Ye say honestly. Rest you merry!

Rom. Stay, fellow; I can read. *He reads.*

"Signior Martino and his wife and daughters;
County Anselmo and his beauteous sisters;
The lady widow of Vitruvio;
Signior Placentio and his lovely nieces;
Mercutio and his brother Valentine;
Mine uncle Capulet, his wife, and daughters;
My fair niece Rosaline and Livia;
Signior Valentio and his cousin Tybalt;
Lucio and the lively Helena."

[*Gives back the paper.*] A fair assembly. Whither should they come?

Serv. Up.

Rom. Whither?

Serv. To supper, to our house.

Rom. Whose house?

Serv. My master's.

Rom. Indeed, I should have asked you that before.

Serv. Now I'll tell you without asking. My master is the great rich Capulet; and if you be not of the house of Montagues, I pray come and crush a cup of wine. Rest you merry! *Exit.*

Ben. At this same ancient feast of Capulet's
Sups the fair Rosaline whom thou so lovest,
With all the admired beauties of Verona.
Go thither, and with unattainted eye
Compare her face with some that I shall show,

ROMEO: Yes, I can read misery for myself in my future.

SERVANT: Maybe you have learned to read the future without an astrology book. But can you read anything you see?

ROMEO: Yes, if I know the language used to write it.

SERVANT: You're an honest fellow, but a silly one. Since you cannot read, I'll find someone who can.

ROMEO: Don't leave. I was only joking. I can read. (Reads CAPULET guest list.) "Mister Martino and his wife and daughters; Count Anselme and his lovely sisters; the lady widow of Vitruvio; Mr. Placentio and his pretty nieces; Mercutio and his brother Valentine; my uncle Capulet, his wife, and daughters; my fair niece Rosaline; Livia; Mr. Valentio and his cousin Tybalt; Lucio and the lively Helena." (Gives back the paper.) That's an interesting group of people. Where are they invited?

SERVANT: Up.

ROMEO: Where?

SERVANT: They've been invited up to our house for supper.

ROMEO: Whose house?

SERVANT: My master's house.

ROMEO: I should have asked you that before.

SERVANT: Now I'll tell you without asking. My master is rich Lord Capulet and if you are not one of the enemy Montagues, come and drink with us. May you continue to be happy.

(The SERVANT leaves.)

BEN: Romeo, your beloved, Rosaline, is going to be at the Capulet party. If you go to the party and really take a look at the other women honestly, you can compare Rosaline's beauty with the others. I shall point them out to you.

And I will make thee think thy swan a crow.
Rom. When the devout religion of mine eye
Maintains such falsehood, then turn tears to fires;
And these, who, often drowned, could never die,
Transparent heretics, be burnt for liars!
One fairer than my love? The all-seeing sun
Ne'er saw her match since first the world begun.
Ben. Tut! you saw her fair, none else being by,
Herself poised with herself in either eye;
But in that crystal scales let there be weighed
Your lady's love against some other maid
That I will show you shining at this feast,
And she shall scant show well that now shows best.
Rom. I'll go along, no such sight to be shown,
But to rejoice in splendor of mine own.

[*Exeunt.*]

[Scene III. Capulet's house.]

Enter *Capulet's Wife,* and *Nurse.*

Wife. Nurse, where's my daughter? Call her forth to
me.
Nurse. Now, by my maidenhead at twelve year old,
I bade her come. What, lamb! what, ladybird!
God forbid! Where's this girl? What, Juliet!

Enter *Juliet.*

Jul. How now? Who calls?
Nurse. Your mother.
Jul. Madam, I am here. What is your will?
Wife. This is the matter—Nurse, give leave awhile,

I will make you think that Rosaline, whom you think resembles a swan, looks more like a crow.

ROMEO: If what my eyes see were not true, then truths we take for granted would be false. Tears would turn to fires; the drowned could never die, and nonconformists would be burnt as liars. There is no one fairer than my love. And the sun has never seen anyone to equal her beauty since the world began.

BEN: Romeo, when you first saw Rosaline, there was no other woman around so she was all you saw. But if we match her with others at this party, your eyes will see that she is not the most beautiful.

ROMEO: All right, I'll go to the party, but I don't believe that what you say will happen. I'll go, but only to reaffirm my belief that she is the only woman for me.

ACT I

(Scene 3: A room in CAPULET'S house.)

(Enter LADY CAPULET and NURSE.)

LADY CAP: Nurse, where is my daughter? Would you call her here for me?

NURSE: Now, by my soul, I'll ask her to come. (Calls to JULIET.) My lamb! My lady bird! God forbid that any harm should come to her. Where is that girl? Oh Juliet!

(Enter JULIET.)

JULIET: What is it? Who is calling for me?

NURSE: Your mother.

JULIET: Mother, I am here. What do you want?

LADY CAP: I'll tell you what I want to talk with you about. (To NURSE.) Nurse, would you leave us alone for a while?

We must talk in secret. Nurse, come back again;
I have remembered me, thou's hear our counsel.
Thou knowest my daughter's of a pretty age.
Nurse. Faith, I can tell her age unto an hour.
Wife. She's not fourteen.
Nurse. I'll lay fourteen of my teeth—
And yet, to my teen be it spoken, I have but four—
She's not fourteen. How long is it now
to Lammastide?
Wife. A fortnight and odd days.
Nurse. Even or odd, of all days in the year,
Come Lammas Eve at night shall she be fourteen.
Susan and she (God rest all Christian souls!)
Were of an age. Well, Susan is with God;
She was too good for me. But, as I said,
On Lammas Eve at night shall she be fourteen;
That shall she, marry; I remember it well.
'Tis since the earthquake now eleven years;
And she was weaned (I never shall forget it),
Of all the days of the year, upon that day;
For I had then laid wormwood to my dug,
Sitting in the sun under the dovehouse wall.
My lord and you were then at Mantua—
Nay, I do bear a brain—But, as I said,
When it did taste the wormwood on the nipple
Of my dug and felt it bitter, pretty fool,
To see it tetchy and fall out with the dug!
Shake, quoth the dovehouse! 'Twas no need, I trow,
To bid me trudge.
And since that time it is eleven years,
For then she could stand alone; nay, by the rood,
She could have run and waddled all about;
For even the day before, she broke her brow;
And then my husband (God be with his soul!

ACT I, Scene 3

This is just between mother and daughter. Oh! Nurse, come back here. You can be part of this conversation. You know that Juliet is old enough to be thinking of marriage.

NURSE: I can tell her age practically to the hour.

LADY CAP: She is not yet fourteen.

NURSE: I'll wager fourteen of my teeth—although I only have four teeth—that she isn't fourteen yet. How many days is it until the holy feast day on August first?

LADY CAP: Around two weeks, more or less.

NURSE: Regardless, July 31 is young Juliet's fourteenth birthday. My daughter Susan, God rest her soul, and Juliet were the same age. Susan is in heaven with God now. She was too good to live on this earth and as I said, July 31 is Juliet's fourteenth birthday. I remember it well. I remember there was an earthquake on her third birthday and on that day Juliet was weaned. I remember it all clearly because I put a bitter potion on my breast so she would stop nursing. At the time I was sitting in the sun under the dovehouse wall. You and Lord Capulet were at Mantua. I have a good memory. But as I said, when Juliet tasted the bitter potion on my breast, she spit it out and would nurse no longer. Suddenly the dovehouse began to shake. Nobody had to tell me to get out of there. And since that time eleven years have passed. By the time she was three, Juliet could stand up by herself, and she could run and walk about. Even on the day before her third birthday she cut her forehead running. And my husband—God rest his soul—

'A was a merry man) took up the child.
"Yea," quoth he, "dost thou fall upon thy face?
Thou wilt fall backward when thou hast more wit,
Wilt thou not, Jule?" and, by my holidam,
The pretty wretch left crying, and said "Ay."
To see now how a jest shall come about!
I warrant, an I should live a thousand years,
I never should forget it. "Wilt thou not, Jule?" quoth he,
And, pretty fool, it stinted, and said "Ay."
Wife. Enough of this. I pray thee hold thy peace.
Nurse. Yes, madam. Yet I cannot choose but laugh
To think it should leave crying and say "Ay."
And yet, I warrant, it had upon it brow
A bump as big as a young cock'rel's stone;
A perilous knock; and it cried bitterly.
"Yea," quoth my husband, "fallst upon thy face?
Thou wilt fall backward when thou comest to age,
Wilt thou not, Jule?" It stinted, and said "Ay"
Jul. And stint thou too, I pray thee, nurse, say I.
Nurse. Peace, I have done. God mark thee to his grace!
Thou wast the prettiest babe that e'er I nursed.
An I might live to see thee married once,
I have my wish.
Wife. Marry, that "marry" is the very theme
I came to talk of. Tell me, daughter Juliet,
How stands your disposition to be married?
Jul. It is an honor that I dream not of.
Nurse. An honor? Were not I thine only nurse,
I would say thou hadst sucked wisdom from thy teat.
Wife. Well, think of marriage now. Younger than you,
Here in Verona, ladies of esteem,
Are made already mothers. By my count,
I was your mother much upon these years
That you are now a maid. Thus then in brief:

picked her up as she cried and he joked with her. "Yes," he said, " you fell flat on your face. When you are grown up and smarter, you will fall backward. Won't you, little Juliet?" And by what is holy to me, I remember the pretty little babe stopped crying and said, "Yes." And if I live for a thousand years, I will always remember it. His joking made her stop crying.

LADY CAP: I have heard enough. Please be quiet now.

NURSE: Yes, madam, but I have to laugh when I remember when little Juliet stopped crying even though she had a bump as big as an egg on her head. It was a bad bump and she cried bitterly. And my husband said, "Did you fall on your face? You will fall backward when you get older. Won't you, Juliet?" And the crying stopped, and she said, "Yes."

JULIET: Stop, please, I beg you.

NURSE: All right, I'll be quiet. God has smiled on you and you were the prettiest baby I ever nursed. I hope I get to see you married once—and I'll have my wish.

LADY CAP: In fact, marriage is the very thing I came to talk about. Tell me, my daughter, how do you feel about being married?

JULIET: Marriage is not an honor that I dream about.

NURSE: An honor? I know that I am the only one who nursed you. You couldn't have gotten that kind of nonsense from my breast.

LADY CAP: Well, think of marriage now. Young ladies here in Verona, who are younger than you, are already mothers. By the time I was about your age, I was a mother. So then, here is my point—

The valiant Paris seeks you for his love.
Nurse. A man, young lady! lady, such a man
As all the world—why he's a man of wax.
Wife. Verona's summer hath not such a flower.
Nurse. Nay, he's a flower, in faith—a very flower.
Wife. What say you? Can you love the gentleman?
This night you shall behold him at our feast.
Read o'er the volume of young Paris' face,
And find delight writ there with beauty's pen;
Examine every several lineament,
And see how one another lends content;
And what obscured in this fair volume lies
Find written in the margent of his eyes.
This precious book of love, this unbound lover,
To beautify him only lacks a cover.
The fish lives in the sea, and 'tis much pride
For fair without the fair within to hide.
That book in many's eyes doth share the glory,
That in gold clasps locks in the golden story;
So shall you share all that he doth possess,
By having him making yourself no less.
Nurse. No less? Nay, bigger! Women grow by men.
Wife. Speak briefly, can you like of Paris' love?
Jul. I'll look to like, if looking liking move;
But no more deep will I endart mine eye
Than your consent gives strength to make it fly.

Enter a *Servingman.*

Serv. Madam, the guests are come, supper served up, you called, my young lady asked for, the nurse cursed in the pantry, and everything in extremity. I must hence to wait. I beseech you follow straight.

ACT I, Scene 3

the valiant Count Paris wants you for his wife.

NURSE: A man, young lady, and such a man! Paris is sheer perfection—the very model of a man in all the world.

LADY CAP: He is handsomer than all the finest flowers in Verona!

NURSE: Yes, he is indeed a flower, a true flower.

LADY CAP: What do you say, Juliet? Can you love this man Paris? You will have the chance to see him at our party tonight. Look at his face carefully. Examine every feature and see how each feature adds to his character. What you don't find on the outside you will find written in his eyes. See him as a precious book of love that only needs a cover. Beautiful fish live in the beautiful sea —one splendid thing inside the other. Paris is like a glorious book that will become more precious because of you, the golden clasp, who embraces the golden story. If you become his wife you will share in all the beauty and grace he possesses, and you will be enhanced by this union.

NURSE: You will certainly be no less. You will probably be more as his wife. You will grow bigger from your pregnancies.

LADY CAP: Yes or no, Juliet? Will you consider Paris?

JULIET: I will certainly look at him, if that will make me love him. But I will not try any harder than looking. Just because you gave your consent does not mean that this arrangement is going to work out, Mother.

(Enter SERVANT.)

SERVANT: Lady Capulet, the guests have arrived; dinner is served; someone is asking to see Juliet. We need the Nurse's help in the kitchen and I must ask you, please, to follow me at once, Madam.

Wife. We follow thee. *Exit* [*Servingmen*]. Juliet, the County stays.
Nurse. Go, girl, seek happy nights to happy days.
Exeunt.

[Scene IV. A street near the Capulet house.]

Enter *Romeo, Mercutio, Benvolio,* with five or six other *Maskers*; *Torchbearers.*

Rom. What, shall this speech be spoke for our excuse?
Or shall we on without apology?
Ben. The date is out of such prolixity.
We'll have no Cupid hoodwinked with a scarf,
Bearing a Tartar's painted bow of lath,
Scaring the ladies like a crowkeeper;
Nor no without-book prologue, faintly spoke
After the prompter, for our entrance;
But, let them measure us by what they will,
We'll measure them a measure, and be gone.
Rom. Give me a torch. I am not for this ambling;
Being but heavy, I will bear the light.
Mer. Nay, gentle Romeo, we must have you dance.
Rom. Not I, believe me. You have dancing shoes
With nimble soles; I have a soul of lead
So stakes me to the ground I cannot move.
Mer. You are a lover. Borrow Cupid's wings
And soar with them above a common bound.
Rom. I am too sore enpierced with his shaft
To soar with his light feathers, and so bound
I cannot bound a pitch above dull woe.
Under love's heavy burden do I sink.

LADY CAP: We're coming this minute.

(SERVANT leaves.)

Juliet, Count Paris is waiting for you.

NURSE: Go ahead, Juliet; have a good time tonight so that your future days will be happy.

(They leave.)

ACT I

(Scene 4: A street near the CAPULET house.)

(Enter ROMEO, MERCUTIO, BENVOLIO, with five or six other people in masks, TORCHBEARERS.)

ROMEO: Shall we formally introduce ourselves at the Capulet's party or shall we just go in unannounced?

BEN: No, nobody wastes their time on formalities like that any more. It's out of style. Besides, we don't want to be introduced by someone dressed like Cupid with a blindfold and bow and arrow, who frightens the ladies like a scarecrow. Nor do we need a person repeating a memorized guest list from a prompter when we enter. We are only in masks, our costumes are not conspicuous, and no one's going to pay any attention to us after our entrance. Forget about formalities and let them take us for what they please. We will dance a little bit and then we'll leave.

ROMEO: Let me carry the torch. I don't feel like taking part in this lighthearted dancing. I am still sad about Rosaline so give me the torch.

MERC: Come on, Romeo, you must dance.

ROMEO: No, please leave me alone. You are the ones who are in a good mood so why don't you dance? I have a heavy heart and simply cannot move with any joy.

MERC: You are a lover—we all know that! So just borrow Cupid's wings and take off!

ROMEO: Because Cupid's arrow has pierced me, I cannot fly any distance at all. I am so impaired that I cannot even jump because I am sinking under love's heavy burden.

Romeo and Juliet ACT.I SC.IV

Mer. And, to sink in it, should you burden love—
Too great oppression for a tender thing.
Rom. Is love a tender thing? It is too rough,
Too rude, too boist'rous, and it pricks like thorn.
Mer. If love be rough with you, be rough with love.
Prick love for pricking, and you beat love down.
Give me a case to put my visage in.
A visor for a visor! What care I
What curious eye doth quote deformities?
Here are the beetle brows shall blush for me.
Ben. Come, knock and enter, and no sooner in
But every man betake him to his legs.
Rom. A torch for me! Let wantons light of heart
Tickle the senseless rushes with their heels;
For I am proverbed with a grandsire phrase,
I'll be a candle-holder and look on;
The game was ne'er so fair, and I am done.
Mer. Tut! dun's the mouse, the constable's own word!
If thou art Dun, we'll draw thee from the mire
Of, save your reverence, love, wherein thou stickst
Up to the ears. Come, we burn daylight, ho!
Rom. Nay, that's not so.
Mer. I mean, sir, in delay
We waste our lights in vain, like lamps by day.
Take our good meaning, for our judgment sits
Five times in that ere once in our five wits.
Rom. And we mean well, in going to this masque;
But 'tis no wit to go.
Mer. Why, may one ask?
Rom. I dreamt a dream tonight.
Mer. And so did I.
Rom. Well, what was yours?
Mer. That dreamers often lie.
Rom. In bed asleep, while they do dream things true.

MERC: Because you are sinking in it, you are turning love into something oppressive. But love is a tender thing, Romeo.

ROMEO: You say that love is tender, but the truth is that love hurts.

MERC: If it's so rough for you, then be rough with love! Beat love down. Somebody give me a mask to wear for the party. What do I care if some perceptive guests recognize this ugly face? The brows drawn on the mask will look embarrassed for me.

BEN: Let's go. We will knock on the door, get inside, and it's every man for himself.

ROMEO: I need a torch. Let those who are light-hearted do the dancing. I am going to follow the old proverb that advises some of us to be observers. I am too tired to play any kind of game.

MERC: Be quiet as a mouse, as the constable said. If you don't make a spectacle of yourself, we'll be able to help you when you are up to your ears in the swamp called love.

ROMEO: No, that isn't so.

MERC: What I mean, Romeo, is that by standing here we are wasting our time as much as we would if we burned lamps in the daylight. Listen to what I say and understand what I mean. We are judged by our reputation five times more than we are judged by our intelligence.

ROMEO: Our intentions are good in going to the party, but it probably isn't a very smart thing to do.

MERC: May I ask why?

ROMEO: Because I had a dream last night.

MERC: And so did I.

ROMEO: Well, what was your dream about?

MERC: That people who dream often lie.

ROMEO: Yes, they lie in bed asleep, and make their fantasies come true in their dreams.

Mer. O, then I see Queen Mab hath been with you.
She is the fairies' midwife, and she comes
In shape no bigger than an agate stone
On the forefinger of an alderman,
Drawn with a team of little atomies
Athwart men's noses as they lie asleep;
Her wagon spokes made of long spinners' legs,
The cover, of the wings of grasshoppers;
Her traces, of the smallest spider's web;
Her collars, of the moonshine's wat'ry beams;
Her whip, of cricket's bone; the lash, of film;
Her wagoner, a small grey-coated gnat,
Not half so big as a round little worm
Pricked from the lazy finger of a maid;
Her chariot is an empty hazelnut,
Made by the joiner squirrel or old grub,
Time out o' mind the fairies' coachmakers.
And in this state she gallops night by night
Through lovers' brains, and then they dream of love;
O'er courtiers' knees, that dream on curtsies straight;
O'er lawyers' fingers, who straight dream on fees;
O'er ladies' lips, who straight on kisses dream,
Which oft the angry Mab with blisters plagues,
Because their breaths with sweetmeats tainted are.
Sometime she gallops o'er a courtier's nose,
And then dreams he of smelling out a suit;
And sometime comes she with a tithe-pig's tail
Tickling a parson's nose as 'a lies asleep,
Then dreams he of another benefice.
Sometime she driveth o'er a soldier's neck,
And then dreams he of cutting foreign throats,
Of breaches, ambuscadoes, Spanish blades,
Of healths five fathom deep; and then anon

ACT I, Scene 4

MERC: Oh then, I see that Queen Mab, the queen of the fairies, has visited you. She acts as a midwife to the fairies, and she is no bigger than a large, jeweled ring on the forefinger of a city councilman, pulled by a team of tiny creatures, astride the noses of men as they sleep. Her wagon spokes are made of long spiders' legs; the wagon's cover is made of grasshoppers' wings: her harness is made of the smallest spider's web; her collars, of misty moonbeams; her whip is the bone of a cricket; the lash, of spider's thread; her driver is a small, gray-coated gnat who is only half as large as a small, round worm that is said to grow on the fingers of lazy young girls. The chariot is an empty hazelnut, made by a squirrel or a grub, both known for their woodworking abilities, who, since the beginning of time, made the fairies' coaches. And in her magnificence she gallops every night through the lovers' brains, and then they dream of love; she drives her wagon over the royal attendants' knees and then they dream of bowing properly; over lawyers' fingers who immediately afterward dream of how much money they will make; over ladies' lips, who quickly dream of kisses; but often the Fairy Queen Mab will cause those lips to blister because the ladies' breaths are heavy from eating too many sweets. She gallops over a royal attendant's nose, and then he dreams of smelling out special favors from the royal monarch. Sometimes she tickles the parson's nose with the tail of the pig which is a contribution from one of his parishoners. Then he dreams of making a good living from having a steady income. Sometimes she drives over the neck of a soldier, and then he dreams of cutting foreign throats, and of breaches in defense, ambushes, and Spanish swords; of tall drinks, and then soon

Drums in his ear, at which he starts and wakes,
And being thus frighted, swears a prayer or two
And sleeps again. This is that very Mab
That plaits the manes of horses in the night
And bakes the elflocks in foul sluttish hairs,
Which once untangled much misfortune bodes.
This is the hag, when maids lie on their backs,
That presses them and learns them first to bear,
Making them women of good carriage.
This is she—
Rom. Peace, peace, Mercutio, peace!
Thou talkst of nothing.
Mer. True, I talk of dreams;
Which are the children of an idle brain,
Begot of nothing but vain fantasy;
Which is as thin of substance as the air,
And more inconstant than the wind, who woos
Even now the frozen bosom of the North
And, being angered, puffs away from thence,
Turning his face to the dew-dropping South.
Ben. This wind you talk of blows us from ourselves.
Supper is done, and we shall come too late.
Rom. I fear, too early; for my mind misgives
Some consequence, yet hanging in the stars,
Shall bitterly begin his fearful date
With this night's revels and expire the term
Of a despised life, closed in my breast,
By some vile forfeit of untimely death.
But he that hath the steerage of my course
Direct my sail! On, lusty gentlemen!
Ben. Strike, drum.
They march about the stage. [*Exeunt.*]

he hears drums which frighten and waken him; and being frightened, he says a prayer or two, and falls asleep again. This is the same Mab, the Fairy Queen, who braids the horses' manes every night and mats the tangled hairs which, when untangled, tell of bad things to come. This is the nightmare, when young women lie on their backs, that teaches them to support the weight of a lover, which makes them women of good standing. This is she who improves the posture of these women as well. This is she—

ROMEO: Calm down, Mercutio. You're getting excited over nothing.

MERC: Yes, it's true I talk about dreams, which are the product of an idle brain—they are nothing but fantasy, as thin as the air and as changeable as the wind that courts the frozen North. And in an angry moment, it turns its face to the rainy South.

BEN: All this talk of winds is delaying our arrival. Supper will be over, and we will be there too late to eat.

ROMEO: I think we will be too early. I have the feeling that something awful is going to happen starting at the Capulet party which will cause my life to end too soon. But fate has guided my life up till now and will continue to do so. Let's go, gentlemen.

BEN: Strike the drum.

(They march about the stage. They leave.)

[Scene V. Capulet's house.]
Servingmen come forth with napkins.

1.Serv. Where's Potpan, that he helps not to take away? He shift a trencher! he scrape a trencher!

2.Serv. When good manners shall lie all in one or two men's hands, and they unwashed too, 'tis a foul thing.

1.Serv. Away with the joint-stools, remove the court-cupboard, look to the plate. Good thou, save me a piece of marchpane and, as thou lovest me, let the porter let in Susan Grindstone and Nell. Anthony, and Potpan!

2.Serv. Ay, boy, ready.

1.Serv. You are looked for and called for, asked for and sought for, in the great chamber.

3.Serv. We cannot be here and there too. Cheerly, boys! Be brisk awhile, and the longer liver take all.

Exeunt.

[*Maskers* appear with *Capulet, his* Wife, Juliet, all the *Guests,* and *Servants.*]

Cap. Welcome, gentlemen! Ladies that have their toes
Unplagued with corns will have a bout with you.
Ah ha, my mistresses! which of you all
Will now deny to dance? She that makes dainty,
She I'll swear hath corns. Am I come near ye now?
Welcome, gentlemen! I have seen the day
That I have worn a visor and could tell
A whispering tale in a fair lady's ear,
Such as would please. 'Tis gone, 'tis gone, 'tis gone!
You are welcome, gentlemen! Come, musicians, play.
A hall, a hall! give room! and foot it, girls.

Music plays, and they dance.

ACT I

(Scene 5: A hall in CAPULET'S house.)

(MUSICIANS are waiting. Enter SERVANTS with napkins.)

SERV. 1: Where's the fool who's supposed to help me who isn't here yet? He's supposed to move and scrape these wooden platters.

SERV.2: It's too bad that we have to rely upon men who are ill-mannered and unwashed.

SERV.1: Take the stools away, get the sideboard out of the way, tend to the silver platters; and if you have any feeling for me, save me a piece of candy. And, if you care about me, let in the other servants. Let the Porter bring in Susan Grindstone and Nell. (Calls to other SERVANTS.) Anthony and Potpan!

SERV.2: All right, boy, I'm ready.

SERV.1: Everybody's looking for you, calling for you, and searching for you in the large dining hall.

SERV. 3: We can't be every place at once. Let's be cheerful, boys, and move as quickly as we can. And the one who lives the longest will have it all.

(SERVANTS leave.)

(Enter LORD CAPULET, with JULIET, LADY CAPULET, GUESTS and SERVANTS.)

LORD CAP: Welcome, gentlemen! The ladies who don't have corns on their feet will dance with you. Ah ha, ladies! Which of you will refuse to dance? She who pretends to be shy must, I swear, have corns. Have I come close to the truth now? Welcome, gentlemen! I remember when I was young and wore a mask at a ball such as this, and whispered something pleasant in a pretty lady's ear. Those days are gone forever. You are welcome, gentlemen! Come musicians play. Clear the hall for dancing. Let's get those feet moving, girls!

(Music plays, and they dance.)

More light, you knaves! and turn the tables up,
And quench the fire, the room is grown too hot.
Ah, sirrah, this unlooked-for sport comes well.
Nay, sit, nay, sit, good cousin Capulet,
For you and I are past our dancing days.
How long is't now since last yourself and I
Were in a mask?
2.Cap. By'r Lady, thirty years.
Cap. What, man? 'Tis not so much, 'tis not so much!
'Tis since the nuptial of Lucentio,
Come Pentecost as quickly as it will,
Some five-and-twenty years, and then we masked.
2.Cap. 'Tis more, 'tis more! His son is elder, sir;
His son is thirty.
Cap. Will you tell me that?
His son was but a ward two years ago.
Rom. [*To a Servingman*] What lady's that, which doth enrich the hand
Of yonder knight?
Serv. I know not, sir.
Rom. O, she doth teach the torches to burn bright!
It seems she hangs upon the cheek of night
Like a rich jewel in an Ethiop's ear—
Beauty too rich for use, for earth too dear!
So shows a snowy dove trooping with crows
As yonder lady o'er her fellows shows.
The measure done, I'll watch her place of stand
And, touching hers, make blessed my rude hand.
Did my heart love till now? Forswear it, sight!
For I ne'er saw true beauty till this night.
Tyb. This, by his voice, should be a Montague.
Fetch me my rapier, boy. What, dares the slave
Come hither, covered with an antic face,
To fleer and scorn at our solemnity?

Let's have more light, you rascals, and move the tables out of the way. Put out the fire because the room is too hot. The party crashers are here with their masks on. My dear relative, good cousin, Capulet, let us sit down because you and I are past our dancing days. How long has it been since you and I were wearing masks?

CAP.2: It's been about thirty years.

LORD CAP: What do you mean, man? It hasn't been that long. We last wore masks as young men at Lucentio's wedding which will be twenty-five years ago this Pentecost.

CAP.2: No, it's longer than that because Lucentio's son is thirty years old.

LORD CAP: Are you sure? His son was still a child two years ago.

ROMEO: (To a SERVANT.) Who is that lady who gives richness to the hand of that knight by simply holding it?

SERVANT: I don't know, sir.

ROMEO: Oh, she is so radiant that she could teach the torches how to burn! When you contrast her fairness against the darkness of night, she is like a rich jewel in an Ethiopian's ear—her beauty is not of this world. To see her with the others is like watching a snowy dove tripping among black crows. When the music is over, I will watch where she is standing and by touching her hand I will bless mine. Did my heart ever love till now? My eyes deceived me because I never saw true beauty till this night.

TYBALT: (Overhearing ROMEO.) I can tell by his voice, this man who is speaking is a Montague. Get me my sword, boy. How does he dare to come here, with a mask on his face, to mock and ridicule us at our party?

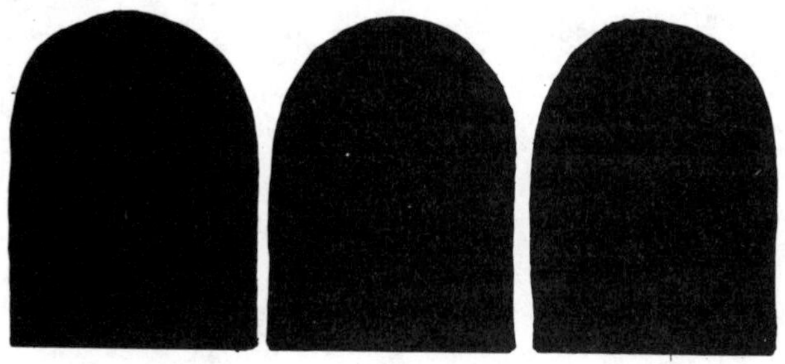

Now, by the stock and honor of my kin,
To strike him dead I hold it not a sin.
Cap. Why, how now, kinsman? Wherefore storm you so?
Tyb. Uncle, this is a Montague, our foe;
A villain, that is hither come in spite
To scorn at our solemnity this night.
Cap. Young Romeo is it?
Tyb. 'Tis he, that villain Romeo.
Cap. Content thee, gentle coz, let him alone.
'A bears him like a portly gentleman,
And, to say truth, Verona brags of him
To be a virtuous and well-governed youth.
I would not for the wealth of all this town
Here in my house do him disparagement.
Therefore be patient, take no note of him.
It is my will; the which if thou respect,
Show a fair presence and put off these frowns,
An ill-beseeming semblance for a feast.
Tyb. It fits when such a villain is a guest.
I'll not endure him.
Cap. He shall be endured.
What, goodman boy? I say he shall. Go to!
Am I the master here, or you? Go to!
You'll not endure him? God shall mend my soul!
You'll make a mutiny among my guests!
You will set cock-a-hoop! you'll be the man!
Tyb. Why, uncle, 'tis a shame.
Cap. Go to, go to!
You are a saucy boy. Is't so, indeed?
This trick may chance to scathe you. I know what.
You must contrary me! Marry, 'tis time.—
Well said, my hearts!—You are a princox—go!

Now, in honor of my relatives, I will use my sword to strike him dead and not consider it sinful.

LORD CAP: Why, Tybalt! Why are you getting so agitated?

TYBALT: Uncle, that guest over there is a Montague. He is a villain like the others, and he has come here to make fun of the festivities tonight.

LORD CAP: Is it young Romeo?

TYBALT: Yes, it is that villain Romeo.

LORD CAP: Calm yourself, gentle nephew, and leave him alone. He is acting like a gentleman and, to tell you the truth, they say very good things about him in Verona. He is a good and well-behaved young man. I would not for all the money in this town insult him in my home. Therefore, be patient and ignore him. It is my decision, and if you respect me, you will stop acting this way and act appropriately. You are a guest at my party!

TYBALT: But the way I act *is* appropriate when such a villain is a guest in this house. I won't stand for this.

LORD CAP: Oh, yes you will! Remember, boy, I say that you will. And am I the master here, or are you? You're telling me you won't tolerate him? God help me, you'll cause a riot here, if given your way. You are reckless and uncontrolled. You will make a shambles of this party because of your arrogance!

TYBALT: Why Uncle, it's a shame that you should take this attitude.

LORD CAP: Go, you insolent boy. This habit you have of quarreling may bring harm to you. I know what I'm talking about. Everything I say you argue with. By the Virgin Mary, I've had enough. And I mean what I say. You are a conceited and overbearing boy. Go!

Be quiet, or—More light, more light!—For shame!
I'll make you quiet; what!—Cheerly, my hearts!
Tyb. Patience perforce with willful choler meeting
Makes my flesh tremble in their different greeting.
I will withdraw; but this intrusion shall,
Now seeming sweet, convert to bitter gall. *Exit.*
Rom. If I profane with my unworthiest hand
This holy shrine, the gentle fine is this:
My lips, two blushing pilgrims, ready stand
To smooth that rough touch with a tender kiss.
Jul. Good pilgrim, you do wrong your hand too much,
Which mannerly devotion shows in this;
For saints have hands that pilgrims' hands do touch,
And palm to palm is holy palmers' kiss.
Rom. Have not saints lips, and holy palmers too?
Jul. Ay, pilgrim, lips that they must use in prayer.
Rom. O, then, dear saint, let lips do what hands do!
They pray; grant thou, lest faith turn to despair.
Jul. Saints do not move, though grant for prayers' sake.
Rom. Then move not while my prayer's effect I take.
Thus from my lips, by thine my sin is purged. [*Kisses her.*]
Jul. Then have my lips the sin that they have took.
Rom. Sin from my lips? O trespass sweetly urged!
Give me my sin again. [*Kisses her.*]
Jul. You kiss by the book.
Nurse. Madam, your mother craves a word with you.
Rom. What is her mother?
Nurse. Marry, bachelor,
Her mother is the lady of the house.
And a good lady, and a wise and virtuous.
I nursed her daughter that you talked withal.
I tell you, he that can lay hold of her
Shall have the chinks.
Rom. Is she a Capulet?

Be quiet, Tybalt, or—hey! Let's have more light in here. Servants!—So, Tybalt, I'll have no more of this, and I want you to stop making such a fuss. (Turns to GUESTS.) Are you having a good time? Enjoy yourselves.

TYBALT: Such enforced restraint in such an unbearable situation makes me shake all over. I'll back down now; but later this seemingly sweet resignation will turn to bitter fury. (TYBALT leaves.)

ROMEO: (To JULIET) If I dare dishonor you with my unworthy hand it would be a sin, for you are like a holy shrine. Were I to touch you, my lips, like two blushing pilgrims, stand ready to smooth my rough touch with a tender kiss.

JULIET: Good Pilgrim, you make too much of the roughness of your hand, for you are truly extending good manners and devotion. Remember that pilgrims touch the hands of saints and palm touching palm is like a holy pilgrim's kiss.

(They touch palms.)

ROMEO: But saints have lips, don't they? And don't holy pilgrims have lips, too?

JULIET: Oh, yes, pilgrims have lips, but those are used in prayer.

ROMEO: Well then, dear saint, let lips do what hands do. Let them also touch. Hands pray and lips pray. So please grant me that. Otherwise you will turn my faith into unhappiness.

JULIET: Remember that saints do not interfere in the affairs of humans. However, they may be convinced by prayer to grant wishes.

ROMEO: Then don't move, dear saint, and grant the wishes of my prayer. From my lips to yours, my sin will be washed away. (Kisses JULIET.)

JULIET: Then kiss my lips for the sin they have taken. Now my lips have taken the sin away from your lips.

ROMEO: You have taken the sin from my lips? Then do it again and give me back my sin again. (Kisses JULIET again.)

JULIET: You kiss as if you had studied the art of kissing and know all the rules.

NURSE: Juliet, your mother wants to talk to you.

ROMEO: Who is her mother?

NURSE: By the Virgin Mary, young man, her mother is Lady Capulet, who is good and wise and virtuous. I am the Nurse of Juliet, the girl you spoke with out here. I can tell you this: whoever marries her will be very rich because her father's a wealthy man.

ROMEO: Is Juliet the daughter of the Capulets?

O dear account! my life is my foe's debt.
Ben. Away, be gone, the sport is at the best.
Rom. Ay, so I fear; the more is my unrest.
Cap. Nay, gentlemen, prepare not to be gone;
We have a trifling foolish banquet towards.
They whisper in his ear.
Is it e'en so? Why then, I thank you all.
I thank you, honest gentlemen. Good night.
More torches here! [*Exeunt Maskers.*] Come on then, let's to bed.
Ah, sirrah, by my fay, it waxes late;
I'll to my rest. *Exeunt [all but Juliet and Nurse].*
Jul. Come hither, nurse. What is yond gentleman?
Nurse. The son and heir of old Tiberio.
Jul. What's he that now is going out of door?
Nurse. Marry, that, I think, be young Petruchio.
Jul. What's he that follows there, that would not dance?
Nurse. I know not.
Jul. Go ask his name—If he be married,
My grave is like to be my wedding bed.
Nurse. His name is Romeo, and a Montague,
The only son of your great enemy.
Jul. My only love, sprung from my only hate!
Too early seen unknown, and known too late!
Prodigious birth of love it is to me
That I must love a loathed enemy.
Nurse. What's this? what's this?
Jul. A rhyme I learnt even now
Of one I danced withal.
one calls within, "Juliet."
Nurse. Anon, anon!
Come, let's away; the strangers all are gone.
Exeunt.

Oh—I can't stand this. What a price to pay! My happiness is in the hands of my enemy.

BEN: (Approaches ROMEO.) Go home, Romeo. This a good time for you to leave!

ROMEO: I am afraid you are right and my fears would increase if I were to stay longer!

LORD CAP: Wait, gentlemen. Don't leave just yet. We have some light refreshments coming. (Someone whispers in CAPULET's ear that there are no refreshments.) (To the whisperer.) Oh, is that so? (To the GUESTS) Why, then I thank you all. Thank you, honest gentlemen, and I bid you all good night. Let's have some torchlight over here! (Guests leave.) It's time for bed. It's getting late. I need some rest. (All leave but JULIET and NURSE.)

JULIET: Nurse, come here and tell me who that gentleman is over there?

NURSE: That is the oldest son of the old man, Tiberio.

JULIET: And who is that who is just going out the door?

NURSE: I think that is young Petruchio.

JULIET: And who is the man over there who refused to dance? (She points to ROMEO.)

NURSE: I don't know.

JULIET: Ask him what his name is. I will die if he is already married. My wedding bed will be a grave if I have to marry someone else.

NURSE: (Giving in to JULIET's persistence) His name is Romeo and he is the only son of the Montagues who are the great enemies of your family.

JULIET: Oh, no! The only person that I choose to love has come from the only family we despise. I didn't see this coming at all, and now that I know who he is, it is too late, for I have already fallen in love with him. My love for him is monstrous and can only bring bad luck because I love a hated enemy.

NURSE: What are you talking about? What are you saying?

JULIET: I was just reciting a little poem about someone I danced with.

(A voice from the house calls, "Juliet.")

NURSE: Right away, right away. Come let's go. Everyone has left. (They leave.)

[PROLOGUE]

[Enter *Chorus.*]

Chor. Now old desire doth in his deathbed lie,
And young affection gapes to be his heir;
That fair for which love groaned for and would die,
With tender Juliet matched, is now not fair.
Now Romeo is beloved, and loves again,
Alike bewitched by the charm of looks;
But to his foe supposed he must complain,
And she steal love's sweet bait from fearful hooks.
Being held a foe, he may not have access
To breathe such vows as lovers use to swear,
And she as much in love, her means much less
To meet her new beloved anywhere;
But passion lends them power, time means, to meet,
Temp'ring extremities with extreme sweet.

[*Exit.*]

[ACT II]

[Scene I. A lane by the wall of Capulet's orchard.]

Enter *Romeo* alone.

Rom. Can I go forward when my heart is here?
Turn back, dull earth, and find thy center out.
[*Climbs the wall and leaps down within it.*]

ACT II
PROLOGUE

(Enter CHORUS.)

CHORUS: Romeo's desire for Rosaline has died now that he has seen Juliet whose beauty pales all others in comparison. Now Romeo's love is returned and the ardor and admiration between the two is reciprocated. Each is bewitched by the charm of the other's face. If Romeo should complain of the pain of loving her, he should remember that Juliet, too, faces danger for loving him. Because she is a member of the enemy Capulets, he may not have the opportunity to say the things to her that lovers do. Juliet returns his feelings deeply but, because she is a girl, does not have the freedom to meet him wherever she pleases. However, passion lends them the power and the determination to find a way to meet. The complexities of this relationship are lessened by the sweetness they experience once they are together.

(CHORUS leaves.)

ACT II

(Scene 1: A lane by the wall of CAPULET'S orchard.)

(Enter ROMEO, alone.)

ROMEO: How can I go anywhere when my heart is here? I cannot leave because the center of my universe is here. (He climbs the wall and jumps down the other side into the orchard.)

[*Enter Benvolio and Mercutio*]

Ben. Romeo! my cousin Romeo! Romeo!
Mer. He is wise,
And, on my life, hath stol'n him home to bed.
Ben. He ran this way, and leapt this orchard wall.
Call, good Mercutio.
Mer. Nay, I'll conjure too.
Romeo! humors! madman! passion! lover!
Appear thou in the likeness of a sigh;
Speak but one rhyme, and I am satisfied!
Cry but "Ay me!" pronounce but "love" and "dove";
Speak to my gossip Venus one fair word,
One nickname for her purblind son and heir,
Young Adam Cupid, he that shot so trim
When King Cophetua loved the beggar maid!
He heareth not, he stirreth not, he moveth not;
The ape is dead, and I must conjure him.
I conjure thee by Rosaline's bright eyes,
By her high forehead and her scarlet lip,
By her fine foot, straight leg, and quivering thigh,
And the demesnes that there adjacent lie,
That in thy likeness thou appear to us!
Ben. An if he hear thee, thou wilt anger him.
Mer. This cannot anger him. 'Twould anger him
To raise a spirit in his mistress' circle
Of some strange nature, letting it there stand
Till she had laid it and conjured it down.
That were some spite; my invocation
Is fair and honest: in his mistress' name,
I conjure only but to raise up him.
Ben. Come, he hath hid himself among these trees
To be consorted with the humorous night.
Blind is his love and best befits the dark.

ACT II, Scene 1

(Enter BENVOLIO with MERCUTIO. Exit ROMEO.)

BEN: Romeo! My cousin, Romeo! Romeo!

MERC: He is wise, I'm sure, and has gone home to bed.

BEN: He ran this way and jumped over the orchard wall. Call him, Mercutio.

MERC: No, if I do, I'll conjure up a spirit, too. Romeo! Whimisical one! Madman! Passionate lover! Let me just hear your voice. Sigh for me or say a rhyme for me and I'll be satisfied. Just say the words of love, like "Ah me!" or say "love" and "dove." Say one word to Venus, the goddess of love, and give me one nickname for her blindfolded son and heir, Cupid. It was Cupid, the very same who shot his arrows right into the heart of Cophetua, the king who fell in love with a beggar girl, according to that song we've heard and know so well. Apparently, Romeo doesn't hear, he doesn't stir, he doesn't move! Like a trained ape, Romeo is dead and I must conjure up his spirit. What shall I use to do this? I'll use Rosaline's bright eyes and her high forehead, her red lips and her pretty feet, her fine legs, and quivering thighs, and the lovely area near her thighs. Once we have Rosaline's likeness here, Romeo is sure to come running to us.

BEN: If Romeo hears your teasing, Mercutio, he is sure to be angry.

MERC: This won't make him angry. If someone else were making love to Rosaline, now that would certainly make him angry! That would really be an outrage. My intentions in invoking Romeo are fair and honest; and the only reason I am using Rosaline's name is so that Romeo will come out of hiding and show himself to us.

BEN: Come on, Romeo has hidden himself among the trees to keep company with the mood of night. His love is blind, which makes him fit well into the darkness.

Mer. If love be blind, love cannot hit the mark.
Now will he sit under a medlar tree
And wish his mistress were that kind of fruit
As maids call medlars when they laugh alone.
O, Romeo, that she were, O that she were
An open et cetera, thou a pop'rin pear!
Romeo, good night. I'll to my truckle bed;
This field-bed is too cold for me to sleep.
Come, shall we go?
Ben. Go then, for 'tis in vain
To seek him here that means not to be found.
Exeunt.

[Scene II. Capulet's orchard.]

[Enter *Romeo.*]

Rom. He jests at scars that never felt a wound.

[Enter *Juliet* above at a window.]

But soft! What light through yonder window breaks?
It is the East, and Juliet is the sun!
Arise, fair sun, and kill the envious moon,
Who is already sick and pale with grief
That thou her maid art far more fair than she.
Be not her maid, since she is envious;
Her vestal livery is but sick and green,
And none but fools do wear it; cast it off.
It is my lady; O, it is my love!
O that she knew she were!
She speaks, yet she says nothing. What of that?
Her eye discourses; I will answer it.

MERC: If love is blind, it cannot hit what it is aiming for. Now Romeo will probably sit under a tree of small, brown apples which will remind him of the fruit of love. He will wish that Rosaline were as accessible as the fruit of the tree, and he will hope to be the one to pick that fruit. Good night, Romeo. I am on my way to bed because it is too cold out here to sleep. Come, Benvolio, shall we go?

BEN: Yes, let's go because it is useless for us to try to find him here.

(MERCUTIO and BENVOLIO leave. Enter ROMEO.)

ACT II

(Scene 2: CAPULET'S orchard.)

(Enter ROMEO.)

ROMEO: It is easy to laugh at someone else's pain when you have never been hurt yourself. (JULIET appears above at a window.)
Hush, I see light coming through that window up above. The light comes from the east, and Juliet is the sun. Arise, fair sun, and kill the moon who is envious of your light and beauty. You are more fair than she. Do not be loyal to the moon, nor serve her, because the moon is also Diana, the goddess of virginity. The virginal clothes she wears are sick and green and only fools would wear them. Don't wear them. Cast them off! I see my lady, Juliet; I see my love. Oh, if only she knew. She speaks, but I cannot hear her. Why is that? Her eyes seem to say something, too. I will answer her.

I am too bold; 'tis not to me she speaks.
Two of the fairest stars in all the heaven,
Having some business, do entreat her eyes
To twinkle in their spheres till they return.
What if her eyes were there, they in her head?
The brightness of her cheek would shame those stars
As daylight doth a lamp; here eyes in heaven
Would through the airy region stream so bright
That birds would sing and think it were not night.
See how she leans her cheek upon her hand!
O that I were a glove upon that hand,
That I might touch that cheek!
Jul. Ay me!
Rom. She speaks.
O, speak again, bright angel! for thou art
As glorious to this night, being o'er my head,
As is a winged messenger of heaven
Unto the white-upturned wond'ring eyes
Of mortals that fall back to gaze on him
When he bestrides the lazy-pacing clouds
And sails upon the bosom of the air.
Jul. O Romeo, Romeo! Wherefore art thou Romeo?
Deny thy father and refuse thy name!
Or, if thou wilt not, be but sworn my love,
And I'll no longer be a Capulet.
Rom. [*Aside*] Shall I hear more, or shall I speak at this?
Jul. 'Tis but thy name that is my enemy.
Thou art thyself, though not a Montague.
What's Montague? It is nor hand, nor foot,
Nor arm, nor face, nor any other part
Belonging to a man. O, be some other name!
What's in a name? That which we call a rose
By any other name would smell as sweet.
So Romeo would, were he not Romeo called,

ACT II, Scene 2

No, I will seem too bold because I know she is not speaking to me. If two of the fairest stars in all of heaven had to go somewhere else, they would choose Juliet's two eyes for their replacements to twinkle in their place until they could return. Just as daylight puts lamplight to shame—so would the brightness of her cheek put the stars to shame. Her eyes in heaven would radiate such light that the birds would sing and think that it were not night. See how she leans her cheek upon her hand. I wish I were a glove upon that hand so that I could touch her face.

JULIET: Ah me!

ROMEO: I hear her voice. Let me hear it again, bright angel, because you are as beautiful to me as a winged messenger of heaven sailing through the airy clouds above the white upturned wondering eyes of mortals.

JULIET: Romeo, Romeo, why do you have to be Romeo Montague?★ Turn your back on your father and your family name. Or, if you will not, swear that you love me, and I will give up my family's name.

ROMEO: (Aside.) Shall I wait to hear more, or should I speak now?

JULIET: It is only your name that is my enemy. You are still my beloved, even though you are a Montague. What is a Montague? It is neither a hand, nor a foot, nor an arm, nor a face, nor any other part belonging to a man. I wish you had some other name. What is in a name? If we were to call a rose something else, it would still smell as sweet. The same is true with you. You would still be Romeo, no matter what your name might be.

★This line is the most popularly quoted from *Romeo and Juliet* and the most misinterpreted as well. In fact, the word **wherefore** means **why,** hence the meaning, "Oh Romeo, Romeo, why are you Romeo Montague?" It does not ask the question, " . . . where are you?"

Retain that dear perfection which he owes
Without that title. Romeo, doff thy name;
And for that name, which is no part of thee,
Take all myself.
Rom. I take thee at thy word.
Call me but love, and I'll be new baptized;
Henceforth I never will be Romeo.
Jul. What man art thou that, thus bescreened in night,
So stumblest on my counsel?
Rom. By a name
I know not how to tell thee who I am.
My name, dear saint, is hateful to myself,
Because it is an enemy to thee.
Had I it written, I would tear the word.
Jul. My ears have yet not drunk a hundred words
Of that tongue's utterance, yet I know the sound.
Art thou not Romeo, and a Montague?
Rom. Neither, fair saint, if either thee dislike
Jul. How camest thou hither, tell me, and wherefore?
The orchard walls are high and hard to climb,
And the place death, considering who thou art,
If any of my kinsmen find thee here.
Rom. With love's light wings did I o'erperch these walls;
For stony limits cannot hold love out,
And what love can do, that dares love attempt.
Therefore thy kinsmen are no let to me.
Jul. If they do see thee, they will murder thee.
Rom. Alack, there lies more peril in thine eye
Than twenty of their swords! Look thou but sweet,
And I am proof against their enmity.
Jul. I would not for the world they saw thee here.
Rom. I have night's cloak to hide me from their sight;
And but thou love me, let them find me here.

Dear Romeo, give up your name which really does not tell what kind of person you are. And then for having forsaken your name, take all of me.

ROMEO: I believe what you say. Just tell me that you love me. If you will, I will be baptized again and be given a new name. After that I will never again be called Romeo.

JULIET: Who is this I hear, hidden in the darkness? Who is listening to my thoughts?

ROMEO: I don't know how to identify myself. I hate my name because it is the name of your enemy. If I had composed it and written it down on paper, I would tear the word.

JULIET: I haven't heard you speak a hundred words yet, but aren't you Romeo Montague?

ROMEO: I am neither Romeo nor Montague if you dislike either name.

JULIET: How did you get here and why did you come? The orchard walls are high and hard to climb. And considering who you are, you could be killed by my relatives if they found you here.

ROMEO: I used love's light wings to fly over these orchard walls. High stone walls cannot keep love out. Love can do many things, once it tries. So your relatives are no obstacle to me.

JULIET: If they see you here, they will kill you.

ROMEO: I regret that there is more danger in your eyes than in twenty of their swords. Your sweet face will protect me against their hostility.

JULIET: I wouldn't want them to find you for all the world.

ROMEO: The night is like a cloak and I hide in its darkness. They won't see me. Unless you love me, my life isn't worth anything.

My life were better ended by their hate
Than death prorogued, wanting of thy love.
Jul. By whose direction foundst thou out this place?
Rom. By love, that first did prompt me to enquire.
He lent me counsel, and I lent him eyes.
I am no pilot, yet, wert thou as far
As that vast shore washed with the farthest sea,
I would adventure for such merchandise.
Jul. Thou knowest the mask of night is on my face;
Else would a maiden blush bepaint my cheek
For that which thou hast heard me speak tonight.
Fain would I dwell on form—fain, fain deny
What I have spoke; but farewell compliment!
Dost thou love me? I know thou wilt say "Ay";
And I will take thy word. Yet, if thou swearst,
Thou mayst prove false. At lovers' perjuries,
They say Jove laughs. O gentle Romeo,
If thou dost love, pronounce it faithfully.
Or if thou thinkst I am too quickly won,
I'll frown, and be perverse, and say thee nay,
So thou wilt woo; but else, not for the world.
In truth, fair Montague, I am too fond,
And therefore thou mayst think my 'havior light;
But trust me, gentleman, I'll prove more true
Than those that have more cunning to be strange.
I should have been more strange, I must confess,
But that thou overheardst, ere I was ware,
My true love's passion. Therefore pardon me,
And not impute this yielding to light love,
Which the dark night hath so discovered.
Rom. Lady, by yonder blessed moon I swear,
That tips with silver all these fruit-tree tops—
Jul. O, swear not by the moon, the inconstant moon,

If I couldn't have your love, my life would be better ended by their hate.

JULIET: How did you find your way here?

ROMEO: I first asked Cupid. He gave me advice and I showed him the way here. I don't know the ways of the sea, but if you were on the farthest shore of the farthest sea, I would venture forth to find you.

JULIET: I know my face is hidden by the night; otherwise, you would see me blush. The words you have overheard me speak tonight embarrass me. I could have gladly behaved according to social rules and denied that I had said these things, but it is too late for polite behavior. Do you love me? I know you will say yes and I will take you at your word and believe you. But you still might not be telling the truth. The ancient god Jove laughs when lovers lie. Oh, gentle Romeo, if you do love me, then tell me truthfully. But if you think I am easily won, I will change my disposition and be difficult in order to make you court me properly. Of course I would not do that under any other circumstances. In truth, I love you too much and am concerned that you might think my behavior unbecoming. But have faith in me, for I will be more sincere in my love than those who pretend to be indifferent. I should have been more distant, I must confess, but you overheard me before I knew it. You overheard the passion of my love, so pardon me and do not think that what you heard revealed in the darkness was superficial love.

ROMEO: I swear by the blessed moon which paints these fruit trees with silver—

JULIET: Oh, don't swear by the fickle moon. The moon changes each month.

That monthly changes in her circled orb,
Lest that thy love prove likewise variable.
Rom. What shall I swear by?
Jul. Do not swear at all;
Or if thou wilt, swear by thy gracious self,
Which is the god of my idolatry,
And I'll believe thee.
Rom. If my heart's dear love—
Jul. Well, do not swear. Although I joy in thee,
I have no joy of this contract tonight.
It is too rash, too unadvised, too sudden;
Too like the lightning, which doth cease to be
Ere one can say "It lightens." Sweet, good night!
This bud of love, by summer's ripening breath,
May prove a beauteous flow'r when next we meet.
Good night, good night! As sweet repose and rest
Come to thy heart as that within my breast!
Rom. O, wilt thou leave me so unsatisfied?
Jul. What satisfaction canst thou have tonight?
Rom. The exchange of thy love's faithful vow for mine.
Jul. I gave thee mine before thou didst request it;
And yet I would it were to give again.
Rom. Wouldst thou withdraw it? For what purpose, love?
Jul. But to be frank and give it thee again.
And yet I wish but for the thing I have.
My bounty is as boundless as the sea,
My love as deep; the more I give to thee,
The more I have, for both are infinite.
I hear some noise within. Dear love, adieu!
[*Nurse*] *calls within.*
Anon, good nurse! Sweet Montague, be true.
Stay but a little, I will come again. [*Exit.*]

So don't swear by the moon unless your love is going to be changeable, too.

ROMEO: What shall I swear by?

JULIET: Don't swear at all. Or if you do swear by anything, swear by your gracious self, because I idolize you. You are my god and I believe you.

ROMEO: If you feel this way—

JULIET: Well, do not swear. Although I enjoy you, I would not be pleased with a marriage contract tonight. It is too quick; we haven't had a chance to consider what we are doing. It reminds me too much of lightning which disappears before you can say, "Look at the lightning." Good night, my sweetheart. The next time we meet this bud of love will have had a chance to ripen into a beautiful flower. Good night, good night. May you feel the same sense of peace as I do.

ROMEO: Will you leave me so unsatisfied?

JULIET: What more can you expect from me tonight?

ROMEO: Let us exchange vows of love.

JULIET: I gave you mine before you even asked for it. And yet I wish I could give it again.

ROMEO: Would you take your vow back? Why would you do that?

JULIET: Just to be generous and give it to you again. The thing that I want is what I already have: your love. The gift of your love is as boundless as the sea, and the more I love you, the deeper my love becomes. The more I give to you, the more I have, because my love and the sea are both infinite. I hear some noise inside. Goodbye, dear love.

(NURSE calls from within.)

In a moment, good Nurse. Sweet Montague, be patient. Stay here awhile and I will return quickly.

(Exit JULIET.)

Rom. O blessed, blessed night! I am afeard,
Being in night, all this is but a dream,
Too flattering-sweet to be substantial.

[Re-enter *Juliet* above.]

Jul. Three words, dear Romeo, and good night indeed.
If that thy bent of love be honorable,
Thy purpose of marriage, send me word tomorrow,
By one that I'll procure to come to thee,
Where and what time thou wilt perform the rite;
And all my fortunes at thy foot I'll lay
And follow thee my lord throughout the world.
Nurse. (Within) Madam!
Jul. I come, anon.—But if thou meanst not well,
I do beseech thee—
Nurse. (Within) Madam!
Jul. By-and-by I come.—
To cease thy suit and leave me to my grief.
Tomorrow will I send.
Rom. So thrive my soul—
Jul. A thousand times good night! *Exit.*
Rom. A thousand times the worse, to want thy light!
Love goes toward love as schoolboys from their books;
But love from love, towards school with heavy looks.

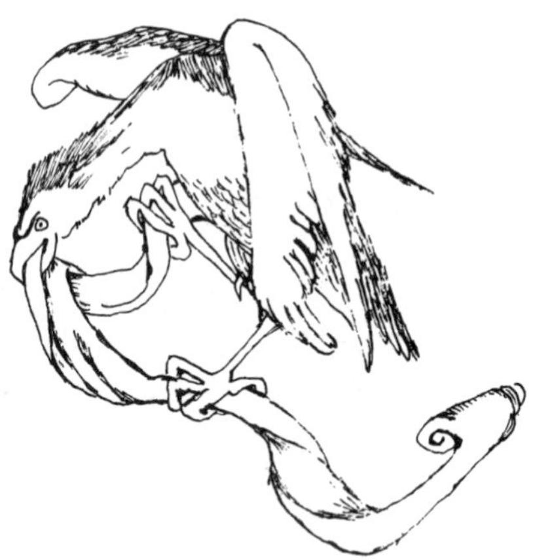

Enter *Juliet* again [, above].

Jul. Hist! Romeo, hist! O for a falc'ner's voice
To lure this tassel-gentle back again!
Bondage is hoarse and may not speak aloud;
Else would I tear the cave where Echo lies,
And make her airy tongue more hoarse than mine

ACT II, Scene 2

ROMEO: Oh blessed, blessed night. I am afraid that all of this is just a dream and too sweet too be real.

(JULIET reenters.)

JULIET: Let me say just a few words more, dear Romeo, and then I'll say good night. If you have honorable intentions, and if you intend to marry me, send me the word tomorrow. I will send a messenger to learn when and where the ceremony will take place. And when that happens, everything I have in the world will be yours and I will follow you, my lord, throughout the world.

NURSE: (From within.) Miss Juliet!

JULIET: (Calling to NURSE.) I am coming at once. (To ROMEO.) But if your intentions are not honorable, I beg you . . .

NURSE: (From within.) Miss Juliet!

JULIET: (To NURSE.) I'm coming, I'm coming! (To ROMEO.) I beg you to stop courting me and then leave me alone in my grief. I will send the messenger to you tomorrow.

ROMEO: I want your messenger to find me tomorrow as much as I want my soul to be saved.

JULIET: A thousand times good night!

(Exit JULIET.)

ROMEO: It is a thousand times worse to want you and be denied. Love is drawn to love as powerfully as schoolboys are repelled by their books. And when love leaves love it is with the same intensity schoolboys feel when they are forced to go to school.

(JULIET reenters.)

JULIET: Oh, if I had the powerful voice of a falconer, I could call my falcon Romeo back again. But I dare not speak aloud because my mother and father might hear. Otherwise, I would find Echo in her cave and make her hoarse

With repetition of my Romeo's name.
Romeo!
Rom. It is my soul that calls upon my name.
How silver-sweet sound lovers' tongues by night,
Like softest music to attending ears!
Jul. Romeo!
Rom. My sweet?
Jul. What o'clock tomorrow
Shall I send to thee?
Rom. By the hour of nine.
Jul. I will not fail. 'Tis twenty years till then.
I have forgot why I did call thee back.
Rom. Let me stand here till thou remember it.
Jul. I shall forget, to have thee still stand there,
Rememb'ring how I love thy company.
Rom. And I'll still stay, to have thee still forget,
Forgetting any other home but this.
Jul. 'Tis almost morning. I would have thee gone—
And yet no farther than a wanton's bird,
That lets it hop a little from her hand,
Like a poor prisoner in his twisted gyves,
And with a silk thread plucks it back again,
So loving-jealous of his liberty.
Rom. I would I were thy bird.
Jul. Sweet, so would I.
Yet I should kill thee with much cherishing.
Good night, good night! Parting is such sweet sorrow,
That I shall say good night till it be morrow. [*Exit.*]
Rom. Sleep dwell upon thine eyes, peace in thy breast!
Would I were sleep and peace, so sweet to rest!
Hence will I to my ghostly father's cell,
His help to crave and my dear hap to tell.
Exit.

by making her repeat my Romeo's name.

ROMEO: Juliet is my soul, and I hear my soul call my name. The voices of lovers make a silvery-sweet sound at night. It is soft music to the ears of those who listen.

JULIET: Romeo?

ROMEO: What is it, my sweet?

JULIET: When shall I send my messenger to you tomorrow?

ROMEO: Nine o'clock in the morning.

JULIET: I will not fail. It will seem like twenty years until then. My wits fail me. I have forgotten why I called you back.

ROMEO: Let me stand here until you remember.

JULIET: If you stand here, I will forget again because I love having you here with me.

ROMEO: And I will stay, though you will still forget; and I will forget that I have any other home but this—here and now.

JULIET: It is almost morning. I wish you would go although I would only want you to go as far as a spoiled child's pet bird. And this small bird, on its leash of silk thread, can only go as far as the child will allow because she pulls it back again—so jealous is she of its liberty.

ROMEO: I wish I were that bird.

JULIET: My sweet, so do I. But I am afraid that I would kill you with love. Good night. Good night. Parting is such sweet sorrow that I shall say good night till it is tomorrow. (JULIET leaves.)

ROMEO: May your eyes be filled with sleep and may you feel peace in your heart. I wish I were both sleep and peace so that I could experience such a sweet resting place. From here I will go to my father confessor to ask for his help and to tell him about my good fortune. (ROMEO leaves.)

[Scene III. Friar Laurence's cell.]

Enter *Friar* [*Laurence*] alone, with a basket.

Friar. The grey-eyed morn smiles on the frowning night,
Chequ'ring the Eastern clouds with streaks of light;
And flecked darkness like a drunkard reels
From forth day's path and Titan's fiery wheels.
Now, ere the sun advance his burning eye
The day to cheer and night's dank dew to dry,
I must up-fill this osier cage of ours
With baleful weeds and precious-juiced flowers.
The earth that's nature's mother is her tomb,
What is her burying grave, that is her womb;
And from her womb children of divers kind
We sucking on her natural bosom find;
Many for many virtues excellent,
None but for some, and yet all different.
O, mickle is the powerful grace that lies
In plants, herbs, stones, and their true qualities;
For naught so vile that on the earth doth live
But to the earth some special good doth give;
Nor aught so good but, strained from that fair use,
Revolts from true birth, stumbling on abuse.
Virtue itself turns vice, being misapplied,
And vice sometime's by action dignified.
Within the infant rind of this small flower
Poison hath residence, and medicine power;
For this, being smelt, with that part cheers each part;
Being tasted, slays all senses with the heart.
Two such opposed kings encamp them still
In man as well as herbs—grace and rude will;

ACT II

(Scene 3: FRIAR LAURENCE'S cell.)

(Enter FRIAR LAURENCE carrying a basket.)

FRIAR: The gray light of day follows the darkness of night. The dark skies are streaked with light from the sun's rays. Now, before it gets too light and the dew dries up, I must fill this willow basket with weeds and flowers. The earth acts both as a womb by helping new life grow and a tomb, for it is the final resting place for things that die. The earth gives birth to many different kinds of life, each one having its own special qualities. There is a mighty power to be found in herbs, plants, and stones. All Creation is made for the good of man, no matter what it may be. It may seem vile or it may be benign. Inside this tiny flower is both poison and medicine. If you smell this flower, its fragrance will cure your sickness; but if you taste it, it will kill you. In both man and herbs, both goodness and evil exist.

And where the worser is predominant,
Full soon the canker death eats up that plant.

Enter *Romeo.*

Rom. Good morrow, father.
Friar. Benedicite!
What early tongue so sweet saluteth me?
Young son, it argues a distempered head
So soon to bid good morrow to thy bed.
Care keeps his watch in every old man's eye,
And where care lodges sleep will never lie;
But where unbruised youth with unstuffed brain
Doth couch his limbs, there golden sleep doth reign.
Therefore thy earliness doth me assure
Thou art uproused with some distemp'rature;
Or if not so, then here I hit it right—
Our Romeo hath not been in bed tonight.
Rom. That last is true, the sweeter rest was mine.
Friar. God pardon sin! Wast thou with Rosaline?
Rom. With Rosaline, my ghostly father? No.
I have forgot that name, and that name's woe.
Friar. That's my good son! But where hast thou been then?
Rom. I'll tell thee ere thou ask it me again.
I have been feasting with mine enemy,
Where on a sudden one hath wounded me
That's by me wounded. Both our remedies
Within thy help and holy physic lies.
I bear no hatred, blessed man, for, lo,
My intercession likewise steads my foe.
Friar. Be plain, good son, and homely in thy drift.
Riddling confession finds but riddling shrift.
Rom. Then plainly know my heart's dear love is set

If evil outweighs goodness in the plant or the man, it will kill the organism.

(Enter ROMEO.)

ROMEO: Good day, Father.

FRIAR: God bless you. Who is saying such a sweet good morning to me so early? To rise so early is the proof of someone who isn't feeling good. Old people are often full of care and they especially have trouble sleeping because they worry so much. But young people with empty brains only have to lie down and they are quickly in a golden sleep. That's why I am sure that your early awakening was caused by some disorder. But if that is not the case with you, then it must mean that you have not been in bed yet tonight.

ROMEO: It's true. I didn't sleep last night, but I had a sweet rest.

FRIAR: May God pardon your sins. Were you with Rosaline?

ROMEO: You ask if I was with Rosaline, my father confessor? The answer is no. I have forgotten her name and all the grief I felt because of her.

FRIAR: That's good, my son. But then where have you been?

ROMEO: I'll tell you before you ask me again. I went to a party given by my enemy where another and I wounded each other. You have the remedy for us both with your holy medicine. I do not bear hatred for my enemy, so please understand, blessed man, that I am asking for your help on behalf of my enemy as well as myself.

FRIAR: Be more direct, my good son. Tell your story in plain English. When you confess your sins in riddles, I must absolve you of those sins in riddles.

ROMEO: Then, in plain words, I want you to know that the dear love of my heart

On the fair daughter of rich Capulet;
As mine on hers, so hers is set on mine,
And all combined, save what thou must combine
By holy marriage. When, and where, and how
We met, we wooed, and made exchange of vow,
I'll tell thee as we pass; but this I pray,
That thou consent to marry us today.
Friar. Holy Saint Francis! What a change is here!
Is Rosaline, that thou didst love so dear,
So soon forsaken? Young men's love then lies
Not truly in their hearts, but in their eyes.
Jesu Maria! What a deal of brine
Hath washed thy sallow cheeks for Rosaline!
How much salt water thrown away in waste,
To season love, that of it doth not taste!
The sun not yet thy sighs from heaven clears,
Thy old groans ring yet in mine ancient ears.
Lo, here upon thy cheek the stain doth sit
Of an old tear that is not washed off yet.
If e'er thou wast thyself, and these woes thine,
Thou and these woes were all for Rosaline.
And art thou changed? Pronounce this sentence then:
Women may fall when there's no strength in men.
Rom. Thou chidst me oft for loving Rosaline.
Friar. For doting, not for loving, pupil mine.
Rom. And badest me bury love.
Friar. Not in a grave
To lay one in, another out to have.
Rom. I pray thee chide not. She whom I love now
Doth grace for grace and love for love allow.
The other did not so.
Friar. O, she knew well
Thy love did read by rote, that could not spell.
But come, young waverer, come go with me.

is the fair daughter of the rich Lord Capulet. My heart is set on hers and hers on mine. We are committed to one another except for having the blessings of the church upon our marriage. I'll tell you later when, where, and how we met and exchanged vows of love; but I hope that you'll agree to marry us today.

FRIAR: Holy Saint Francis! You have certainly changed, Romeo! You loved Rosaline so dearly once, and now you've forgotten her. The love that young men feel is not in their hearts but in their eyes. Jesu Maria! So many saltwater tears have washed down your cheeks for Rosaline and were wasted. All these tears do not seem to have affected you. Your sighs are still heard in heaven and your groans still ring in my old ears. The stain of an old tear is still on your cheek. Before, all of your problems and grief were for Rosaline. And are you changed now? You must agree to this proverb, then: Women may fall when there's no strength in men.

ROMEO: You often scolded me for loving Rosaline.

FRIAR: For being infatuated with Rosaline, not for loving her, my dear pupil.

ROMEO: And you told me to bury this love.

FRIAR: I didn't intend for you to bury one in the grave so you could love another girl.

ROMEO: Don't joke with me. The person whom I love now loves me back. The other did not.

FRIAR: Oh, Rosaline knew that your love was insincere and empty. But come, my changeable young man, come with me.

In one respect I'll thy assistant be;
For this alliance may so happy prove
To turn your households' rancor to pure love.

Rom. O, let us hence! I stand on sudden haste.

Friar. Wisely, and slow. They stumble that run fast.

Exeunt.

[Scene IV. A street.]

Enter Benvolio and *Mercutio.*

Mer. Where the devil should this Romeo be?
Came he not home tonight?

Ben. Not to his father's. I spoke with his man.

Mer. Why, that same pale hard-hearted wench, that Rosaline,
Torments him so that he will sure run mad.

Ben. Tybalt, the kinsman to old Capulet,
Hath sent a letter to his father's house.

Mer. A challenge, on my life.

Ben. Romeo will answer it.

Mer. Any man that can write may answer a letter.

Ben. Nay, he will answer the letter's master, how he dares, being dared.

Mer. Alas, poor Romeo, he is already dead! stabbed with a white wench's black eye; shot through the ear with a love song; the very pin of his heart cleft with the blind bow-boy's butt-shaft; and is he a man to encounter Tybalt?

Ben. Why, what is Tybalt?

Mer. More than Prince of Cats, I can tell you. O, he's the courageous captain of compliments. He fights as you sing pricksong—keeps time, distance, and proportion;

I will help you for one reason—that this union will prove to be so happy, it will change the hatred in both your households to pure love.

ROMEO: Please, let's go quickly.

FRIAR: Better to be slow than quick. The ones who run too quickly are sure to stumble. (They leave.)

ACT II

(Scene 4: A street.)

(Enter BENVOLIO and MERCUTIO.)

MERC: Where the devil can Romeo be? Do you know if he went home last night?

BEN: He didn't go to his father's house. I spoke with his servant.

MERC: Well, that same Rosaline, that pale, hard-hearted girl torments Romeo's mind so much that it will certainly drive him crazy.

BEN: I found out that Tybalt, a relative of the Capulets, sent a letter to Romeo at his father's house.

MERC: I will wager it was a challenge to a duel.

BEN: Romeo will answer it.

MERC: Any man who can write can answer a letter.

BEN: You know what I mean. Romeo will accept Tybalt's challenge and ask Tybalt directly how he had the nerve to dare him.

MERC: Alas, poor Romeo is as good as dead! He has been stabbed by a fair girl's dark eyes, shot through the ear with Cupid's love song. The very center of his heart has been split in two with one of Cupid's lightest arrows. And is Romeo man enough to fight Tybalt?

BEN: Why? What makes Tybalt so special? Who is he?

MERC: He is more than Prince of Cats. He is quite the beast. He is the captain of the club. He understands everything about the formalities of dueling and knows how to defend against attack. He knows everything about fencing, about turning, distance,

rests me his minim rest, one, two, and the third in your bosom! the very butcher of a silk button, a duelist, a duelist! a gentleman of the very first house, of the first and second cause. Ah, the immortal *passado!* the *punto reverso!* the *hay!*

Ben. The what?

Mer. The pox of such antic, lisping, affecting fantasticoes—these new tuners of accent! "By Jesu, a very good blade! a very tall man! a very good whore!" Why, is not this a lamentable thing, grandsire, that we should be thus afflicted with these strange flies, these fashion-mongers, these *pardona-mi's,* who stand so much on the new form that they cannot sit at ease on the old bench? O, their bones, their bones!

Enter *Romeo.*

Ben. Here comes Romeo! here comes Romeo!

Mer. Without his roe, like a dried herring. O flesh, flesh, how art thou fishified! Now is he for the numbers that Petrarch flowed in. Laura, to his lady, was but a kitchen wench (marry, she had a better love to berhyme her), Dido a dowdy, Cleopatra a gypsy, Helen and Hero hildings and harlots, Thisbe a grey eye or so, but not to the purpose. Signior Romeo, *bon jour!* There's a French salutation to your French slop. You gave us the counterfeit fairly last night.

Rom. Good morrow to you both. What counterfeit did I give you?

Mer. The slip, sir, the slip. Can you not conceive?

Rom. Pardon, good Mercutio. My business was great, and in such a case as mine a man may strain courtesy.

Mer. That's as much as to say, such a case as yours constrains a man to bow in the hams.

and with a musical rest of one and two, he stabs your chest on the count of three. He is so precise in his fencing, he can cut the silk button off your shirt with his rapier. He is an expert of the best fencing school. He is insulted easily and is quick to turn the insult into a provocation for dueling. When he is through with you, my friend, then you have had it, especially when he says the *hay*—which is the cry when the home thrust is made. It comes from the Italian, "You've got it!"

BEN: The what?

MERC: (Ignoring BENVOLIO's question) I wish a plague would take those affected people who use all that faddish language. Listen to how they talk: "By Jesu, a very good blade! a very tall man, a very good whore!" Don't you think it is pitiful, my grand sir, Benvolio, that we should have to tolerate these parasities? They are slaves to fashion and make themselves miserable because they cannot be comfortable with the old ways of doing things. Instead they are wretched just to keep in style.

(Enter ROMEO.)

BEN: Here comes Romeo! Here comes Romeo!

MERC: He looks like a dried out herring that has spawned. I wonder if he is full of verses like the poet and courtly lover Petrarch, who wrote sonnets for Laura. But Rosaline makes Laura look like a mere kitchen maid (though a great poet wrote rhymes for her). For sure Rosaline puts them all to shame: Dido, Queen of Carthage; Cleopatra; Helen of Troy; Hero (Leander's lover); and Thisbe (beloved of Pyramus) — all unattractive and immoral women. Certainly they are nothing next to Rosaline! Signior Romeo—bon jour! That's a suitable French greeting in honor of your stylish French baggy breeches. You gave us the slip last night, you tricky fellow.

ROMEO: Good morning to both of you. How did I give you the slip last night?

MERC: Come on, now—the slip, the slip. You know what I'm talking about. You understand.

ROMEO: Pardon me, my good Mercutio, but I had such pressing business to attend to that I can be forgiven my lack of courtesy.

MERC: That's the same as saying that you're having trouble bowing.

Rom. Meaning, to curtsy.

Mer. Thou hast most kindly hit it.

Rom. A most courteous exposition.

Mer. Nay, I am the very pink of courtesy.

Rom. Pink for flower.

Mer. Right.

Rom. Why, then is my pump well-flowered.

Mer. Well said! Follow me this jest now till thou hast worn out thy pump, that, when the single sole of it is worn, the jest may remain, after the wearing, solely singular.

Rom. O single-soled jest, solely singular for the singleness!

Mer. Come between us, good Benvolio! My wits faint.

Rom. Switch and spurs, switch and spurs! or I'll cry a match.

Mer. Nay, if our wits run the wild-goose chase, I am done; for thou hast more of the wild goose in one of thy wits than, I am sure, I have in my whole five. Was i with you there for the goose?

Rom. Thou wast never with me for anything when thou wast not there for the goose.

Mer. I will bite thee by the ear for that jest.

Rom. Nay, good goose, bite not!

Mer. Thy wit is a very bitter sweeting; it is a most sharp sauce.

Rom. And is it not, then, well served in to a sweet goose?

Mer. O, here's a wit of cheveril, that stretches from an inch narrow to an ell broad!

Rom. I stretch it out for that word "broad," which, added to the goose, proves thee far and wide a broad goose.

Mer. Why, is not this better now than groaning for

ROMEO: You mean I look slightly stooped and cannot curtsy.

MERC: That's exactly right. You've hit it.

ROMEO: You have expressed my situation most courteously.

MERC: You bet! I am the very pink of courtesy.

ROMEO: You're pink like a flower.

MERC: You're correct.

ROMEO: Why, that is the same as my shoe, which is pinked with a decorative pattern of punched holes.

MERC: Say, that's pretty good. Now, just hang on and let's follow this joke through, because when your pinked shoe sole is worn through then only the soul of the joke will still remain.

ROMEO: If you want my opinion, I think that your joke is the kind that makes people groan. It's pretty weak.

MERC: Benvolio, you'd better come between us. I think my wits are failing me and I'm not quite so funny anymore.

ROMEO: Come on, try harder, Mercutio. Urge your wits on. If you don't then I will claim myself the winner of this battle of wits.

MERC: If you run this wild goose chase, I am done for because you have more sharpness in one of your wits than I have in all five of mine. Did I hit home when I said the word *goose*?

ROMEO: You have always been with me for everything including the goose.

MERC: I will bite you on your ear for that remark.

ROMEO: You had better not bite—good goose!

MERC: Your wit is like a sweet, flavored apple, well served in a very sharp sauce.

ROMEO: And doesn't a sour sauce go well when served with a sweet goose?

MERC: Your wit is like an elastic kidskin that stretches from one to forty-five inches.

ROMEO: Yes indeed—my wit can be stretched, and because of this, I make of you a wider and broader goose for everyone to behold.

MERC: Now isn't this more fun than groaning about

love? Now art thou sociable, now art thou Romeo; now art thou what thou art, by art as well as by nature. For this driveling love is like a great natural that runs lolling up and down to hide his bauble in a hole.

Ben. Stop there, stop there!

Mer. Thou desirest me to stop in my tale against the hair.

Ben. Thou wouldst else have made thy tale large.

Mer. O, thou art deceived! I would have made it short; for I was come to the whole depth of my tale, and meant indeed to occupy the argument no longer.

Enter *Nurse* and her *Man* [*Peter*].

Rom. Here's goodly gear!

Mer. A sail, a sail!

Ben. Two, two! a shirt and a smock.

Nurse. Peter!

Peter. Anon.

Nurse. My fan, Peter.

Mer. Good Peter, to hide her face; for her fan's the fairer of the two.

Nurse. God ye good morrow, gentlemen.

Mer. God ye good-den, fair gentlewoman.

Nurse. Is it good-den?

Mer. 'Tis no less, I tell ye; for the bawdy hand of the dial is now upon the prick of noon.

Nurse. Out upon you! What a man are you!

Rom. One, gentlewoman, that God hath made for himself to mar.

Nurse. By my troth, it is well said. "For himself to mar," quoth 'a? Gentlemen, can any of you tell me where I may find the young Romeo?

Rom. I can tell you; but young Romeo will be older

love? Now you are sociable and now you are Romeo. You are your old self with all that nature has given you plus social refinement. A man must be true to himself and his nature. For drooling love is like a big idiot, trying to hide his jester stick, with his tongue hanging out.

BEN: Let's stop it right there. Stop it.

MERC: Do you want me to stop what comes naturally in this pun and go against the grain?

BEN: Yes, I do want you to stop. Otherwise, you will make this story obscene!

MERC: Oh, you're getting the wrong idea. I would not have made it obscene because I was coming to the end of my tale.I didn't intend to stretch things out.

(Enter NURSE and PETER.)

ROMEO: Here comes someone we can tease and have fun with.

MERC: Look at the Nurse's headdress! It looks like a huge sail billowing in the wind.

BEN: I see two people—a man and a woman.

NURSE: Peter, would you please come here?

PETER: What do you wish?

NURSE: Give me my fan, Peter.

MERC: That's a good idea, Peter. Do give her the fan so she can hide her face. The fan looks better than she does.

NURSE: Good morning, gentlemen.

MERC: Good afternoon, fair lady.

NURSE: Is it afternoon now?

MERC: It isn't earlier than noon. Look at the hands of the sun dial. They are pointing directly at noon. Are the hands someplace that suggest something else to you?

NURSE: Do I hear a double meaning from you? What kind of man are you, anyway?

ROMEO: Mercutio is the kind of man who sometimes has a foul mouth.

NURSE: Truly, I do agree with you. He does have a foul mouth. Gentlemen, can any of you tell me where I may find the young Romeo?

ROMEO: I can tell you. But Romeo will be older

when you have found him than he was when you sought him. I am the youngest of that name, for fault of a worse.

Nurse. You say well.

Mer. Yea, is the worst well? Very well took, i' faith! wisely, wisely.

Nurse. If you be he, sir, I desire some confidence with you.

Ben. She will endite him to some supper.

Mer. A bawd, a bawd, a bawd! So ho!

Rom. What hast thou found?

Mer. No hare, sir; unless a hare, sir, in a lenten pie, that is something stale and hoar ere it be spent.

He walks by them and sings.

An old hare hoar,
And an old hare hoar,
Is very good meat in Lent;
But a hare that is hoar
Is too much for a score
When it hoars ere it be spent.

Romeo, will you come to your father's? We'll to dinner thither.

Rom. I will follow you.

Mer. Farewell, ancient lady. Farewell, [*sings*] lady, lady, lady. *Exeunt Mercutio, Benvolio.*

Nurse. Marry, farewell! I pray you, sir, what saucy merchant was this that was so full of his ropery?

Rom. A gentleman, nurse, that loves to hear himself talk and will speak more in a minute than he will stand to in a month.

Nurse. An 'a speak anything against me, I'll take him down, an 'a were lustier than he is, and twenty such

when you find him than when you started looking for him. I am the youngest with that name for lack of a worse name.

NURSE: You express yourself well.

MERC: How can the worst be well? You really don't know what you're talking about— I'm sure, I'm sure.

NURSE: If you are Romeo, I'd like to speak with you.

BEN: She will invite him to supper.

MERC: She's a go-between—a real go-between. As the hunter shouts, "So ho! So ho!" when he spies game, I see what's going on here.

ROMEO: What have you found?

MERC: Well, sir, I haven't found a hare in a meatless Lenten pie, unless it is one of those old rabbits bought on the black market and you know it is mouldy even before it is eaten! (He walks by them and sings.)

An old hare hoar,
And an old hare hoar,
Is very good meat in Lent;
But a hare that is hoar
Is too much for a score
When it hoars ere it be spent.

Romeo, will you join us for dinner at your father's?

ROMEO: I will follow you.

MERC: Farewell, old woman. Farewell, (sings) lady, lady, lady.

(Exit MERCUTIO and BENVOLIO.)

NURSE: Truly, farewell. Please tell me, Romeo, who was that obnoxious person?

ROMEO: He is a gentleman who loves to hear himself talk, who will boast of more in a minute than he can possibly live up to in a month.

NURSE: And if he says anything against me, I'll go after him because I am tougher than he is and twenty more

Jacks; and if I cannot, I'll find those that shall. Scurvy knave! I am none of his flirt-gills; I am none of his skains-mates. And thou must stand by too, and suffer every knave to use me at his pleasure!

Peter. I saw no man use you at his pleasure. If I had, my weapon should quickly have been out, I warrant you. I dare draw as soon as another man, if I see occasion in a good quarrel, and the law on my side.

Nurse. Now, afore God, I am so vexed that every part about me quivers. Scurvy knave! Pray you, sir, a word; and, as I told you, my young lady bid me enquire you out. What she bid me say, I will keep to myself; but first let me tell ye, if ye should lead her into a fool's paradise, as they say, it were a very gross kind of behavior, as they say; for the gentlewoman is young; and therefore, if you should deal double with her, truly it were an ill thing to be offered to any gentlewoman, and very weak dealing.

Rom. Nurse, commend me to thy lady and mistress. I protest unto thee—

Nurse. Good heart, and i' faith I will tell her as much. Lord, Lord! she will be a joyful woman.

Rom. What wilt thou tell her, nurse? Thou dost not mark me.

Nurse. I will tell her, sir, that you do protest, which, as I take it, is a gentlemanlike offer.

Rom. Bid her devise
Some means to come to shrift this afternoon;
And there she shall at Friar Laurence' cell
Be shrived and married. Here is for thy pains.

Nurse. No, truly, sir; not a penny.

Rom. Go to! I say you shall.

Nurse. This afternoon, sir? Well, she shall be there.

Rom. And stay, good nurse, behind the abbey wall.
Within this hour my man shall be with thee

like him. And if I can't do it, I'll find those who will. That rotten man! I'm not one of his loose women. I'm not one of his cutthroats. And Peter, you stood by while this took place and let his foul mouth insult me.

PETER: I didn't hear anybody insult you. If I had I would have quickly pulled out my sword, I can assure you. I will always draw my weapon as quickly as any man, if it's called for in a quarrel, and the law is on my side.

NURSE: Now, before God, I am so angry that every part of me is quivering. That rotten good-for-nothing. Romeo, I would like to have a word with you. As I told you, my young lady wants me to ask you for a message which I'm supposed to keep confidential. But I want to tell you that you had better not lead her astray. It would be the cruelest behavior on your part because Juliet is so young. And if you deceive her, it would be a terrible thing to do to any gentlewoman and contemptible besides.

ROMEO: Nurse, please send my kindest regards to the lady, your mistress, and I want you to know—

NURSE: (Interrupting) Good heart, in faith I will carry your respects to her, and I know this will make her very happy.

ROMEO: What will you tell her, Nurse? You are not listening to me.

NURSE: I'll tell her, sir, that you are making an honorable offer to her as a gentleman would.

ROMEO: Tell her to find a way to come to confession this afternoon so that she may be absolved of sins and then be married. Here is something for your trouble.

NURSE: No, sir, I will not take a penny.

ROMEO: Don't say another word. I want you to take the money.

NURSE: So you will expect her this afternoon at Friar Laurence's. Well, she will be there.

ROMEO: Stay behind the abbey wall, good Nurse. My servant will join you within the hour

And bring thee cords made like a tackled stair,
Which to the high topgallant of my joy
Must be my convoy in the secret night.
Farewell. Be trusty, and I'll quit thy pains.
Farewell. Commend me to thy mistress.

Nurse. Now God in heaven bless thee! Hark you, sir.

Rom. What sayst thou, my dear nurse?

Nurse. Is your man secret? Did you ne'er hear say,
Two may keep counsel, putting one away?

Rom. I warrant thee my man's as true as steel.

Nurse. Well, sir, my mistress is the sweetest lady. Lord, Lord! when 'twas a little prating thing—O, there is a nobleman in town, one Paris, that would fain lay knife aboard; but she, good soul, had as lief see a toad, a very toad, as see him. I anger her sometimes, and tell her that Paris is the properer man; but I'll warrant you, when I say so, she looks as pale as any clout in the versal world. Doth not rosemary and Romeo begin both with a letter?

Rom. Ay, nurse, what of that? Both with an R.

Nurse. Ah, mocker! that's the dog's name. R is for the —No; I know it begins with some other letter; and she hath the prettiest sententious of it, of you and rosemary, that it would do you good to hear it.

Rom. Commend me to thy lady.

Nurse. Ay, a thousand times. [*Exit Romeo.*] Peter!

Peter. Anon.

Nurse. Peter, take my fan, and go before, and apace.

Exeunt.

and bring you a rope ladder which will carry me to the highest point of my joy in the secret night. Farewell. Make sure I can depend upon you, and I will reward your trouble. Farewell and pay my respects to your mistress.

NURSE: May God in heaven bless you. Hear me, sir.

ROMEO: What did you say, dear Nurse?

NURSE: Is your man trustworthy? Did you ever hear it said that two can keep a secret when only one of them knows it?

ROMEO: I assure you that my servant is as true as steel is strong, and he can be trusted.

NURSE: Well, sir, my mistress, Juliet, is the sweetest lady. Lord, lord! when she was a little baby, what a dear. Oh, there is a nobleman in town whose name is Paris and how he would like to win her heart. But she, good soul, would rather see a toad than see him. I anger her sometimes when I tell her that Paris is more handsome than you, but I can assure you that when I make remarks like that, she looks as pale as any piece of cloth in the universe. Tell me something—is it true that the flower rosemary, which symbolizes remembrance, and your name, Romeo, both begin with the same letter?

ROMEO: Well, Nurse, what about it? They both start with an R.

NURSE: You are making fun of me! *R* is the dog's letter because R sounds like a dog's growling. I am trying to think of something else, but I cannot quite remember. Juliet has made up such pretty sayings about you and the flower of remembrance that it would please you to hear them.

ROMEO: Give my regards to your lady.

NURSE: I will, a thousand times. (Exit ROMEO.) Peter, come here.

PETER: I'm coming.

NURSE: Peter, take my fan and let's go quickly.

(NURSE and PETER leave.)

[Scene V. Capulet's orchard.]

Enter *Juliet.*

Jul. The clock struck nine when I did send the nurse;
In half an hour she promised to return.
Perchance she cannot meet him. That's not so.
O, she is lame! Love's heralds should be thoughts,
Which ten times faster glide than the sun's beams
Driving back shadows over lowering hills.
Therefore do nimble-pinioned doves draw Love,
And therefore hath the wind-swift Cupid wings.
Now is the sun upon the highmost hill
Of this day's journey, and from nine till twelve
Is three long hours; yet she is not come.
Had she affections and warm youthful blood,
She would be as swift in motion as a ball;
My words would bandy her to my sweet love,
And his to me.
But old folks, many feign as they were dead—
Unwieldy, slow, heavy and pale as lead.

Enter *Nurse* [and *Peter*].

O God, she comes! O honey nurse, what news?
Hast thou met with him? Send thy man away.
Nurse. Peter, stay at the gate.
[*Exit Peter.*]
Jul. Now, good sweet nurse—O Lord, why lookst thou sad?
Though news be sad, yet tell them merrily;
If good, thou shamest the music of sweet news
By playing it to me with so sour a face.

ACT II

(Scene 5: CAPULET'S orchard.)

(Enter JULIET.)

JULIET: I sent the Nurse at nine o'clock and she promised to return in half an hour. Maybe she couldn't meet him. No, that isn't true. Oh, she is lame! Lovers' messengers should be thoughts, not people, for thoughts move ten times faster than sunbeams, driving the shadows over the darkening hills. This should be, and if it were so, the swift-winged doves would carry love and bring Cupid quickly through the wind. Now the sun is directly overhead so it is noon. It is three hours since the Nurse left, and she still has not returned. If she were young and in love, she would be as quick as a rolling ball, and my sweet Romeo would have already known my thoughts and I would have known his. But old folks act as if they were dead—clumsy and slow, heavy, and pale as lead.

(Enter NURSE with PETER.)

Oh God, here she comes. Oh, sweet Nurse, what news do you have for me? Have you met with Romeo? Please, send Peter away.

NURSE: Peter, leave us and wait at the gate. (Exit PETER.)

JULIET: Now then, good sweet Nurse— Oh Lord, why do you look so sad? If your news is sad, tell it cheerfully. If your news is good, you're ruining it with your sour face.

Nurse. I am aweary, give me leave awhile.
Fie, how my bones ache! What a jaunce have I had!
Jul. I would thou hadst my bones, and I thy news.
Nay, come, I pray thee speak. Good, good nurse, speak.
Nurse. Jesu, what haste! Can you not stay awhile?
Do you not see that I am out of breath?
Jul. How art thou out of breath when thou hast breath
To say to me that thou art out of breath?
The excuse that thou dost make in this delay
Is longer than the tale thou dost excuse.
Is thy news good or bad? Answer to that.
Say either, and I'll stay the circumstance.
Let me be satisfied, is't good or bad?
Nurse. Well, you have made a simple choice; you know not how to choose a man. Romeo? No, not he. Though his face be better than any man's, yet his leg excels all men's; and for a hand and a foot, and a body, though they be not to be talked on, yet they are past compare. He is not the flower of courtesy, but, I'll warrant him, as gentle as a lamb. Go thy ways, wench; serve God. What, have you dined at home?
Jul. No, no. But all this did I know before.
What says he of our marriage? What of that?
Nurse. Lord, how my head aches! What a head have I!
It beats as it would fall in twenty pieces.
My back o't' other side—ah, my back, my back!
Beshrew your heart for sending me about
To catch my death with jauncing up and down!
Jul. I'faith, I am sorry that thou art not well.
Sweet, sweet, sweet nurse, tell me, what says my love?
Nurse. Your love says, like an honest gentleman, and a courteous, and a kind, and a handsome, and, I warrant, a virtuous—Where is your mother?
Jul. Where is my mother? Why, she is within.

ACT II, Scene 5

NURSE: I'm weary. Let me alone for a while. My, how my bones ache! I have certainly had a rough journey today, running to and fro.

JULIET: I wish you had my young bones and I had your news. Now come, please talk to me, good, kind, sweet Nurse, talk to me.

NURSE: In the name of Jesus, what is the hurry? Can't you wait awhile? Can't you see how out of breath I am?

JULIET: How can you be out of breath when you have enough breath to say you're out of breath? Your excuses take more time to tell than the news you are supposed to tell me. Is your news good or bad? Answer me. Say either one, and I'll wait for details. But satisfy my curiosity—do you have good news or bad news?

NURSE: Well, you have made a foolish choice. You don't know how to choose a man. How could you have chosen Romeo? It should never have been Romeo, although his face is handsomer than any other man's and his legs, hands, feet, and body are beyond compare. He is not the perfect gentleman, but I'll guarantee him to be as gentle as a lamb. Juliet, you should serve God by becoming a nun. What's this—did you have lunch at home?

JULIET: No, I didn't. But you're telling me things about Romeo I already knew. Tell me what he says about our wedding! What about that?

NURSE: Lord, do I have a headache! What a terrible headache I have! My head is pounding as if it's going to break into twenty pieces. My back also hurts—oh, my back, my back! Curse your heart for sending me out and killing me by making me run around so.

JULIET: Truly, I am sorry you aren't well. Sweet, kind, thoughtful Nurse, tell me: What does my lover say?

NURSE: Your love, who is honest and courteous and kind and handsome, and I guarantee virtuous—he says—Where is your mother?

JULIET: Why are you asking me where my mother is? Why, she is inside.

Where should she be? How oddly thou repliest!
"Your love says, like an honest gentleman,
'Where is your mother?' "
Nurse. O God's Lady dear!
Are you so hot? Marry come up, I trow.
Is this the poultice for my aching bones?
Henceforward do your messages yourself.
Jul. Here's such a coil! Come, what says Romeo?
Nurse. Have you got leave to go to shrift today?
Jul. I have.
Nurse. Then hie you hence to Friar Laurence' cell;
There stays a husband to make you a wife.
Now comes the wanton blood up in your cheeks;
They'll be in scarlet straight at any news.
Hie you to church; I must another way,
To fetch a ladder, by the which your love
Must climb a bird's nest soon when it is dark.
I am the drudge, and toil in your delight;
But you shall bear the burden soon at night.
Go; I'll to dinner; hie you to the cell.
Jul. Hie to high fortune! Honest nurse, farewell.
Exeunt.

[Scene VI. Friar Laurence's cell.]

Enter *Friar* [Laurence] and *Romeo.*

Friar. So smile the heavens upon this holy act
That after-hours with sorrow chide us not!
Rom. Amen, amen! But come what sorrow can,
It cannot countervail the exchange of joy
That one short minute gives me in her sight.
Do thou but close our hands with holy words,
Then love-devouring death do what he dare—

Where should she be? You're so hard to understand. First you tell me that Romeo is an honest gentleman, and then you ask me where my mother is!

NURSE: By the Virgin Mary, are you that eager? I've lost all patience with you! I'm insulted. Is this the way you treat my aching bones? From now on carry your own messages.

JULIET: You are making such a fuss. Now tell me, what did Romeo say?

NURSE: Do you have permission to go to confession today?

JULIET: Yes, I have permission.

NURSE: Then hurry to Friar Laurence's cell where Romeo waits to make you his bride. Now I see the blood rushing to your cheeks. You will blush quickly at any news about the ceremony. You hurry to church while I go someplace else to find a ladder that Romeo will use tonight when he climbs to your bedroom. I have to do some heavy work, but I work so that you will be happy. However, tonight you will have new responsibilities as a wife. I'm going to dinner; you hurry to Friar Laurence's cell.

JULIET: I am so lucky. Thank you, good Nurse, and farewell.

(NURSE and JULIET leave.)

ACT II

(Scene 6: FRIAR LAURENCE'S cell.)

(Enter FRIAR LAURENCE and ROMEO.)

FRIAR: May the heavens smile upon this marriage so that there will be no sorrow afterwards.

ROMEO: Amen, amen. But whatever sorrow might come, it cannot outweigh the joy I have of seeing Juliet for one short minute. As long as we are married, I don't mind dying.

It is enough I may but call her mine.
Friar. These violent delights have violent ends
And in their triumph die, like fire and powder,
Which, as they kiss, consume. The sweetest honey
Is loathsome in his own deliciousness
And in the taste confounds the appetite.
Therefore love moderately: long love doth so;
Too swift arrives as tardy as too slow.

Enter *Juliet.*

Here comes the lady. O, so light a foot
Will ne'er wear out the everlasting flint.
A lover may bestride the gossamer
That idles in the wanton summer air,
And yet not fall; so light is vanity.
Jul. Good even to my ghostly confessor.
Friar. Romeo shall thank thee, daughter, for us both.
Jul. As much to him, else is his thanks too much.
Rom. Ah, Juliet, if the measure of thy joy
Be heaped like mine, and that thy skill be more
To blazon it, then sweeten with thy breath
This neighbor air, and let rich music's tongue
Unfold the imagined happiness that both
Receive in either by this dear encounter.
Jul. Conceit, more rich in matter than in words,
Brags of his substance, not of ornament.
They are but beggars that can count their worth;
But my true love is grown to such excess
I cannot sum up sum of half my wealth.
Friar. Come, come with me, and we will make short work;
For, by your leaves, you shall not stay alone
Till Holy Church incorporate two in one.

[*Exeunt.*]

It is enough that I may call Juliet mine.

FRIAR: When delight burns with such passion, it will end in the same way—much like the way a match lights gunpowder. The sweetest honey can still make you sick. Despite how good it tastes, it will destroy the appetite. Therefore, love in moderation, because that is how true love lasts. It is just as bad to be fast as it is to be too slow. (Enter JULIET.)
Here comes Lady Juliet now. When I look at her it is easy to believe that Romeo will never tire of her and will feel an everlasting passion for her. A lover may ride a cobweb that floats in the summer air and yet not fall because his earthly joy keeps him afloat.

JULIET: Good afternoon, Father Confessor.

FRIAR: Romeo will thank you, Juliet, for both of us.

JULIET: May Romeo enjoy himself this evening, too, or else he won't have much to be thankful for.

ROMEO: Ah, Juliet, if you are as happy as I am, and if you are able to describe that joy, then say it sweetly and express how happy we will both be because of our blessed wedding here today.

JULIET: True understanding involves much more than just words, which are mere decorations. People who count their worth in money are truly beggars. My love has grown to such magnitude that I cannot add up even half of my wealth.

FRIAR: Come, come with me, and we will get this over with, quickly. With your permission, you two cannot be left alone until the Holy Church marries you.

(They leave.)

[ACT III]

[Scene I. A public place.]

Enter *Mercutio, Benvolio, and Men.*

Ben. I pray thee, good Mercutio, let's retire.
The day is hot, the Capulet's abroad,
And if we meet, we shall not scape a brawl,
For now, these hot days, is the mad blood stirring.

Mer. Thou art like one of these fellows that, when he enters the confines of a tavern, claps me his sword upon the table and says "God send me no need of thee!" and by the operation of the second cup draws him on the drawer, when indeed there is no need.

Ben. Am I like such a fellow?

Mer. Come, come, thou art as hot a Jack in thy mood as any in Italy; and as soon moved to be moody, and as soon moody to be moved.

Ben. And what to?

Mer. Nay, an there were two such, we should have none shortly, for one would kill the other. Thou! why, thou wilt quarrel with a man that hath a hair more or a hair less in his beard than thou hast. Thou wilt quarrel with a man for cracking nuts, having no other reason but because thou hast hazel eyes. What eye but such an eye would spy out such a quarrel? Thy head is as full of quarrels as an egg is full of meat; and yet thy head hath been

ACT III

(Scene 1: A public place.)

(Enter MERCUTIO, BENVOLIO, PAGE, and MEN.)

BEN: Please, good Mercutio, let's go home. It's so hot today,and the Capulets are out walking the streets. If we run into them, there will certainly be a fight. You know how easy it is to lose one's temper when the weather is this warm.

MERC: You're just like one of those men who walks into a tavern, slaps his sword down on the table, and says out loud, "I hope I won't have to use this!" But by the time he has had his second drink, he's drawing that same sword on the harmless waiter who brought him those refreshments.

BEN: Do you really think I'm like that?

MERC: Your temper is as hot as anyone's in Italy, and you get angry when you're crossed, too.

BEN: What do I get angry about?

MERC: If there were two people like you, we wouldn't have any because one would kill the other. As for you, you would quarrel over trivial things—like over who has one hair more or less in his beard than you have. And you would quarrel with a man who is cracking some nuts open for no better reason than the fact that you have hazel eyes. Who but you would find such a silly reason to fight? Do you realize what stupid things you've fought about? Your head is as full of quarrels as an egg is full of food; but your head has been beaten as addle as an egg for quarreling. Thou hast quarreled with a man for coughing in the street, because he hath wakened thy dog that hath lain asleep in the sun. Didst thou not fall out with a tailor for wearing his new doublet before Easter? with another for tying his new shoes with old riband? And yet thou wilt tutor me from quarreling!

Ben. An I were so apt to quarrel as thou art, any man should buy the fee simple of my life for an hour and a quarter.

Mer. The fee simple? O simple!

Enter *Tybalt* and others.

Ben. By my head, here come the Capulets.

Mer. By my heel, I care not.

Tyb. Follow me close, for I will speak to them.
Gentlemen, good den. A word with one of you.

Mer. And but one word with one of us?
Couple it with something; make it a word and a blow.

Tyb. You shall find me apt enough to that, sir, an you will give me occasion.

Mer. Could you not take some occasion without giving?

Tyb. Mercutio, thou consortest with Romeo.

Mer. Consort? What, dost thou make us minstrels? An thou make minstrels of us, look to hear nothing but discords. Here's my fiddlestick; here's that shall make you dance. Zounds, consort!

Ben. We talk here in the public haunt of men.
Either withdraw unto some private place
And reason coldly of your grievances,
Or else depart. Here all eyes gaze on us.

Mer. Men's eyes were made to look, and let them gaze.
I will not budge for no man's pleasure, I.

beaten so much, it's as muddled as a rotten egg. You have quarreled with that man who coughed in the street because he woke up your dog sleeping in the sun. And didn't you argue with a tailor because he wore the outfit he made for himself before Easter? And didn't you fight with another man because he tied his shoes with old laces? And yet you think you have the right to teach *me* how to avoid quarreling?

BEN: If I were as quarrelsome as you, I probably wouldn't live longer than an hour and a quarter. My life wouldn't be worth anything.

MERC: You said it. You wouldn't be worth a thing. (Enter TYBALT and others.)

BEN: Oh, I see the Capulets coming.

MERC: I don't care. I'm staying right here.

TYBALT: (To his men.) Stay close to me because I'm going to talk to them. (To MERCUTIO and BENVOLIO.) Gentlemen, good afternoon. I would like to have a word with one of you.

MERC: Is it only one word that you want with one of us? Why don't you add something to that one word? How about a word and a slash of your sword?

TYBALT: I will be more than willing to do that, sir, if you give me a reason.

MERC: I'm sure you could find a reason if none were given to you.

TYBALT: Look, Mercutio, I know you play around with Romeo—

MERC: "Play around?" What do you think we are—silly musicians? If you think we're like that, prepare to fight. My sword shall make you dance. Can you believe what he said, Benvolio? That we are musicians?

BEN: Do you realize we are in public? You two should either go someplace private and get your complaints out in the open or else leave. Everyone is looking at us here.

MERC: Men's eyes were made to look, so let them look. I won't budge to make some other man happy.

Enter *Romeo.*

Tyb. Well, peace be with you, sir. Here comes my man.
Mer. But I'll be hanged, sir, if he wear your livery.
Marry, go before to field, he'll be your follower!
Your worship in that sense may call him man.
Tyb. Romeo, the love I bear thee can afford
No better term than this: thou art a villain.
Rom. Tybalt, the reason that I have to love thee
Doth much excuse the appertaining rage
To such a greeting. Villain am I none.
Therefore farewell. I see thou knowst me not.
Tyb. Boy, this shall not excuse the injuries
That thou hast done me; therefore turn and draw.
Rom. I do protest I never injured thee,
But love thee better than thou canst devise
Till thou shalt know the reason of my love;
And so, good Capulet, which name I tender
As dearly as mine own, be satisfied.
Mer. O calm, dishonorable, vile submission!
Alla stoccata carries it away. [*Draws.*]
Tybalt, you ratcatcher, will you walk?
Tyb. What wouldst thou have with me?
Mer. Good King of Cats, nothing but one of your nine lives. That I mean to make bold withal, and, as you shall use me hereafter, dry-beat the rest of the eight. Will you pluck your sword out of his pilcher by the ears? Make haste, lest mine be about your ears ere it be out.
Tyb. I am for you. [*Draws.*]
Rom. Gentle Mercutio, put thy rapier up.
Mer. Come, sir, your *passado!* [*They fight.*]
Rom. Draw, Benvolio; beat down their weapons.

ACT III, Scene 1

(Enter ROMEO.)

TYBALT: Well, sir, may the rest of your day be pleasant. Here comes my man.

MERC: Don't address Romeo as if he were a servant. Go on, go someplace where you two can have a duel, and he'll follow you there. But in no other sense can he be called your follower.

TYBALT: Romeo, I hate you so intensely that the best name I can call you is a villain.

ROMEO: Tybalt, the affection I feel for you overshadows the rage I would normally feel when greeted in that insulting way. I am not a villain. Therefore, good-bye. You really don't know me at all.

TYBALT: Listen, boy. You're not going to weasel your way out of this. Your presence at the party last night insulted me. Turn around and draw your sword.

ROMEO: I must say in my own defense that I never insulted you, Tybalt. In fact, I like you more than you can understand right now, and sometime soon you will understand the reason for my good feelings toward you. Therefore, good Capulet, and that is a name I regard as highly as my own name, please calm yourself.

MERC: What do you mean, "Calm yourself"? You're submitting to this wretch? Tybalt's fencing skills have made a coward of you, Romeo. (He draws his sword.) Tybalt, you ratcatcher, would you like to take a walk with me?

TYBALT: Why? What would be the purpose of such a walk?

MERC: I just want to kill you. Do you think you can get your sword out of its scabbard? You'd better hurry or else mine will be out first.

TYBALT: I am ready for you. (He draws his sword.)

ROMEO: Gentle Mercutio, please don't fight.

MERC: Come on Tybalt, let's see your lunge.

ROMEO: Oh, Benvolio, help! Draw your sword and beat down their weapons.

Gentlemen, for shame! forbear this outrage!
Tybalt, Mercutio, the Prince expressly hath
Forbid this bandying in Verona streets.
Hold, Tybalt! Good Mercutio!

Tybalt under Romeo's arm thrusts Mercutio in, and flies [*with his Men*].

Mer. I am hurt.
A plague o' both your houses! I am sped.
Is he gone and hath nothing?

Ben. What, art thou hurt?

Mer. Ay, ay, a scratch, a scratch. Marry, 'tis enough.
Where is my page? Go, villain, fetch a surgeon.

[*Exit Page.*]

Rom. Courage, man. The hurt cannot be much.

Mer. No, 'tis not so deep as a well, nor so wide as a church door; but 'tis enough, 'twill serve. Ask for me to-morrow, and you shall find me a grave man. I am peppered, I warrant, for this world. A plague o' both your houses! Zounds, a dog, a rat, a mouse, a cat, to scratch a man to death! A braggart, a rogue, a villain, that fights by the book of arithmetic! Why the devil came you between us? I was hurt under your arm.

Rom. I thought all for the best.

Mer. Help me into some house, Benvolio,
Or I shall faint. A plague o' both your houses!
They have made worms' meat of me. I have it,
And soundly too. Your houses!

Exit [*supported by Benvolio*].

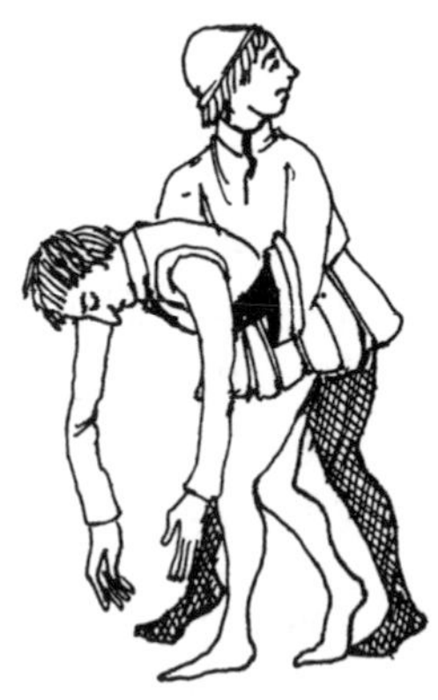

Rom. This gentleman, the Prince's near ally,
My very friend, hath got his mortal hurt
In my behalf—my reputation stained
With Tybalt's slander—Tybalt, that an hour
Hath been my kinsman. O sweet Juliet,

Tybalt and Mercutio, this is horrible. Remember that Prince Escalus very clearly outlawed this kind of fighting on the city streets. Stop it, you two!

(TYBALT under ROMEO's arm stabs MERCUTIO and flees with his followers.)

MERC: I have been stabbed! I wish a plague on both your houses! I am done for! How is it possible that I lie here dying and Tybalt left without a wound?

BEN: What's wrong, Mercutio? Are you hurt?

MERC: Yes, yes, I've been scratched—but a scratch is enough. Where is my servant? Go, you good-for-nothing servant, get a doctor. (Exit PAGE.)

ROMEO: Have courage, Mercutio, you can't be hurt too badly.

MERC: No, the wound isn't as deep as a well or wide as a church door, but it's enough. I won't be alive tomorrow. I have been hurt badly. Again, I curse the Capulet and Montague families. Ask for me tomorrow and you will find me a grave man. I am finished for this world. A plague on both your houses! I swear—a dog, a rat, a mouse, or a cat could all scratch a man to death. But I have been slain by a braggart, a rogue, a villain, who fights by precise rules. Why the devil did you step between Tybalt and me when we were fighting, Romeo? Tybalt struck me then under your arm.

ROMEO: I thought I was doing the right thing.

MERC: Benvolio, help me into some house or I shall faint. Again, I wish a plague on both your houses! The worms will feast on my corpse. This a terrible wound. (MERCUTIO leaves with BENVOLIO's help.)

ROMEO: Mercutio, friend to both the Prince and me, died for me because Tybalt slandered and humiliated me. This is the same Tybalt who has been my cousin for only one hour. Dear sweet Juliet,

Thy beauty hath made me effeminate
And in my temper softened valor's steel!

Enter *Benvolio.*

Ben. O Romeo, Romeo, brave Mercutio's dead!
That gallant spirit hath aspired the clouds,
Which too untimely here did scorn the earth.
Rom. This day's black fate on more days doth depend;
This but begins the woe others must end.

Enter *Tybalt.*

Ben. Here comes the furious Tybalt back again.
Rom. Alive in triumph, and Mercutio's slain?
Away to heaven respective lenity,
And fire-eyed fury be my conduct now!
Now, Tybalt, take the "villain" back again
That late thou gavest me, for Mercutio's soul
Is but a little way above our heads,
Staying for thine to keep him company.
Either thou or I, or both, must go with him.
Tyb. Thou, wretched boy, that didst consort him here,
Shalt with him hence.
Rom. This shall determine that.
They fight. Tybalt falls.
Ben. Romeo, away, be gone!
The citizens are up, and Tybalt slain.
Stand not amazed. The Prince will doom thee death
If thou art taken. Hence, be gone, away!
Rom. O, I am fortune's fool!
Ben. Why dost thou stay?
Exit Romeo.

your love has made me womanish and weak.

(Reenter BENVOLIO.)

BEN: O Romeo, Romeo, brave Mercutio is dead! His gallant spirit is now in heaven which scorned the earth and took him before his time.

ROMEO: This day's black fate is just the beginning. Others must end this grief.

(Reenter TYBALT.)

BEN: Oh no, here comes Tybalt again and he is furious.

ROMEO: It is absolutely inconceivable that Tybalt should be alive and Mercutio dead. I can no longer forgive Tybalt just because he is Juliet's cousin. Now, Tybalt, take your insults back, and do it now! Mercutio's soul is waiting for yours to keep him company. And I promise that either you, or I, or both of us will do just that.

TYBALT: You sickening wretch, you who were a friend to Mercutio here, shall go with him there.

ROMEO: Our fight will determine if you are right or wrong.

(They fight; TYBALT falls.)

BEN: Get out of here, Romeo, get out of here! The townspeople are coming, and Tybalt is dead. Don't stand around here looking dazed. The Prince will sentence you to death if he finds you here. Go, get out of here, move!

ROMEO: Oh, I am fortune's fool! What has fate done to me?

BEN: Why are you still here?

(Exit ROMEO.)

Enter *Citizens.*

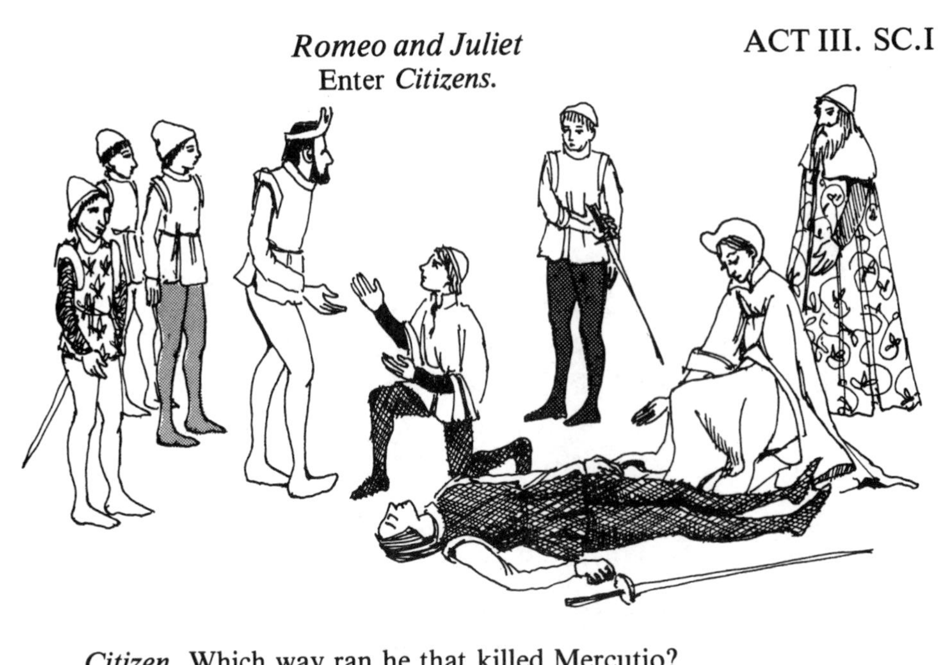

Citizen. Which way ran he that killed Mercutio?
Tybalt, that murderer, which way ran he?
Ben. There lies that Tybalt.
Citizen. Up, sir, go with me.
I charge thee in the Prince's name obey.

Enter *Prince* [with his *Train*], *Old Montague, Capulet,* their *Wives,* and [others].

Prince. Where are the vile beginners of this fray?
Ben. O noble Prince, I can discover all
The unlucky manage of this fatal brawl.
There lies the man, slain by young Romeo,
That slew thy kinsman, brave Mercutio.
Cap. Wife. Tybalt, my cousin! O my brother's child!
O Prince! O cousin! O husband! O, the blood is spilled
Of my dear kinsman! Prince, as thou art true,
For blood of ours shed blood of Montague.
O cousin, cousin!
Prince. Benvolio, who began this bloody fray?
Ben. Tybalt, here slain, whom Romeo's hand did slay.
Romeo, that spoke him fair, bid him bethink
How nice the quarrel was, and urged withal
Your high displeasure. All this—uttered
With gentle breath, calm look, knees humbly bowed—
Could not take truce with the unruly spleen
Of Tybalt deaf to peace, but that he tilts
With piercing steel at bold Mercutio's breast;
Who, all as hot, turns deadly point to point,
And, with a martial scorn, with one hand beats
Cold death aside and with the other sends

ACT III, Scene 1

(Enter CITIZENS.)

CIT.1: We're looking for Tybalt, who killed Mercutio. Which way did he go?

BEN: That's Tybalt there, lying dead on the ground.

CIT.1: I arrest you, sir, in the name of the law. Don't give me any trouble.

(Enter PRINCE, with his retinue; LORD MONTAGUE, LORD CAPULET, their WIVES, and others.)

PRINCE: Where are the people who began this fight?

BEN: O noble Prince, I can tell you everything that happened. Tybalt, who killed your cousin, brave Mercutio, was himself murdered by young Romeo.

LADY CAP: O Tybalt, my nephew! O Prince! O husband! My dear nephew's blood has been spilled. If you are fair, Prince, you must take the life of young Romeo Montague since the blood of a young Capulet has been shed.

PRINCE: Benvolio, who started the fight?

BEN: Tybalt did. Romeo tried to convince Tybalt that their quarrel was trivial and he even said how displeased you would be, Prince, over this quarrel. Romeo said this calmly and humbly, but his words had no effect on Tybalt's fiery temper. Tybalt just ignored Romeo and started fighting with Mercutio, who was equally as angry and matched

It back to Tybalt, whose dexterity
Retorts it. Romeo he cries aloud,
"Hold, friends! friends, part!" and swifter than his tongue,
His agile arm beats down their fatal points,
And 'twixt them rushes; underneath whose arm
An envious thrust from Tybalt hit the life
Of stout Mercutio, and then Tybalt fled,
But by-and-by comes back to Romeo,
Who had but newly entertained revenge,
And to't they go like lightning; for, ere I
Could draw to part them, was stout Tybalt slain;
And, as he fell, did Romeo turn and fly.
This is the truth, or let Benvolio die.
Cap. Wife. He is a kinsman to the Montague;
Affection makes him false, he speaks not true.
Some twenty of them fought in this black strife,
And all those twenty could but kill one life.
I beg for justice, which thou, Prince, must give.
Romeo slew Tybalt; Romeo must not live.
Prince. Romeo slew him; he slew Mercutio.
Who now the price of his dear blood doth owe?
Mon. Not Romeo, Prince; he was Mercutio's friend;
His fault concludes but what the law should end,
The life of Tybalt.
Prince. And for that offense
Immediately we do exile him hence.
I have an interest in your hate's proceeding,
My blood for your rude brawls doth lie a-bleeding;
But I'll amerce you with so strong a fine
That you shall all repent the loss of mine.
I will be deaf to pleading and excuses;
Nor tears nor prayers shall purchase out abuses.
Therefore use none. Let Romeo hence in haste,

ACT III, Scene 1

Tybalt lunge for lunge. Romeo tried again to stop the fight and ran between Tybalt and Mercutio, but Tybalt managed to thrust his sword into Mercutio under Romeo's arm. Then Tybalt ran away, but came back for Romeo, who by now was obsessed with avenging Mercutio's death. Everything happened so fast! Before I could draw my sword to separate them, Tybalt was dead. As he fell, Romeo ran away. If this isn't the truth, then let me die.

LADY CAP: Benvolio is prejudiced. He is a relative of the Montagues, and he's lying. Prince, you must be fair. It took twenty Montagues to kill my nephew. I beg for justice which you must give. Romeo killed Tybalt, and for that Romeo must not live.

PRINCE: Yes, Romeo did kill Tybalt, but Tybalt killed Mercutio. Who now must pay for Tybalt's death?

LORD MONT: Not Romeo, Prince. Romeo was a good friend to Mercutio. Romeo only did to Tybalt what the law would have done anyway—to end the life of Tybalt.

PRINCE: For his crime, Romeo is to be exiled. I now am involved in this feud because Mercutio was one of my relatives, but I will fine you so heavily that you will all regret my bereavement. I will not listen to any more excuses, and don't think that tears or prayers will make everything all right. Romeo had better leave town quickly,

Else, when he is found, that hour is his last.
Bear hence this body, and attend our will.
Mercy but murders, pardoning those that kill.

Exeunt.

[Scene II. Capulet's orchard.]

Enter *Juliet* alone.

Jul. Gallop apace, you fiery-footed steeds,
Towards Phoebus' lodging! Such a wagoner
As Phaeton would whip you to the West
And bring in cloudy night immediately.
Spread thy close curtain, love-performing night,
That runaways' eyes may wink, and Romeo
Leap to these arms untalked of and unseen.
Lovers can see to do their amorous rites
By their own beauties; or, if love be blind,
It best agrees with night. Come, civil night,
Thou sober-suited matron, all in black,
And learn me how to lose a winning match,
Played for a pair of stainless maidenhoods.
Hood my unmanned blood, bating in my cheeks,
With thy black mantle; till strange love, grown bold,
Think true love acted simple modesty.
Come, night; come, Romeo; come, thou day in night;
For thou wilt lie upon the wings of night
Whiter than new snow upon a raven's back.
Come, gentle night; come, loving, black-browed night;
Give me my Romeo; and, when he shall die,
Take him and cut him out in little stars,
And he will make the face of heaven so fine
That all the world will be in love with night

or else he will be killed on sight. Let's get this body out of here, and obey my wishes. Mercy is a murderer, if it pardons those who kill.

(They leave.)

ACT III

(Scene 2: CAPULET'S orchard.)

(Enter JULIET, alone.)

JULIET: Gallop swiftly, you powerful steeds with feet of fire, rushing toward the sun god's temple. If Phaethon, the reckless son of Phoebus, had been driving the chariot, it would have been night already since he could not control the horses as they streaked across the sky. Concealing night, come spread your dark curtain to hide our embraces so that prying eyes will be closed and will not see. That is when Romeo can come to my arms, silently and unseen. Lovers can find each other in the darkness because their beauty radiates light. If love is blind, it agrees with the night. Come, obliging night, like a matron dressed in black, and teach me to yield in the game of love with my innocence as the prize. Blindfold the untamed love that flushes in my cheeks with your black shawl until chaste and true love erupts in passion. Come to me, night, and come to me, Romeo, for you illuminate the darkness of night and you will lie upon the wings of night, whiter than new snow on a raven's back. Come, gentle night; come loving, black night; and bring me my Romeo; and when he dies, take him back and use his luminous light for the little stars in the heavens. He will make night so beautiful that the universe will fall in love with the darkness

And pay no worship to the garish sun.
O, I have bought the mansion of a love,
But not possessed it; and though I am sold,
Not yet enjoyed. So tedious is this day
As is the night before some festival
To an impatient child that hath new robes
And may not wear them. O, here comes my nurse,

Enter *Nurse,* wringing her hands, with the ladder of cords in her lap.

And she brings news; and every tongue that speaks
But Romeo's name speaks heavenly eloquence.
Now, nurse, what news? What hast thou there? the cords
That Romeo bid thee fetch?
Nurse. Ay, ay, the cords.
Jul. Ay me! what news? Why dost thou wring thy hands?
Nurse. Ah, well-a-day! he's dead, he's dead, he's dead!
We are undone, lady, we are undone!
Alack the day! he's gone, he's killed, he's dead!
Jul. Can heaven be so envious?
Nurse. Romeo can,
Though heaven cannot. O Romeo, Romeo!
Who ever would have thought it? Romeo!
Jul. What devil art thou that dost torment me thus?
This torture should be roared in dismal hell.
Hath Romeo slain himself? Say thou but "I,"
And that bare vowel "I" shall poison more
Than the death-darting eye of cockatrice.
I am not I, if there be such an "I";
Or those eyes shut that make thee answer "I."
If he be slain, say "I"; or if not, "no."
Brief sounds determine of my weal or woe.

and no longer idolize the gaudy sun. Oh, I have taken the vows of marriage yet not used them. This day comes slowly. I feel like an impatient child who has new party clothes but cannot wear them for it is still not time. Here comes my Nurse.
(Enter NURSE, wringing her hands with the ladder of cords over her arm.) And she will tell me what is going on. Anyone who speaks Romeo's name speaks eloquently. Well, Nurse, tell me what the plans are. What do you have there? Are those the cords that Romeo told you to get?

NURSE: Yes, yes, these are the cords.

JULIET: So what is happening? Why are you so miserable? Why are you wringing your hands?

NURSE: Alas! He's dead, he's dead, he's dead. Our plans are ruined, Lady, our plans are ruined. He's gone, he's killed, he's dead.

JULIET: Can Heaven want him so badly that it would take him now on his wedding day?

NURSE: No, not Heaven. Romeo is the envious one. O Romeo, Romeo. Who would ever have thought this possible? It is Romeo who is envious.

JULIET: What is wrong with you that you would torment me this way? This is the kind of torture one would find in Hell. Did Romeo commit suicide? If you say "yes," just that one little sound will be more deadly to me than the deadly eye of a serpent. If that is true, my life is no longer worth living. So say a brief yes or no. Such little words decide whether I will be happy or miserable.

Nurse. I saw the wound, I saw it with mine eyes,
(God save the mark!) here on his manly breast.
A piteous corse, a bloody piteous corse;
Pale, pale as ashes, all bedaubed in blood,
All in gore blood. I swounded at the sight.
Jul. O, break, my heart! poor bankrout, break at once!
To prison, eyes; ne'er look on liberty!
Vile earth, to earth resign; end motion here,
And thou and Romeo press one heavy bier!
Nurse. O Tybalt, Tybalt, the best friend I had!
O courteous Tybalt! honest gentleman!
That ever I should live to see thee dead!
Jul. What storm is this that blows so contrary?
Is Romeo slaughtered, and is Tybalt dead?
My dear-loved cousin, and my dearer lord?
Then, dreadful trumpet, sound the general doom!
For who is living, if those two are gone?
Nurse. Tybalt is gone, and Romeo banished;
Romeo that killed him, he is banished.
Jul. O God! Did Romeo's hand shed Tybalt's blood?
Nurse. It did, it did! alas the day, it did!
Jul. O serpent heart, hid with a flow'ring face!
Did ever dragon keep so fair a cave?
Beautiful tyrant! fiend angelical!
Dove-feathered raven! wolvish-ravening lamb!
Despised substance of divinest show!
Just opposite to what thou justly seemst—
A damned saint, an honorable villain!
O nature, what hadst thou to do in hell
When thou didst bower the spirit of a fiend
In mortal paradise of such sweet flesh?
Was ever book containing such vile matter
So fairly bound? O, that deceit should dwell
In such a gorgeous palace!

ACT III, Scene 2

NURSE: I saw the wound, I saw it with my own eyes—it was right on his chest. His corpse looked all pitiful and bloody. It was as pale as ashes and all bloody. I fainted at the sight.

JULIET: I hope my heart breaks soon for it is empty now. I hope I die soon. I am now a prisoner of the earth and will have no freedom now that Romeo is dead.

NURSE: O Tybalt, Tybalt! He was the best friend I ever had. He was such a courteous and honest gentleman. O Tybalt! I never thought that I would live to see you dead.

JULIET: Now what are you telling me? Are both Romeo and Tybalt dead? Both are dead—my cousin and my husband? There is no point in living if both are gone.

NURSE: No, Juliet. Tybalt has been killed and Romeo has been sent away. You see, it was Romeo who killed Tybalt so he has been banished for his crime.

JULIET: Oh, God! Do you mean to tell me that Romeo killed Tybalt?

NURSE: Yes, yes. Oh, alas, yes.

JULIET: How could such ugliness be hidden in my happiness as a new bride? Romeo—I curse you with your serpent's heart hidden in your handsome face. You bring to my mind all of those ugly monsters who violate the goodness and virtue of innocent creatures. Was there ever such an evil dragon who lived in such a beautiful cave? Beautiful tyrant! Fiend yet angel! Raven—covered in dove's feathers! Wolf in lamb's clothing! You look divine but inside you are ugly. You are the opposite of what you appear—a damned saint, an honorable villain! O Nature, what did you do in Hell when you disguised such a fiendish spirit inside such a good and sweet body? Was there ever such a beautifully bound book that contained such vile content? Oh, how horrible that such deception should live in such a gorgeous palace.

Nurse. There's no trust,
No faith, no honesty in men; all perjured,
All forsworn, all naught, all dissemblers.
Ah, where's my man? Give me some aqua vitae.
These griefs, these woes, these sorrows make me old.
Shame come to Romeo!
Jul. Blistered be thy tongue
For such a wish! He was not born to shame.
Upon his brow shame is ashamed to sit;
For 'tis a throne where honor may be crowned
Sole monarch of the universal earth.
O, what a beast was I to chide at him!
Nurse. Will you speak well of him that killed your cousin?
Jul. Shall I speak ill of him that is my husband?
Ah, poor my lord, what tongue shall smooth thy name
When I, thy three-hours' wife, have mangled it?
But wherefore, villain, didst thou kill my cousin?
That villain cousin would have killed my husband.
Back, foolish tears, back to your native spring!
Your tributary drops belong to woe,
Which you, mistaking, offer up to joy.
My husband lives, that Tybalt would have slain;
And Tybalt's dead, that would have slain my husband.
All this is comfort; wherefore weep I then?
Some word there was, worser than Tybalt's death,
That murdered me. I would forget it fain;
But O, it presses to my memory
Like damned guilty deeds to sinners' minds!
"Tybalt is dead, and Romeo—banished."
That "banished," that one word "banished,"
Hath slain ten thousand Tybalts. Tybalt's death
Was woe enough, if it had ended there;
Or, if sour woe delights in fellowship

ACT III, Scene 2

NURSE: Men are untrustworthy, faithless, and dishonest. They are all corrupt, all hypocrites. Ah, where is Peter? Give me something strong to drink. All this grief, this sorrow, and this tragedy make me feel old. I hope that shame will come to Romeo.

JULIET: May your tongue break out in blisters for such an unfair wish. Romeo has always been honorable, so honorable that shame has no place in his life. Oh, what is wrong with me that I criticized him? I am a beast.

NURSE: Are you praising the man who killed your cousin?

JULIET: How can I speak badly of my husband? If I, his bride of only three hours, speak ill of him, who will speak well? But why, evil Romeo, why did you kill my cousin Tybalt? I'll tell you why. Because evil Tybalt would have killed Romeo, that's why. I am so confused—but I know that my tears should be tears of joy for Romeo's triumph rather than be tears of misery for Tybalt's death. There is no doubt; Tybalt would have killed Romeo if he had had a chance. If this is so comforting, why am I crying then? I think it is because I heard some word you said, Nurse, that was even worse than Tybalt's death. That word is killing me. I wish I could forget it. Now I know: it was that Romeo has been banished. For me the word "banished" is worse than if ten thousand Tybalts had been killed. It would have been bad enough if you had only said that Tybalt is dead. Or if misery loves company,

And needly will be ranked with other griefs,
Why followed not, when she said "Tybalt's dead,"
Thy father, or thy mother, nay, or both,
Which modern lamentation might have moved?
But with a rearward following Tybalt's death,
"Romeo is banished"—to speak that word
Is father, mother, Tybalt, Romeo, Juliet,
All slain, all dead. "Romeo is banished"—
There is no end, no limit, measure, bound,
In that word's death; no words can that woe sound.
Where is my father and my mother, nurse?
Nurse. Weeping and wailing over Tybalt's corse.
Will you go to them? I will bring you thither.
Jul. Wash they his wounds with tears? Mine shall be spent,
When theirs are dry, for Romeo's banishment.
Take up those cords. Poor ropes, you are beguiled,
Both you and I, for Romeo is exiled.
He made you for a highway to my bed;
But I, a maid, die maiden-widowed.
Come, cords; come, nurse. I'll to my wedding bed;
And death, not Romeo, take my maidenhead!
Nurse. Hie to your chamber. I'll find Romeo
To comfort you. I wot well where he is.
Hark ye, your Romeo will be here at night.
I'll to him; he is hid at Laurence' cell.
Jul. O, find him! give this ring to my true knight
And bid him come to take his last farewell.

Exeunt.

and if you had said that my parents had been killed, too, that would have been truly worse. But to say that Romeo is banished destroys everything and everyone near and dear to me—my father, mother, Tybalt, Romeo, even myself. "Romeo has been banished"—there are no ways to describe the misery of those words. Nurse, can you tell me where my parents are at this moment?

NURSE: They are grieving over Tybalt's death. Do you wish to see them? I will take you to them.

JULIET: I am sure they are crying a great deal. But my tears will still fall when theirs are dry, because I cry for Romeo's banishment. Never mind about those cords you brought. They will serve no purpose now. I think I'll go to bed, and I hope that Death will take me since Romeo will not.

NURSE: Yes, Juliet, go to your room. I'll find Romeo—I know where he is hiding—and I'll bring him here to console you. Listen to me: your Romeo will be here with you tonight. I'll go to him—he's hiding at Friar Laurence's cell.

JULIET: Oh, find him, yes! And give him this ring. Yes, tell him to come so we can say good-bye before he has to leave Verona.

(They leave.)

[Scene III. Friar Laurence's cell.]

Enter *Friar* [*Laurence*].

Friar. Romeo, come forth; come forth, thou fearful
man.
Affliction is enamored of thy parts,
And thou art wedded to calamity.

Enter *Romeo.*

Rom. Father, what news? What is the Prince's doom?
What sorrow craves acquaintance at my hand
That I yet know not?
Friar. Too familiar
Is my dear son with such sour company.
I bring thee tidings of the Prince's doom.
Rom. What less than doomsday is the Prince's doom?
Friar. A gentler judgment vanished from his lips—
Not body's death, but body's banishment.
Rom. Ha, banishment? Be merciful, say "death";
For exile hath more terror in his look,
Much more than death. Do not say "banishment."
Friar. Hence from Verona art thou banished.
Be patient, for the world is broad and wide.
Rom. There is no world without Verona walls,
But purgatory, torture, hell itself.
Hence banished is banisht from the world,
And world's exile is death. Then "banishment"
Is death mistermed. Calling death "banishment,"
Thou cuttst my head off with a golden axe
And smilest upon the stroke that murders me.
Friar. O deadly sin! O rude unthankfulness!

ACT III, Scene 3

ACT III

(Scene 3: FRIAR LAURENCE's cell.)

(Enter FRIAR LAURENCE.)

FRIAR: Romeo, come here, come here, you frightened man. It seems as if everything that's bad has happened to you.

(Enter ROMEO.)

ROMEO: What news do you have for me, Father? What is the Prince's judgment about me? What other sorrow is about to overtake me that I don't know about yet?

FRIAR: You have had too much sorrow already! I must give you word of the Prince's judgment.

ROMEO: What could be less than doomsday for me?

FRIAR: He has issued a more gentle judgment. He doesn't want you dead but he does want your banishment.

ROMEO: Banishment! Be merciful and say "death" instead. Exile is more horrible for me than death. Don't say "banishment."

FRIAR: From now on you are banished from Verona, but be calm. The world is a very big place.

ROMEO: There is no world outside of Verona's walls but purgatory, torture, and hell itself. So to be banished is to be exiled from the world, and exile from the world is the same as death. The word "banishment" really is an improper term for death. Calling death "banishment" gives it a fancy name, like cutting off my head with a golden axe and smiling on the stroke that murders me.

FRIAR: Your ingratitude is a sin! Of all the rude thanklessness I've ever heard!

Thy fault our law calls death; but the kind Prince,
Taking thy part, hath rushed aside the law,
And turned that black word death to banishment.
This is dear mercy, and thou seest it not.
Rom. 'Tis torture, and not mercy. Heaven is here,
Where Juliet lives; and every cat and dog
And little mouse, every unworthy thing,
Live here in heaven and may look on her;
But Romeo may not. More validity,
More honorable state, more courtship lives
In carrion flies than Romeo. They may seize
On the white wonder of dear Juliet's hand
And steal immortal blessing from her lips,
Who, even in pure and vestal modesty,
Still blush, as thinking their own kisses sin;
But Romeo may not—he is banished.
This may flies do, when I from this must fly;
They are free men, but I am banished.
And sayst thou yet that exile is not death?
Hadst thou no poison mixed, no sharp-ground knife?
No sudden mean of death, though ne'er so mean,
But "banished" to kill me—"banished"?
O friar, the damned use that word in hell;
Howling attends it! How hast thou the heart,
Being a divine, a ghostly confessor,
A sin-absolver, and my friend professed,
To mangle me with that word "banished"?
Friar. Thou fond mad man, hear me a little speak.
Rom. O, thou wilt speak again of banishment.
Friar. I'll give thee armor to keep off that word;
Adversity's sweet milk, philosophy,
To comfort thee, though thou art banished.
Rom. Yet "banished"? Hang up philosophy!
Unless philosophy can make a Juliet,

Our law says that what you have done is punishable by death, but the kind Prince on your behalf set aside that law and turned that horrible word "death" to "banishment." And you can't see that this is an extraordinary act of mercy?

ROMEO: It is torture, and not mercy. Heaven is here in Verona where Juliet lives; and every cat and dog and little mouse, every unworthy thing lives here in heaven and may look at her. But I cannot if I am banished. The lowest garbage flies have more worth than I have because they can give their gallant attentions to Juliet. They can touch the white wonder of her hand and steal immortal blessings from her lips that are pure and virginal—those lips that still blush, thinking that their own kisses are sinful. But I may not do those things for I am banished. Flies can do this while I am forced to fly from here. Flies are free but I am banished. And you say that exile isn't death? Have you no poison or sharp knife to kill me? Do you have anything less painful than banishment that can kill me instantly? Oh, Friar, that word is howled by the damned in hell. How do you have the heart, as my confessor, as the person who forgives my sins, as someone who calls himself my friend, to mangle me with the word "banished"?

FRIAR: Listen to me, you foolish man.

ROMEO: Don't start again! I know you will speak of banishment.

FRIAR: I will give you the strength to deal with that word. There is always a worse situation than your own. If you can just be philosophical about the situation, it will comfort you even though you are banished.

ROMEO: Still "banished." I hear that word again. Don't talk to me about philosophy—unless your philosophy can create a Juliet,

Displant a town, reverse a prince's doom,
It helps not, it prevails not. Talk no more.

Friar. O, then I see that madmen have no ears.

Rom. How should they, when that wise men have no eyes?

Friar. Let me dispute with thee of thy estate.

Rom. Thou canst not speak of that thou dost not feel.
Wert thou as young as I, Juliet thy love,
An hour but married, Tybalt murderèd,
Doting like me, and like me banishèd,
Then mightst thou speak, then mightst thou tear thy hair,
And fall upon the ground, as I do now,
Taking the measure of an unmade grave.

Nurse knocks [*within*].

Friar. Arise; one knocks. Good Romeo, hide thyself.

Rom. Not I; unless the breath of heartsick groans
Mist-like infold me from the search of eyes. *Knock.*

Friar. Hark, how they knock! Who's there? Romeo, arise;
Thou wilt be taken.—Stay awhile!—Stand up; *Knock.*
Run to my study.—By-and-by!—God's will,
What simpleness is this.—I come, I come! *Knock.*
Who knocks so hard? Whence come you? What's your will?

Nurse. [*Within*] Let me come in, and you shall know my errand.
I come from Lady Juliet.

Friar. Welcome then.

Enter *Nurse.*

Nurse. O holy friar, O, tell me, holy friar,
Where is my lady's lord, where's Romeo?

or uproot a town, or reverse a Prince's sentence. If it cannot do these things, then it doesn't help. Don't talk to me anymore.

FRIAR: Oh, then I see that crazy men don't listen and you are one of them.

ROMEO: Why should madmen have ears when men who are supposed to be wise have no eyes to see a situation clearly?

FRIAR: Let me discuss this matter with you. In my opinion you are luckier than you realize.

ROMEO: You don't have the right to express an opinion about emotions that you don't feel. If you were as young as I, and if you loved Juliet, then you could speak. If, after being married one hour, you had murdered her cousin Tybalt; and if, like me, you were banished—*then* and only then would you have the right to speak. You would probably tear your hair out and fall on the ground the way I do, with the feeling that you were measuring yourself for your own grave.

(NURSE knocks within.)

FRIAR: Get up off the floor, Romeo. Someone is knocking. Hide yourself, good Romeo.

ROMEO: I will not hide myself. If my love hides me then I will be hidden. Otherwise, I don't care. (Knock.)

FRIAR: Listen to that loud knocking! Who is there? Romeo, please get up. You will be taken away by the authorities. Be reasonable. Stand up (Knock.) and run into my study. Soon God's will shall help. What foolishness is this? I'm coming, I'm coming. (Knock.) Who knocks so hard? What do you want?

NURSE: (Outside.) Let me come in and I'll tell you why I am here. Lady Juliet sent me.

FRIAR: I welcome you then. (Enter NURSE.)

NURSE: Oh, holy Friar, oh tell me, holy Friar, where is my lady's Lord Romeo?

Friar. There on the ground, with his own tears made drunk.
Nurse. O, he is even in my mistress' case,
Just in her case! O woeful sympathy!
Piteous predicament! Even so lies she,
Blubb'ring and weeping, weeping and blubbering.
Stand up, stand up! Stand, an you be a man.
For Juliet's sake, for her sake, rise and stand!
Why should you fall into so deep an O?
Rom. (*Rises*) Nurse—
Nurse. Ah sir! ah sir! Well, death's the end of all.
Rom. Spakest thou of Juliet? How is it with her?
Doth not she think me an old murderer,
Now I have stained the childhood of our joy
With blood removed but little from her own?
Where is she? and how doth she? and what says
My concealed lady to our canceled love?
Nurse. O, she says nothing, sir, but weeps and weeps;
And now falls on her bed, and then starts up,
And Tybalt calls; and then on Romeo cries,
And then down falls again.
Rom. As if that name,
Shot from the deadly level of a gun,
Did murder her; as that name's cursed hand
Murdered her kinsman. O tell me, friar, tell me,
In what vile part of this anatomy
Doth my name lodge? Tell me, that I may sack
The hateful mansion. [*Draws his dagger.*]
Friar. Hold thy desperate hand.
Art thou a man? Thy form cries out thou art;
Thy tears are womanish, thy wild acts denote
The unreasonable fury of a beast.
Unseemly woman in a seeming man!
Or ill-beseeming beast in seeming both!

ACT III, Scene 3

FRIAR: He is there on the ground, drunk with his own tears.

NURSE: Oh, he is in the same condition as my mistress. What a pitiful predicament! She lies on her bed blubbering and weeping, weeping and blubbering. Stand up, stand up, Romeo, if you are a man. For Juliet's sake, rise and stand and stop your moaning.

ROMEO: (Rises.) Nurse—

NURSE: Ah sir! Ah sir! Well, death is the end of everything.

ROMEO: Are you talking about Juliet? How is she? Does she think of me as a brutal murderer, now that I have stained the beginnings of our joy and done it with the blood of her close cousin? Where is she? How is she? And what does my secret bride say about the condition of our endangered love?

NURSE: She doesn't say anything, sir. She just keeps crying and falls on her bed and then gets up and calls to Tybalt, and then to Romeo, and then falls down on her bed again.

ROMEO: She must feel that my name, like a shot from a gun, has murdered her as surely as my hand murdered her cousin. Oh, tell me, Friar, where in my body does my name exist so that I can destroy it? (Draws his dagger.)

FRIAR: Stop it! Hold off with such desperate actions. Are you a man? You look like a man, but you act like a woman with your tears. Your wild acts make you sound like an unreasonable, furious beast. You appear to be an unbecoming woman in the body of a man, or a strange, confined beast which is neither man nor woman.

Thou hast amazed me. By my holy order,
I thought thy disposition better tempered.
Hast thou slain Tybalt? Wilt thou slay thyself?
And slay thy lady too that lives in thee,
By doing damned hate upon thyself?
Why railst thou on thy birth, the heaven, and earth?
Since birth and heaven and earth, all three do meet
In thee at once; which thou at once wouldst lose.
Fie, fie, thou shamest thy shape, thy love, thy wit,
Which, like a usurer, aboundst in all,
And usest none in that true use indeed
Which should bedeck thy shape, thy love, thy wit.
Thy noble shape is but a form of wax,
Digressing from the valor of a man;
Thy dear love sworn but hollow perjury,
Killing that love which thou hast vowed to cherish;
Thy wit, that ornament to shape and love,
Misshapen in the conduct of them both,
Like powder in a skilless soldier's flask,
Is set afire by thine own ignorance,
And thou dismembered with thine own defense.
What, rouse thee, man! Thy Juliet is alive,
For whose dear sake thou wast but lately dead.
There art thou happy. Tybalt would kill thee,
But thou slewest Tybalt. There art thou happy.
The law, that threatened death, becomes thy friend
And turns it to exile. There art thou happy.
A pack of blessings light upon thy back;
Happiness courts thee in her best array;
But, like a misbehaved and sullen wench,
Thou poutst upon thy fortune and thy love.
Take heed, take heed, for such die miserable.
Go get thee to thy love, as was decreed,
Ascend her chamber, hence and comfort her.

You amaze me. By all that is invested in me I thought you were more sensible and had a more even disposition. You killed Tybalt, didn't you? Now you want to kill yourself, too, and by doing so, you will destroy Juliet who loves you. Remember that suicide is an unforgivable sin. Why do you complain and carry on so much about your birth and heaven and earth? All three, birth, heaven, and earth—are part of you as a human being and you would lose them all by your behavior. You shame your shape as a man, your love, and your judgment. You are like a moneylender who brings shame upon himself. You have the noble shape of a man, but inside you lack a man's valor and integrity. You make a lie of your love and you kill the love you vowed to cherish. Your judgment, the complement to your shape and love, is warped. Like an inexperienced soldier you have misused your ability and have been badly injured by your own weapon. It is time to straighten out, man. Remember, you should be grateful that Juliet is alive and you yourself could easily have been murdered by Tybalt's sword.That should make you happy! Tybalt could have killed you, but you killed him. That should make you happy! Moreover, the law has befriended you and instead of giving you the death sentence has turned it into exile. That should make you happy! You have a pack of blessings on your back and you ignore them. You misbehave, you are sullen. You frown upon your good fortune and your love. Listen to me and pay attention—such ingrates as you die miserable. Now move yourself and go to Juliet as we arranged. Go to her chamber and comfort her.

But look thou stay not till the watch be set,
For then thou canst not pass to Mantua,
Where thou shalt live till we can find a time
To blaze your marriage, reconcile your friends,
Beg pardon of the Prince, and call thee back
With twenty hundred thousand times more joy
Than thou wentst forth in lamentation.
Go before, nurse. Commend me to thy lady,
And bid her hasten all the house to bed,
Which heavy sorrow makes them apt unto.
Romeo is coming.
Nurse. O Lord, I could have stayed here all the night
To hear good counsel. O, what learning is!
My lord, I'll tell my lady you will come.
Rom. Do so, and bid my sweet prepare to chide.
Nurse offers to go and turns again.
Nurse. Here is a ring she bid me give you, sir.
Hie you, make haste, for it grows very late. *Exit.*
Rom. How well my comfort is revived by this!
Friar. Go hence; good night; and here stands all your
state:
Either be gone before the watch be set,
Or by the break of day disguised from hence.
Sojourn in Mantua. I'll find out your man,
And he shall signify from time to time
Every good hap to you that chances here.
Give me thy hand. 'Tis late. Farewell; good night.
Rom. But that a joy past joy calls out on me,
It were a grief so brief to part with thee.
Farewell.

Exeunt.

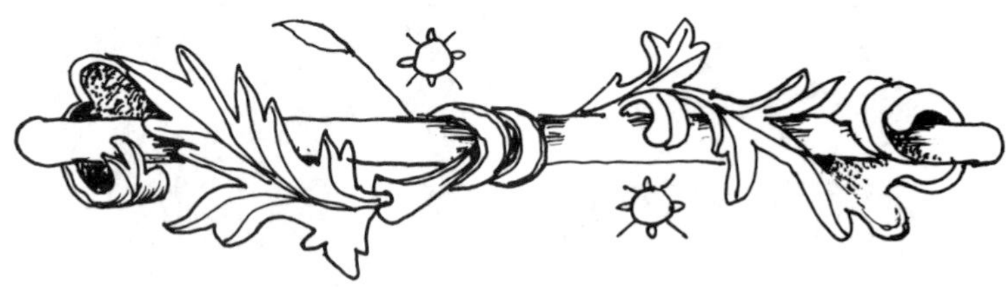

But be careful of the guards on duty at the gates of Verona. If you encounter them, you will not be able to leave for Mantua. The time will be right to announce your marriage when you reconcile both your families and beg the Prince for his pardon. Then you will return with twenty hundred thousand times more joy than when you left in sadness. Leave right now, dear Nurse, ahead of Romeo, and give my regards to Juliet. Ask her to hurry everyone in the household to bed—which they will be inclined to do because of their great sorrow over Tybalt. Romeo will follow you.

NURSE: Oh Lord, I could have stayed here all night to hear such good advice. Oh, but learning is so wonderful. My lord Romeo, I'll tell my lady you will come.

ROMEO: Do so, and tell my sweet lady to be prepared to scold me.

(NURSE offers to go and turns again.)

NURSE: Here is a ring Juliet gave me to give to you, sir. Do hurry because it's getting late. (NURSE leaves.)

ROMEO: I feel like a new man because of this ring from my beloved. My happiness is revived.

FRIAR: Get started now, Romeo—good night. And remember that your whole situation depends upon your leaving Verona when it is safe at the gates. Take care. Stay in Mantua. I'll locate your servant Balthasar and will give him whatever good news may develop here from time to time. Give me your hand; it's getting late. Farewell and good night.

ROMEO: It is only because the most incredible joy calls out to me that I am able to leave you. Otherwise it would fill me with grief to part with you so hastily. Farewell.

(They leave.)

[Scene IV. Capulet's house.]

Enter *Old Capulet,* his *Wife,* and *Paris.*

Cap. Things have fall'n out, sir, so unluckily
That we have had no time to move our daughter.
Look you, she loved her kinsman Tybalt dearly,
And so did I. Well, we were born to die.
'Tis very late; she'll not come down tonight.
I promise you, but for your company,
I would have been abed an hour ago.
Par. These times of woe afford no time to woo.
Madam, good night. Commend me to your daughter.
Lady. I will, and know her mind early tomorrow;
Tonight she's mewed up to her heaviness.
Paris offers to go and Capulet calls him again.
Cap. Sir Paris, I will make a desperate tender
Of my child's love. I think she will be ruled
In all respects by me; nay more, I doubt it not.
Wife, go you to her ere you go to bed;
Acquaint her here of my son Paris' love
And bid her (mark you me?) on Wednesday next—
But, soft! what day is this?
Par. Monday, my lord.
Cap. Monday! ha, ha! Well, Wednesday is too soon.
A Thursday let it be—a Thursday, tell her,
She shall be married to this noble earl.
Will you be ready? Do you like this haste?
We'll keep no great ado—a friend or two;
For hark you, Tybalt being slain so late,
It may be thought we held him carelessly,
Being our kinsman, if we revel much.

ACT III

(Scene 4: CAPULET'S house.)

(Enter LORD CAPULET, his WIFE, and PARIS.)

LORD CAP: So many things have happened, Paris, that have been so unfortunate, that my wife and I have not had the time to try to prepare Juliet for your proposal of marriage. You see—she loved her cousin Tybalt dearly, and so did I. It is difficult to speak to her for she mourns him deeply. Well, death is a part of all our lives. It's very late, so Juliet will not come down tonight. I assure you that if it hadn't been for your company, I would have been in bed an hour ago.

PARIS: It is not the time to court someone's affection during such sad times. Good night, Madam Capulet. Give my regards to your daughter.

LADY CAP: I will, and tomorrow I will talk with her. Tonight she is full grief and completely taken up with it.

(PARIS offers to go and LORD CAPULET calls him again.)

LORD CAP: Sir Paris, I am going to make what seems like a reckless offer of Juliet's love. In this situation I think she will do as I ask. I have no doubt of it. Wife, go to her before you go to bed, tell her about Paris's love for her and tell her that I have decided that on Wednesday—wait, what day is it today?

PARIS: Monday, my lord.

LORD CAP: Monday! Well, then, Wednesday is too soon. Let it be Thursday. Tell her she will be married to this noble earl on Thursday. Will you be ready, Paris? Does this seem too fast for you? We won't have a big ceremony—just a friend or two. After all, we must consider that Tybalt was recently killed. Having a party so soon after Tybalt's death would seem disrespectful.

Therefore we'll have some half a dozen friends,
And there an end. But what say you to Thursday?
Par. My lord, I would that Thursday were tomorrow.
Cap. Well, get you gone. A Thursday be it then.
Go you to Juliet ere you go to bed;
Prepare her, wife, against this wedding day.
Farewell, my lord.—Light to my chamber, ho!
Afore me, it is so very very late
That we may call it early by-and-by.
Good night.

Exeunt.

[Scene V. Capulet's orchard.]

Enter *Romeo* and *Juliet* aloft, at the window.

Jul. Wilt thou be gone? It is not yet near day.
It was the nightingale, and not the lark,
That pierced the fearful hollow of thine ear.
Nightly she sings on yond pomegranate tree.
Believe me, love, it was the nightingale.
Rom. It was the lark, the herald of the morn;
No nightingale. Look, love, what envious streaks
Do lace the severing clouds in yonder East.
Night's candles are burnt out, and jocund day
Stands tiptoe on the misty mountain tops.
I must be gone and live, or stay and die.
Jul. Yond light is not daylight; I know it, I.
It is some meteor that the sun exhales
To be to thee this night a torchbearer
And light thee on thy way to Mantua.
Therefore stay yet; thou needst not to be gone.
Rom. Let me be ta'en, let me be put to death.

Therefore we'll invite half a dozen friends and end the matter. But what do you say to Thursday?

PARIS: My lord, it isn't too soon. I wish that Thursday were tomorrow.

LORD CAP: Well, you had better be going. Let it be Thursday then. Before you go to bed, dear wife, you had better go to Juliet. Let her know about our plan for her wedding day. Farewell, my lord. (To SERVANT.)
I need a light so I can find my way to my chamber. I hardly realized that it was so very late. Soon it will be morning. Good night.

(They leave.)

ACT III

(Scene 5: CAPULET'S orchard.)

(Enter ROMEO and JULIET, both at the window on the balcony.)

JULIET: Are you going so soon? It is not daylight yet. It was the nightingale that sings at night and not the morning lark that you heard with such apprehension. I know that nightingale. She sings on that pomegranate tree in the orchard. Believe me, love, it was the nightingale.

ROMEO: It was the lark I heard that announces the morning and not a nightingale. Look, my love, at those unkind streaks of morning that come through the clouds in the East. The night's candles are burnt out and the bright day stands on tiptoes on the misty mountain tops. I must either go and live in Mantua, or stay and die in Verona.

JULIET: That light over there is not daylight. I know it is not. It is a flash of light from a meteor—a fiery streak for you to use as a torch tonight to light your way to Mantua. So please stay awhile; you don't need to leave just yet.

ROMEO: If you feel that way, then let me be taken and let me be put to death.

I am content, so thou wilt have it so.
I'll say yon grey is not the morning's eye,
'Tis but the pale reflex of Cynthia's brow;
Nor that is not the lark whose notes do beat
The vaulty heaven so high above our heads.
I have more care to stay than will to go.
Come, death, and welcome! Juliet wills it so.
How is't, my soul? Let's talk; it is not day.
Jul. It is, it is! Hie hence, be gone, away!
It is the lark that sings so out of tune,
Straining harsh discords and unpleasing sharps.
Some say the lark makes sweet division;
This doth not so, for she divideth us.
Some say the lark and loathed toad changed eyes;
O, now I would they had changed voices too,
Since arm from arm that voice doth us affray,
Hunting thee hence with hunt's-up to the day!
O, now be gone! More light and light it grows.
Rom. More light and light—more dark and dark our woes!

Enter *Nurse,* hastily.

Nurse. Madam!
Jul. Nurse?
Nurse. Your lady mother is coming to your chamber.
The day is broke; be wary, look about. [*Exit.*]
Jul. Then, window, let day in, and let life out.
Rom. Farewell, farewell! One kiss, and I'll descend.
He goeth down.
Jul. Art thou gone so, my lord, my love, my friend?
I must hear from thee every day in the hour,
For in a minute there are many days.

I will be content if that is what you wish. I will say that the greyness comes not from the sun but from the reflection of the moon. And I will say that it is not the morning lark whose notes pierce the heavens above our heads. I am more eager to stay than to go. Come, death—I welcome you because Juliet wants it this way. And does that please you, my sweet soul Juliet? Speak to me; it is not daylight yet.

JULIET: It is day! Yes, it is day! Please leave—go right now. It is the morning lark I hear that sings so out of tune, straining harsh, shrill notes. Some say it sings quiet melodies but that cannot be true because her singing heralds the morning when we must say good-bye. I've heard that the lark and the toad exchanged eyes once upon a time. The toad's large and brilliant eyes would be more appropriate to a bird. How I wish they had changed voices too, because it is the lark's voice we fear—the same lark who hunts you now with the same morning song used to waken hunters. Go now. It is getting lighter and lighter.

ROMEO: As it gets lighter and lighter, our problems grow darker and darker.

(Enter NURSE hastily.)

NURSE: Madam!

JULIET: Nurse—what do you want?

NURSE: Your mother is coming to your room. The morning is here. Be careful and do watch out.

JULIET: As this window lets in the day, it lets out my life.

ROMEO: Good-bye, good-bye. Give me just one kiss and I'll climb down.

(He descends.)

JULIET: Are you gone now, my lord, my love, my friend? I must hear from you every day in the hour—because every minute will seem like days.

O, by this count I shall be much in years
Ere I again behold my Romeo!
Rom. Farewell!
I will omit no opportunity
That may convey my greetings, love, to thee.
Jul. O, thinkst thou we shall ever meet again?
Rom. I doubt it not; and all these woes shall serve
For sweet discourses in our time to come.
Jul. O God, I have an ill-divining soul!
Methinks I see thee, now thou art below,
As one dead in the bottom of a tomb.
Either my eyesight fails, or thou lookst pale.
Rom. And trust me, love, in my eye so do you.
Dry sorrow drinks our blood. Adieu! adieu! *Exit.*
Jul. O Fortune, Fortune! all men call thee fickle.
If thou art fickle, what dost thou with him
That is renowned for faith? Be fickle, Fortune,
For then I hope thou wilt not keep him long
But send him back.
Lady. [*Within*] Ho, daughter! are you up?
Jul. Who is't that calls? It is my lady mother.
Is she not down so late, or up so early?
What unaccustomed cause procures her hither?

Enter *Mother.*

Lady. Why, how now, Juliet?
Jul. Madam, I am not well.
Lady. Evermore weeping for your cousin's death?
What, wilt thou wash him from his grave with tears?
An if thou couldst, thou couldst not make him live.
Therefore have done. Some grief shows much of love;
But much of grief shows still some want of wit.

And if I count the time in this fashion, I will be an old woman when I see my Romeo again.

ROMEO: Farewell! I will take every opportunity to send messages and my love to you.

JULIET: Do you think we will ever meet again?

ROMEO: I have no doubt that we will. All the sorrows we suffer now will provide us with sweet conversations in the future.

JULIET: Oh, God, I foresee evil. I think I see you, there on the ground, as if you were dead at the bottom of a tomb. Either my eyesight fails me or you look pale.

ROMEO: Trust me, dearest, because as I look into your face, you look pale, too. It is only that our sorrow drains the blood from us. Good-bye! Good-bye! (He leaves.)

JULIET: Oh Chance, oh Fate—all men think of you as changeable. If you are so fickle, then perhaps as Romeo and I part, you will change your mind again and send my Romeo back to me.

LADY CAP: (Within.) Hello—my daughter, are you up?

JULIET: Who is that calling? Oh, it is my mother. Either she is terribly late going to bed or she is up very early. This is strange. I wonder what brings her here at this hour?

(Enter LADY CAPULET.)

LADY CAP: How are you, Juliet?

JULIET: I am not well, Mother.

LADY CAP: Are you still crying over your cousin's death? Are you going to wash him from his grave with your tears? And if you tried, you still could not bring him back to life. It is time to get over your sorrow. Some grief is proof of a person's love but too much of it only means that you are unwise.

Jul. Yet let me weep for such a feeling loss.
Lady. So shall you feel the loss, but not the friend
Which you weep for.
Jul. Feeling so the loss,
I cannot choose but ever weep the friend.
Lady. Well, girl, thou weepst not so much for his death
As that the villain lives which slaughtered him.
Jul. What villain, madam?
Lady. That same villain Romeo.
Jul. [*Aside*] Villain and he be many miles asunder.—
God pardon him! I do, with all my heart;
And yet no man like he doth grieve my heart.
Lady. That is because the traitor murderer lives.
Jul. Ay, madam, from the reach of these my hands.
Would none but I might venge my cousin's death!
Lady. We will have vengeance for it, fear thou not.
Then weep no more. I'll send to one in Mantua,
Where that same banished runagate doth live,
Shall give him such an unaccustomed dram
That he shall soon keep Tybalt company;
And then I hope thou wilt be satisfied.
Jul. Indeed I never shall be satisfied
With Romeo till I behold him—dead—
Is my poor heart so for a kinsman vexed.
Madam, if you could find out but a man
To bear a poison, I would temper it;
That Romeo should, upon receipt thereof,
Soon sleep in quiet. O, how my heart abhors
To hear him named and cannot come to him,
To wreak the love I bore my cousin Tybalt
Upon his body that hath slaughtered him!
Lady. Find thou the means, and I'll find such a man.
But now I'll tell thee joyful tidings, girl.

ACT III, Scene 5

JULIET: Please just give me a bit more time to cry over such a heartbreaking loss.

LADY CAP: You should try to think about the friendship which you felt for Tybalt and not about your loss.

JULIET: I feel so deeply about his death that I cannot choose to do anything but weep over him.

LADY CAP: Well, girl, if you want to cry, then you should cry because the villain who slaughtered Tybalt is still alive.

JULIET: What villain are you talking about, Mother?

LADY CAP: I'm talking about the murderer, Romeo.

JULIET: (Aside.) That villain is probably miles from here. God pardon him as I do with all my heart, yet no man gives me more grief than he does.

LADY CAP: That's because that traitor murderer is still alive.

JULIET: I only feel grief, Mother, because Tybalt's murderer is so far away. If he were here, I could get my hands on him and avenge my cousin's death.

LADY CAP: We'll have our revenge on him, don't worry about that. So stop crying. I'll send someone to Mantua, where that banished runaway lives, and we'll see to it that he gets a dose of poison that will quickly put him away with our dead Tybalt. Then I hope you will be satisfied.

JULIET: Indeed, I will never be satisified with Romeo until I see him—dead—is my poor heart for the loss of my cousin. Mother, if you could only find a man to carry the poison, I would put something else in it so that Romeo would soon sleep quietly. Oh, how my heart hates to hear his name and not be able to go to him myself. I want to avenge the love I feel for my cousin on Romeo's body because Romeo slaughtered Tybalt.

LADY CAP: You find a way of doing it and I'll find such a man. But now I want to talk of joyful news, my daughter.

Jul. And joy comes well in such a needy time.
What are they, I beseech your ladyship?
Lady. Well, well, thou hast a careful father, child;
One who, to put thee from thy heaviness,
Hath sorted out a sudden day of joy
That thou expects not nor I looked not for.
Jul. Madam, in happy time! What day is that?
Lady. Marry, my child, early next Thursday morn
The gallant, young, and noble gentleman,
The County Paris, at Saint Peter's Church,
Shall happily make thee there a joyful bride.
Jul. Now by Saint Peter's Church, and Peter too,
He shall not make me there a joyful bride!
I wonder at this haste, that I must wed
Ere he that should be husband comes to woo.
I pray you tell my lord and father, madam,
I will not marry yet; and when I do, I swear
It shall be Romeo, whom you know I hate,
Rather than Paris. These are news indeed!
Lady. Here comes your father. Tell him so yourself,
And see how he will take it at your hands.

Enter *Capulet* and *Nurse.*

Cap. When the sun sets the air doth drizzle dew,
But for the sunset of my brother's son
It rains downright.
How now? a conduit, girl? What, still in tears?
Evermore show'ring? In one little body
Thou counterfeitst a bark, a sea, a wind:
For still thy eyes, which I may call the sea,
Do ebb and flow with tears; the bark thy body is,
Sailing in this salt flood; the winds, thy sighs,
Who, raging with thy tears and they with them,

ACT III, Scene 5

JULIET: And joy comes just when it is most needed. Tell me, please,what is this joyful news?

LADY CAP: Well, well, you have a very caring father, my child, who is concerned about you and your happiness. He has arranged for a special joyous day for you which neither you nor I expected.

JULIET: It sounds like the right thing at the right time. What occasion are you talking about?

LADY CAP: Well, my child, early next Thursday morning the gallant, young, and noble Count Paris will happily make you his joyful bride at Saint Peter's Church.

JULIET: By Saint Peter's Church, and by the saint himself, he will not make me his joyful bride! What is this rush? Why am I expected to be married before my future husband comes to court me? I beg of you to tell my lord and father that I will not marry yet; and when I do, I swear it will be to Romeo, whom you know I hate, rather than to Paris. This certainly is some news, indeed!

LADY CAP: Here comes your father. Tell him so yourself, and see how he will take the news from you.

(Enter LORD CAPULET and NURSE.)

LORD CAP: Ordinarily, when the sun sets, the air drizzles with dew. But when the sun sets for my nephew, it rains heavily because the heavens weep for him. (To JULIET.) What's this? Are you still crying like a fountain? What, still in tears? Weeping forever? In your little body we see a tree, a sea, and the wind: your eyes are the seas which ebb and flow with tears; your body is the tree which sails in this salty flood; and your sighs are the winds which rage with your tears as your tears rage with the winds. It is a vicious cycle.

Without a sudden calm will overset
Thy tempest-tossed body. How now, wife?
Have you delivered to her our decree?
Lady. Ay, sir; but she will none, she gives you thanks.
I would the fool were married to her grave!
Cap. Soft! take me with you, take me with you, wife.
How? Will she none? Doth she not give us thanks?
Is she not proud? Doth she not count her blest,
Unworthy as she is, that we have wrought
So worthy a gentleman to be her bridegroom?
Jul. Not proud you have, but thankful that you have.
Proud can I never be of what I hate,
But thankful even for hate that is meant love.
Cap. How, how, how, how, choplogic? What is this?
"Proud"—and "I thank you"—and "I thank you not"—
And yet "not proud"? Mistress minion you,
Thank me no thankings, nor proud me no prouds,
But fettle your fine joints 'gainst Thursday next
To go with Paris to Saint Peter's Church,
Or I will drag thee on a hurdle thither.
Out, you green-sickness carrion! out, you baggage!
You tallow-face!
Lady. Fie, fie; what, are you mad?
Jul. Good father, I beseech you on my knees,
She kneels down.
Hear me with patience but to speak a word.
Cap. Hang thee, young baggage! disobedient wretch!
I tell thee what—get thee to church a Thursday
Or never after look me in the face.
Speak not, reply not, do not answer me!
My fingers itch. Wife, we scarce thought us blest
That God had lent us but this only child;
But now I see this one is one too much,

Let me caution you; unless there is a sudden calm in the storm the winds will overturn your body, tossed by the storm. (To LADY CAP.) Well, now, my wife, have you told Juliet about our decision?

LADY CAP: Yes, I have, but she doesn't want any part of it. This is the way she thanks you. I would rather the fool were married to her grave instead.

LORD CAP: Wait a moment. I do not understand what is going on here. Do you mean she will have no part of this? Doesn't she thank us? Does she have no pride? Doesn't she consider herself blessed that, unworthy as she is, we have arranged a marriage with a worthy gentleman?

JULIET: I am not proud that you have made these arrangements, but I do thank you for your kindness. I cannot be proud of what I hate, and I hate the thought of marrying Paris. But I am thankful for your love and concern for me.

LORD CAP: How, how, how, have you arrived at this crazy logic? What is this? "Proud"—and "I thank you"—and "I don't thank you"—and yet "not proud"? My little darling, thank me no thankings and proud me no prouds, but prepare yourself to go with Paris to Saint Peter's Church next Thursday. If you don't, I will drag you there, you anemic, sickly lump of flesh, you waxy-faced baggage!

LADY CAP: Stop it, stop it, are you crazy?

JULIET: My good father, I beg you on my knees (she kneels), just be patient long enough for me to speak a word.

LORD CAP: Hang you, young baggage! Disobedient wretch! I'm telling you—you had better get yourself to church on Thursday or never look into my face again. Do not speak, do not reply, do not answer me! My fingers itch to slap you. Wife, we thought we were blessed when God gave us this only child but now I see this one is one too many!

And that we have a curse in having her.
Out on her, hilding!
Nurse. God in heaven bless her!
You are to blame, my lord, to rate her so.
Cap. And why, my Lady Wisdom? Hold your tongue,
Good Prudence. Smatter with your gossips, go!
Nurse. I speak no treason.
Cap. O, God-i-god-en!
Nurse. May not one speak?
Cap. Peace, you mumbling fool!
Utter your gravity o'er a gossip's bowl,
For here we need it not.
Lady. You are too hot.
Cap. God's bread! it makes me mad. Day, night, late, early,
At home, abroad, alone, in company,
Waking or sleeping, still my care hath been
To have her matched; and having now provided
A gentleman of princely parentage,
Of fair demesnes, youthful, and nobly trained,
Stuffed, as they say, with honorable parts,
Proportioned as one's thought would wish a man—
And then to have a wretched puling fool,
A whining mammet, in her fortunes tender,
To answer "I'll not wed, I cannot love;
I am too young, I pray you pardon me"!
But, an you will not wed, I'll pardon you.
Graze where you will, you shall not house with me.
Look to't, think on't; I do not use to jest.
Thursday is near; lay hand on heart, advise;
An you be mine, I'll give you to my friend;
An you be not, hang, beg, starve, die in the streets,
For, by my soul, I'll ne'er acknowledge thee,

We are cursed to have her. Get out, you wretch!

NURSE: My lord, may God in heaven bless her. You are to blame for losing your temper like this and abusing her so.

LORD CAP: And you, Lady Wisdom, hold your tongue for gossiping about things of which you know nothing.

NURSE: I am not speaking out of turn.

LORD CAP: I hope God punishes you for that.

NURSE: May no one speak? Isn't anyone allowed to say a word around you?

LORD CAP: Be quiet, you mumbling fool. Save your wisdom for over the punch bowl, because we certainly don't need it here.

LADY CAP: You are too hot-tempered and out of control.

LORD CAP: I swear it makes me mad when I think that day and night, late and early, at home or abroad, alone and in company, waking or sleeping, I've done everything I could to find a good man for her, and now I've found him—a gentleman of princely parentage—who is wealthy, young, and has good breeding and is of fine character—as fine a man as one would wish for. Now she acts like a whining fool, a mindless puppet, and says she can't get married, she can't love, she's too young and wants me to pardon her. Mind me, Juliet—if you do not get married I will be glad to see the last of you. You will move out of my house and I will never see you again. Think about it, because it is not my habit to joke! Thursday is near, so put your hand on your heart and think about this carefully; and if you choose still to be my daughter, I'll give you to Paris in marriage. But if you don't, you can hang, beg, starve, or die in the streets, for I swear on my soul I will never acknowledge you again.

Nor what is mine shall never do thee good.
Trust to't. Bethink you. I'll not be forsworn. *Exit.*
Jul. Is there no pity sitting in the clouds
That sees into the bottom of my grief?
O sweet my mother, cast me not away!
Delay this marriage for a month, a week;
Or if you do not, make the bridal bed
In that dim monument where Tybalt lies.
Lady. Talk not to me, for I'll not speak a word.
Do as thou wilt, for I have done with thee. *Exit.*
Jul. O God!—O nurse, how shall this be prevented?
My husband is on earth, my faith in heaven.
How shall that faith return again to earth
Unless that husband send it me from heaven
By leaving earth? Comfort me, counsel me.
Alack, alack, that heaven should practice stratagems
Upon so soft a subject as myself!
What sayst thou? Hast thou not a word of joy?
Some comfort, nurse.
Nurse. Faith, here it is.
Romeo is banisht; and all the world to nothing
That he dares ne'er come back to challenge you;
Or if he do, it needs must be by stealth.
Then, since the case so stands as now it doth,
I think it best you married with the County.
O, he's a lovely gentleman!
Romeo's a dishclout to him. An eagle, madam,
Hath not so green, so quick, so fair an eye
As Paris hath. Beshrew my very heart,
I think you are happy in this second match,
For it excels your first; or if it did not,
Your first is dead—or 'twere as good he were
As living here and you no use of him.
Jul. Speakst thou this from thy heart?

You will inherit nothing from me. Be assured of that. You may be certain that I will never break my oath.

(Exit LORD CAPULET.)

JULIET: Is there no pity in the heavens that sees how deep my grief is? Oh, my sweet mother, don't turn me away! Delay this marriage for a month, or a week; because if you do not, I will sicken and die. Then you can make my bridal bed in the burial vault where Tybalt lies.

LADY CAP: Do not talk to me because I will not discuss this further. Do what you want because I am through with you.

(LADY CAP leaves.)

JULIET: Oh, God! Oh, Nurse, how can I prevent all of this? My husband lives and I am married in the eyes of God. Only if Romeo dies and leaves this earth could I be married to another. How could heaven punish one as vulnerable as I? Say something to me, Nurse! Don't you have one word of joy or comfort for me?

NURSE: Here is my advice to you. Romeo is banished and the chances are poor that he will ever come back to claim you. If he returns, he will have to do it illegally and at great peril. Since this is the case, I think it is best for you to marry Count Paris. Oh, he's a lovely gentleman! Romeo is a dishrag compared to him. Even the majestic eagle does not have Paris's beautiful, lively, green eyes. Curse my very heart, but I think you are better off with this second match because it is so much better than your first. But whether or not it is better than your first—consider Romeo as good as dead. Even though he is living in this world he is of no use to you.

JULIET: Are you speaking from your heart?

Nurse. And from my soul too; else beshrew them both.
Jul. Amen!
Nurse. What?
Jul. Well, thou hast comforted me marvelous much.
Go in; and tell my lady I am gone,
Having displeased my father, to Laurence' cell,
To make confession and to be absolved.
Nurse. Marry, I will; and this is wisely done. *Exit.*
Jul. Ancient damnation! O most wicked fiend!
Is it more sin to wish me thus forsworn,
Or to dispraise my lord with that same tongue
Which she hath praised him with above compare
So many thousand times? Go, counselor!
Thou and my bosom henceforth shall be twain.
I'll to the friar to know his remedy.
If all else fail, myself have power to die.
Exit.

NURSE: And from my soul, too! If that is not the truth you may curse both my heart and soul.

JULIET: Amen! So be it.

NURSE: What did you say?

JULIET: Well, you have comforted me so marvellously well that you may go in and tell my mother that I am leaving. Having displeased my father, I am going to Friar Laurence's cell to make confession and be forgiven.

NURSE: I certainly will. What you are doing is very wise.

(Exit NURSE.)

JULIET: Nurse, how could you? you old devil! You wicked fiend! Is it more sinful to encourage me to break my marriage vows to Romeo or to insult him with the same tongue that praised him so many thousand times? Go, my counselor! You may be sure I will never, ever trust you again. I will go to the Friar now to see if he can help me. If all else fails I hope I have the strength to die.

(Exit JULIET.)

[ACT IV]

[Scene I. Friar Laurence's cell.]

Enter *Friar* [*Laurence*] and *County Paris.*

Friar. On Thursday, sir? The time is very short.
Par. My father Capulet will have it so,
And I am nothing slow to slack his haste.
Friar. You say you do not know the lady's mind.
Uneven is the course; I like it not.
Par. Immoderately she weeps for Tybalt's death,
And therefore have I little talked of love;
For Venus smiles not in a house of tears.
Now, sir, her father counts it dangerous
That she do give her sorrow so much sway,
And in his wisdom hastes our marriage
To stop the inundation of her tears,
Which, too much minded by herself alone,
May be put from her by society.
Now do you know the reason of this haste.
Friar. [*Aside*] I would I knew not why it should be slowed.—
Look, sir, here comes the lady toward my cell.

Enter *Juliet.*

Par. Happily met, my lady and my wife!
Jul. That may be, sir, when I may be a wife.

ACT IV

(Scene 1: FRIAR LAURENCE'S cell.)

(Enter FRIAR LAURENCE and PARIS.)

FRIAR: You want the wedding to occur on Thursday? The time is very short.

PARIS: My future father-in-law wants it that way, and I am not about to stand in his way.

FRIAR: But you said you don't know how Juliet feels about all this. That could make it difficult—I don't like to do things so hurriedly.

PARIS: She has cried and cried so much over Tybalt's death that I have not had the chance to talk about love. You know what they say—that Venus, the goddess of love, does not visit those who are unhappy. The point of the matter is that her father thinks her grief is dangerous because she has allowed it to overwhelm her. Therefore, he has wisely hurried our wedding plans to stop Juliet's tears and sorrow. Lord Capulet feels that our marriage will end her loneliness and will force her to be more social. Now you know the reason for this rush.

FRIAR: (Aside.) I know the real reason why this wedding should be delayed, and I wish I didn't—for Juliet is already married to Romeo. Oh, look, Paris, here comes Juliet now.

(Enter JULIET.)

PARIS: I am very happy to see you, Juliet, my future wife.

JULIET: That may be true, Paris, when I become a wife.

Par. That may be must be, love, on Thursday next.
Jul. What must be shall be.
Friar. That's a certain text.
Par. Come you to make confession to this father?
Jul. To answer that, I should confess to you.
Par. Do not deny to him that you love me.
Jul. I will confess to you that I love him.
Par. So will ye, I am sure, that you love me.
Jul. If I do so, it will be of more price,
Being spoke behind your back, than to your face.
Par. Poor soul, thy face is much abused with tears.
Jul. The tears have got small victory by that,
For it was bad enough before their spite.
Par. Thou wrongst it more than tears with that report.
Jul. That is no slander, sir, which is a truth;
And what I spake, I spake it to my face.
Par. Thy face is mine, and thou hast slandered it.
Jul. It may be so, for it is not mine own.
Are you at leisure, holy father, now,
Or shall I come to you at evening mass?
Friar. My leisure serves me, pensive daughter, now.
My lord, we must entreat the time alone.
Par. God shield I should disturb devotion!
Juliet, on Thursday early will I rouse ye.
Till then, adieu, and keep this holy kiss. *Exit.*
Jul. O, shut the door! and when thou hast done so,
Come weep with me—past hope, past cure, past help!
Friar. Ah, Juliet, I already know thy grief;
It strains me past the compass of my wits.
I hear thou must, and nothing may prorogue it,
On Thursday next be married to this County.
Jul. Tell me not, friar, that thou hearst of this,
Unless thou tell me how I may prevent it.
If in thy wisdom thou canst give no help,

PARIS: There is no *maybe* about it, my love; it shall happen Thursday.

JULIET: Since the marriage has to be, then it will be.

FRIAR: That is certainly true.

PARIS: Did you come to Friar Laurence for confession?

JULIET: If I answered you, I would be confessing my sins to you.

PARIS: Make sure you tell him that you love me.

JULIET: I will tell *you* that I love *him*.

PARIS: And I am sure you will say that you love me.

JULIET: If I do, it will be worth more spoken behind your back than if I said it to your face.

PARIS: You poor soul. I can see that your face is swollen from crying.

JULIET: If I am not so lovely now, it is not the fault of the tears. That is the way I was before I began weeping.

PARIS: I do not like the things you are saying about your face. You are unkinder to your face than your tears have been.

JULIET: I am not lying, sir. I spoke the truth, and I am being totally honest with myself.

PARIS: Your face belongs to me now, and I say that you are being unkind.

JULIET: That may be because it does not belong to me anymore. Can you see me now, Friar Laurence, or shall I come to you at evening mass?

FRIAR: No, I am available to see you now. Paris, Juliet and I must speak in private.

PARIS: God forbid I should interfere with Juliet's prayers. Juliet, I will wake you up early on Thursday; till then, farewell, and here is a holy kiss for you.

(PARIS leaves.)

JULIET: Oh, Friar, close the door and come weep with me, for the situation is past hope, past cure, past help!

FRIAR: Ah Juliet, I already know what is bothering you. It upsets me terribly. I hear that on Thursday you are going to be married to Count Paris, and nothing will postpone it.

JULIET: Do not talk to me about the marriage, Friar, unless you can tell me how I can prevent it. If in your wisdom you cannot help me,

Do thou but call my resolution wise
And with this knife I'll help it presently.
God joined my heart and Romeo's, thou our hands;
And ere this hand, by thee to Romeo's sealed,
Shall be the label to another deed,
Or my true heart with treacherous revolt
Turn to another, this shall slay them both.
Therefore, out of thy long-experienced time,
Give me some present counsel; or, behold,
'Twixt my extremes and me this bloody knife
Shall play the umpire, arbitrating that
Which the commission of thy years and art
Could to no issue of true honor bring.
Be not so long to speak. I long to die
If what thou speakst speak not of remedy.
Friar. Hold, daughter. I do spy a kind of hope,
Which craves as desperate an execution
As that is desperate which we would prevent.
If, rather than to marry County Paris,
Thou hast the strength of will to slay thyself,
Then is it likely thou wilt undertake
A thing like death to chide away this shame,
That copest with death himself to scape from it;
And, if thou darest, I'll give thee remedy.
Jul. O, bid me leap, rather than marry Paris,
From off the battlements of yonder tower,
Or walk in thievish ways, or bid me lurk
Where serpents are; chain me with roaring bears,
Or shut me nightly in a charnel house,
O'ercovered quite with dead men's rattling bones,
With reeky shanks and yellow chapless skulls;
Or bid me go into a new-made grave
And hide me with a dead man in his shroud—
Things that, to hear them told, have made me tremble—

then give me your blessing and I will kill myself right now with this knife. God joined my heart and Romeo's; and you, Friar Laurence, joined our hands. And before this hand, already sealed to Romeo's, shall enter into another marriage contract and before my heart dishonestly revolts and turns to another, this knife will stop them both. Watch how this knife shall kill me, if you cannot give me some wise advice and help me out of this situation honorably. Do not be evasive; be forthright, because I desperately want to die if you cannot offer me some cure.

FRIAR: Be patient, Juliet, for I see a kind of hope which calls for a very dangerous plan, but not any worse than marrying Paris. If you would rather kill yourself than marry Paris, however, then you will probably go along with this plan which calls for you to face death. If you desire, I will tell you what I have in mind.

JULIET: I am ready to take *any* risk to avoid marrying Paris. Why, I would jump off a high tower, become a thief, expose myself to snakes. You could chain me to roaring bears or lock me up in a charnel house with dead men's rattling skeletons; reeking bones; and yellow, jawless skulls. Or tell me to hide in a freshly dug grave with a dead man in his shroud. It is strange that when I used to hear these things I would tremble with fear.

And I will do it without fear or doubt,
To live an unstained wife to my sweet love.
Friar. Hold, then. Go home, be merry, give consent
To marry Paris. Wednesday is tomorrow.
Tomorrow night look that thou lie alone;
Let not the nurse lie with thee in thy chamber.
Take thou this vial, being then in bed,
And this distilled liquor drink thou off;
When presently through all thy veins shall run
A cold and drowsy humor; for no pulse
Shall keep his native progress, but surcease;
No warmth, no breath, shall testify thou livest;
The roses in thy lips and cheeks shall fade
To paly ashes, thy eyes' windows fall
Like death when he shuts up the day of life;
Each part, deprived of supple government,
Shall, stiff and stark and cold, appear like death;
And in this borrowed likeness of shrunk death
Thou shalt continue two-and-forty hours,
And then awake as from a pleasant sleep.
Now, when the bridegroom in the morning comes
To rouse thee from thy bed, there art thou dead.
Then, as the manner of our country is,
In thy best robes uncovered on the bier
Thou shalt be borne to that same ancient vault
Where all the kindred of the Capulets lie.
In the mean time, against thou shalt awake,
Shall Romeo by my letters know our drift;
And hither shall he come; and he and I
Will watch thy waking, and that very night
Shall Romeo bear thee hence to Mantua.
And this shall free thee from this present shame,
If no inconstant toy nor womanish fear
Abate thy valor in the acting it.

Now, however, I would gladly do any of them without fear or doubt in order to live as a pure wife to my sweet love.

FRIAR: All right, then, Juliet, I want you to go home and act as if you are happy. Tell your parents that you will marry Paris after all. Tomorrow night, on the eve of your wedding, tell your nurse that you would rather she didn't sleep in your bedroom with you. Then, once you are in bed, drink the contents of this bottle. The liquid inside will run through your veins and make you cold and drowsy. Your pulse and breathing will stop. The coloring in your lips will fade and change to a deathly pallor. Your eyes will close as if you were dead. Your body will be stiff and stark. All these symptoms will continue for forty-two hours, after which time you will awake, just as if you had been sleeping. So when your bridegroom Paris comes to awaken you in the morning you will be "dead." According to our burial laws, you will be dressed in your finest clothes and carried to your family's ancient vault. You will lie uncovered on the bier. Meanwhile, while all this is happening, I will send a letter to Romeo and tell him of our plan. He will return to Verona and accompany me when we witness your wakening in the tomb. Then, dear Juliet, he will carry you off to Mantua. Yes, that is the plan—a plan that shall free you from this shame as long as you show no signs of womanish fear while carrying it out.

Jul. Give me, give me! O, tell not me of fear!
Friar. Hold! Get you gone, be strong and prosperous
In this resolve. I'll send a friar with speed
To Mantua, with my letters to thy lord.
Jul. Love give me strength! and strength shall help afford.
Farewell, dear father.

Exeunt.

[Scene II. Capulet's house.]

Enter *Father Capulet, Mother, Nurse,* and *Servingmen,* two or three.

Cap. So many guests invite as here are writ.
[*Exit a Servingman.*]
Sirrah, go hire me twenty cunning cooks.

Serv. You shall have none ill, sir; for I'll try if they can lick their fingers.

Cap. How canst thou try them so?

Serv. Marry, sir, 'tis an ill cook that cannot lick his own fingers. Therefore he that cannot lick his fingers goes not with me.

Cap. Go, begone. *Exit Servingman.*
We shall be much unfurnished for this time.
What, is my daughter gone to Friar Laurence?
Nurse. Ay, forsooth.
Cap. Well, he may chance to do some good on her.
A peevish self-willed harlotry it is.

Enter *Juliet.*

Nurse. See where she comes from shrift with merry look.

JULIET: Give me that bottle! Give it to me! Don't even mention fear, for I am brave!

FRIAR: All right, you can leave now. Be strong and single-minded when you are following this plan. And I will send one of the other friars to tell Romeo about what we intend to do.

JULIET: Love will give the strength to do what is required. Farewell, dear Friar!

(JULIET and FRIAR leave.)

ACT IV

(Scene 2: CAPULET'S house.)

(Enter LORD CAPULET, LADY CAPULET, NURSE, and two SERVANTS.)

LORD CAP: Make sure you invite the same guests whose names are written on this list.

(Exit FIRST SERVANT.)

And you go find some cooks to prepare today's feast; I should think we will need about twenty good ones.

SERV. 2: You won't have any bad cooks, sir. I'll see if they lick their own fingers.

LORD CAP: What kind of a test is that?

SERV. 2: Well, sir, it's a bad cook who doesn't want to lick his own fingers. Therefore, if someone doesn't lick his own fingers, then he won't be coming back here with me.

LORD CAP: Get out of here, go on. (Exit SECOND SERVANT.)
I don't think we're going to have enough to eat at this wedding. Has anyone seen Juliet? Did she go to Friar Laurence's?

NURSE: Yes, she has.

LORD CAP: Well, I hope he will have some good influence on her, because so far she has been a headstrong and good-for-nothing girl.

(Enter JULIET.)

NURSE: Here she comes. She has returned from confession with a smile on her face.

Cap. How now, my headstrong? Where have you been gadding?
Jul. Where I have learnt me to repent the sin
Of disobedient opposition
To you and your behests, and am enjoined
By holy Laurence to fall prostrate here
To beg your pardon. Pardon, I beseech you!
Henceforward I am ever ruled by you.
Cap. Send for the County. Go tell him of this.
I'll have this knot knit up tomorrow morning.
Jul. I met the youthful lord at Laurence' cell
And gave him what becomed love I might,
Not stepping o'er the bounds of modesty.
Cap. Why, I am glad on't. This is well. Stand up.
This is as't should be. Let me see the County.
Ay, marry, go, I say, and fetch him hither.
Now, afore God, this reverend holy friar,
All our whole city is much bound to him.
Jul. Nurse, will you go with me into my closet
To help me sort such needful ornaments
As you think fit to furnish me tomorrow?
Mother. No, not till Thursday. There is time enough.
Cap. Go, nurse, go with her. We'll to church tomorrow.
Exeunt Juliet and Nurse.
Mother. We shall be short in our provision.
'Tis now near night.
Cap. Tush, I will stir about,
And all things shall be well, I warrant thee, wife.
Go thou to Juliet, help to deck up her.
I'll not to bed tonight; let me alone.
I'll play the housewife for this once. What, ho!
They are all forth; well, I will walk myself
To County Paris, to prepare him up

ACT IV, Scene 2

LORD CAP: How are you, my stubborn daughter? Where have you been?

JULIET: I have been to Friar Laurence's. There I have repented the sin of disobedience to you and your commands. Friar Laurence has told me that I must fall to my knees and beg your forgiveness. Please, dear Father, forgive me, I beg of you. From now on I will do as you say.

LORD CAP: Someone bring Count Paris here, and tell him how Juliet has changed. They will tie the knot tomorrow morning, instead of Thursday.

JULIET: I saw Paris at Friar Laurence's cell today and showed him what love I could, while not stepping over the bounds of modesty.

LORD CAP: I am most pleased to hear that. This is splendid. Get up off the floor, Juliet. Yes, stand up.This is the way a daughter should act. Bring Paris to me. I am so glad you went to the Friar's today. The whole city owes him so much for all his help.

JULIET: Nurse, will you please help me pick out some of the clothes I will need for the wedding tomorrow?

LADY CAP: No, this wedding will not take place till Thursday. Wednesday is too soon.

LORD CAP: Go on, Nurse, go with Juliet. And Wife, we will get Juliet married tomorrow.

(JULIET and NURSE leave.)

LADY CAP: We will not have enough time. And we will not have enough food. It is already late in the day.

LORD CAP: Don't worry, I will take care of everything. Everything will be just fine, I assure you. Now you go help Juliet pick out her clothes. I do not plan on going to bed tonight. Leave me alone. I will play the housewife this time. It seems that all the servants are out so I will have to go to Paris myself and tell him that the wedding has been changed to

Against tomorrow. My heart is wondrous light,
Since this same wayward girl is so reclaimed.
Exeunt.

[Scene III. Juliet's chamber.]

Enter Juliet and *Nurse.*

Jul. Ay, those attires are best; but, gentle nurse,
I pray thee leave me to myself tonight;
For I have need of many orisons
To move the heavens to smile upon my state,
Which, well thou knowest, is cross and full of sin.

Enter *Mother.*

Mother. What, are you busy, ho? Need you my help?
Jul. No, madam; we have culled such necessaries
As are behooveful for our state tomorrow.
So please you, let me now be left alone,
And let the nurse this night sit up with you;
For I am sure you have your hands full all
In this so sudden business.
Mother. Good night.
Get thee to bed and rest, for thou hast need.
Exeunt. [*Mother and Nurse*].
Jul. Farewell! God knows when we shall meet again.
I have a faint cold fear thrills through my veins
That almost freezes up the heat of life.
I'll call them back again to comfort me.
Nurse!—What should she do here?
My dismal scene I needs must act alone.
Come, vial.

tomorrow. I feel so wondrously lighthearted to see this dramatic change in Juliet.

(They leave.)

ACT IV

(Scene 3: JULIET'S chamber.)

(Enter JULIET and NURSE.)

JULIET: I think these dresses will be best. But, please, gentle Nurse, let me be by myself tonight. I have many prayers to offer so that the heavens will smile upon me. For, as you know, what I am doing is full of sin.

(Enter LADY CAP.)

LADY CAP: Are you doing all right? Do you need me to stay and help?

JULIET: No, Mother, we have already chosen those clothes that will be appropriate for the wedding tomorrow. So please, let me be alone and let the Nurse sit up with you tonight since you have your hands full with the wedding being so near.

LADY CAP: Good night. And you should be in bed sleeping, too, for you have a big day tomorrow.

(LADY CAP and NURSE leave.)

JULIET: Farewell! Only God knows when we will all meet again. I have a faint cold fear that runs through my veins and chills me completely. I think I will call them back here to comfort me. Nurse! What could she do to help me? Friar Laurence's plan requires that I act alone. Come, little bottle.

What if this mixture do not work at all?
Shall I be married then tomorrow morning?
No, no! This shall forbid it. Lie thou there.
[*Lays down a dagger.*]
What if it be a poison which the friar
Subtly hath ministered to have me dead,
Lest in this marriage he should be dishonored
Because he married me before to Romeo?
I fear it is; and yet methinks it should not,
For he hath still been tried a holy man.
How if, when I am laid into the tomb,
I wake before the time that Romeo
Come to redeem me? There's a fearful point!
Shall I not then be stifled in the vault,
To whose foul mouth no healthsome air breathes in,
And there die strangled ere my Romeo comes?
Or, if I live, is it not very like
The horrible conceit of death and night,
Together with the terror of the place—
As in a vault, an ancient receptacle
Where for this many hundred years the bones
Of all my buried ancestors are packed;
Where bloody Tybalt, yet but green in earth,
Lies fest'ring in his shroud; where, as they say,
At some hours in the night spirits resort—
Alack, alack, is it not like that I,
So early waking—what with loathsome smells,
And shrieks like mandrakes torn out of the earth,
That living mortals, hearing them, run mad—
O, if I wake, shall I not be distraught,
Environed with all these hideous fears,
And madly play with my forefathers' joints,
And pluck the mangled Tybalt from his shroud,
And, in this rage, with some great kinsman's bone

ACT IV, Scene 3

Oh, I have so many doubts! What if the mixture inside does not work at all? Then will I be married to Paris tomorrow morning? No, no! I have a plan which will serve me if the liquid does not—this dagger which I will keep right by my side. (Lays down a dagger.) Oh, what if Friar Laurence really gave me poison so that he would not be dishonored because he married Romeo and me? I am afraid of that; yet I do not believe it could be. He has always been found to be a holy man, honest and true. What if, when I am laid into the tomb, I waken before Romeo comes to get me? That is a frightening thought! Wouldn't I suffocate in the vault—that foul place where no healthy air comes in—and die there strangled before my Romeo comes? And what if I lived? I would spend my last days with death and night in that place of terror where for hundreds of years the bones of my buried ancestors are packed. There bloody Tybalt, recently buried, lies rotting in his shroud.

As with a club dash out my desp'rate brains?
O, look! methinks I see my cousin's ghost
Seeking out Romeo, that did spit his body
Upon a rapier's point. Stay, Tybalt, stay!
Romeo, I come! this do I drink to thee.
She [*drinks and*] *falls upon her bed within the curtains.*

[Scene IV. Capulet's house]

Enter *Lady of the House* and *Nurse.*

Lady. Hold, take these keys and fetch more spices, nurse.
Nurse. They call for dates and quinces in the pastry.

Enter *Old Capulet.*

Cap. Come, stir, stir, stir! The second cock hath crowed,
The curfew bell hath rung, 'tis three o'clock.
Look to the baked meats, good Angelica;
Spare not for cost.
Nurse. Go, you cot-quean, go,
Get you to bed! Faith, you'll be sick tomorrow
For this night's watching.
Cap. No, not a whit. What, I have watched ere now
All night for lesser cause, and ne'er been sick.
Lady. Ay, you have been a mouse-hunt in your time;
But I will watch you from such watching now.
Exeunt Lady and Nurse.
Cap. A jealous hood, a jealous hood!

ACT IV, Scene 4

This is a place where people say ghosts live; and when people hear the shrieks and experience the awful stench there, they lose their minds. Surely I, too, would go crazy. I might play with the skeletons, take Tybalt's dead body out of its shroud, and then dash my brains out with one of my ancestor's bones. Oh, look! I think I see Tybalt's ghost looking for Romeo, the man who murdered him with a sword. Stop, Tybalt, stop! Romeo, this potion will bring me closer to you! I drink to you.

(JULIET falls upon her bed, within the curtains.)

ACT IV

(Scene 4: CAPULET'S house.)

(Enter LADY CAPULET and NURSE.)

LADY CAP: Stop, Nurse. Take these keys and get more spices.

NURSE: They need more dates and quinces in the kitchen.

(Enter LORD CAPULET.)

LORD CAP: Come on now—stir, stir, stir faster. The second rooster has crowed, the curfew has sounded, and it's three o'clock in the morning. Take care of the meat pies, good Nurse Angelica, and don't be stingy about the cost at a time like this.

NURSE: Lord Capulet, will you please leave? You act like a housewife and you are interfering with our work here. Go, get some rest or you will be sick tomorrow.

LORD CAP: That is not true. Besides, I've been up all night at other times without as good a reason as this, and it hasn't made me sick.

LADY CAP: Yes, but that was because you were a woman-hunter in your time who stalked your prey at night. I will prevent you from doing such hunting now.

(LADY CAPULET and NURSE leave.)

LORD CAP: You are a jealous ninny, my dear wife, a jealous ninny!

Enter three or four [*Servants*], with spits and logs and baskets.

Now, fellow,
What is there?
1. Serv. Things for the cook, sir; but I know not what.
Cap. Make haste, make haste. [*Exit Servant.*] Sirrah, fetch drier logs.
Call Peter; he will show thee where they are.
2. Serv. I have a head, sir, that will find out logs
And never trouble Peter for the matter.
Cap. Mass, and well said; a merry whoreson, ha!
Thou shalt be loggerhead. [*Exit Servant.*] Good faith, 'tis day.
The County will be here with music straight,
For so he said he would. (*Play music.*) I hear him near.
Nurse! Wife! What, ho! What, nurse, I say!

Enter *Nurse.*

Go waken Juliet; go and trim her up.
I'll go and chat with Paris. Hie, make haste,
Make haste! The bridegroom he is come already:
Make haste, I say.

[*Exeunt.*]

[Scene V. Juliet's chamber.]

[Enter *Nurse.*]

Nurse. Mistress! what, mistress! Juliet! Fast, I warrant her, she.
Why, lamb! why, lady! Fie, you slugabed!

ACT IV, Scene 5

(Enter three or four SERVANTS with spits, logs, and baskets.)

LORD CAP: Now, fellow, what do you have?

SERV. 1: I have things for the cook, sir, but I don't know what they are.

LORD CAP: Hurry up, hurry up.

(Exit FIRST SERVANT.)

Now, you, fetch drier logs. Call Peter; he'll show you where they are.

SERV. 2: I have a head for things like that, sir. I can find the logs without bothering Peter.

LORD CAP: By the Holy Church, you've said it well, you rascal! You will be our loghead!

(Exit SECOND SERVANT.)

My goodness, it is daylight. Soon Count Paris will be here with the musicians as he promised. (He hears music.) I hear him near. Nurse! Wife! Where are the two of you? Nurse!

(Enter NURSE.)

Waken Juliet and get her dressed and ready. I'll go and chat with Paris. Hurry now. Hurry! The bridgroom is here already. Hurry, I said!

(Exit LORD CAPULET and NURSE.)

ACT IV

(Scene 5: JULIET'S chamber.)

(Enter NURSE.)

NURSE: Mistress! Mistress! It is time to waken. You are truly fast asleep. Come, my lamb, come my lady, don't be a sleepyhead!

Why, love, I say! madam! sweetheart! Why, bride!
What, not a word? You take your pennyworths now!
Sleep for a week; for the next night, I warrant,
The County Paris hath set up his rest
That you shall rest but little. God forgive me!
Marry, and amen. How sound is she asleep!
I needs must wake her. Madam, madam, madam!
Ay, let the County take you in your bed!
He'll fright you up, i' faith. Will it not be?
[*Opens the curtains.*]
What, dressed and in your clothes and down again?
I must needs wake you. Lady! lady! lady!
Alas, alas! Help, help! my lady's dead!
O well-a-day that ever I was born!
Some aqua vitae, ho! My lord! my lady!

Enter *Mother.*

Mother. What noise is here?
Nurse. O lamentable day!
Mother. What is the matter?
Nurse. Look, look! O heavy day!
Mother. O me, O me! My child, my only life!
Revive, look up, or I will die with thee!
Help, help! Call help.

Enter *Father.*

Father. For shame, bring Juliet forth; her lord is come.
Nurse. She's dead, deceased; she's dead! Alack the day!
Mother. Alack the day, she's dead, she's dead, she's dead!
Cap. Ha! let me see her. Out alas! she's cold,
Her blood is settled, and her joints are stiff;

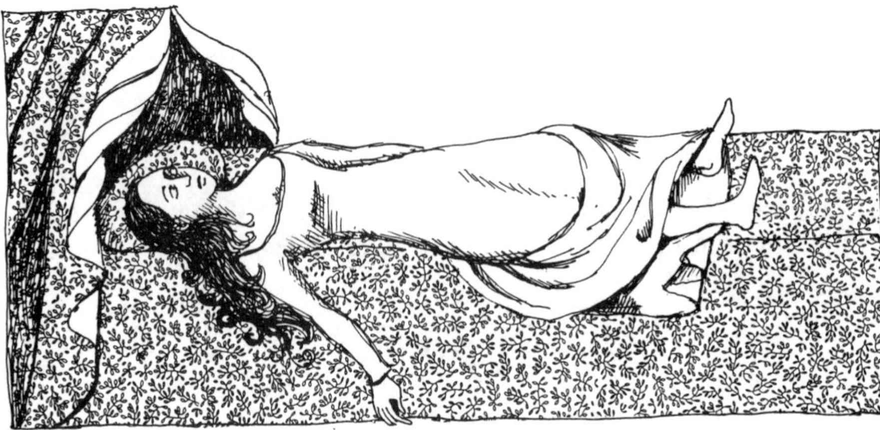

Love, Madam, sweetheart, bride. What, not a word? You are taking your rest now. You should sleep for a week. I am sure Count Paris is determined that you shall not get much rest on your honeymoon. God forgive me! She is so sound asleep. I absolutely must waken her. Madam, madam, madam! The Count will have to marry you in your bed! That should frighten you. Well, what is it going to be? (Opens curtains.) What? You are dressed and in bed with your clothes on? I must waken you. Lady, lady, lady! Oh, God! Help, help! My lady is dead! I regret the day that I was ever born! Some water, water! My lord! My lady! Please come!

(Enter LADY CAPULET.)

LADY CAP: What is this noise all about?

NURSE: Oh, what a lamentable day!

LADY CAP: What is the matter?

NURSE: Look, look! What a hideous day!

LADY CAP: Oh my child! My child, my only life! Wake up, open your eyes, or I will die with you! Help, help! Call for help!

(Enter LORD CAPULET.)

LORD CAP: This is humiliating not to have Juliet out here. This is a shame. Bring Juliet out. Her future husband is here.

NURSE: She's dead, deceased; she's dead! What an unbearable day!

LADY CAP: An unspeakable day. She's dead, she's dead, she's dead.

LORD CAP: Let me see her for myself. Oh God, it's true. She's cold. Her blood is still and her limbs are stiff.

Life and these lips have long been separated.
Death lies on her like an untimely frost
Upon the sweetest flower of all the field.
Nurse. O lamentable day!
Mother. O woeful time!
Cap. Death, that hath ta'en her hence to make me wail,
Ties up my tongue and will not let me speak.

Enter *Friar* [*Laurence*] and the *County* [*Paris*], with *Musicians.*

Friar. Come, is the bride ready to go to church?
Cap. Ready to go, but never to return.
O son, the night before thy wedding day
Hath Death lain with thy wife. See, there she lies,
Flower as she was, deflowered by him.
Death is my son-in-law, Death is my heir;
My daughter he hath wedded. I will die
And leave him all. Life, living, all is Death's.
Par. Have I thought long to see this morning's face,
And doth it give me such a sight as this?
Mother. Accursed, unhappy, wretched, hateful day!
Most miserable hour that e'er time saw
In lasting labor of his pilgrimage!
But one, poor one, one poor and loving child,
But one thing to rejoice and solace in,
And cruel Death hath catched it from my sight!
Nurse. O woe! O woeful, woeful, woeful day!
Most lamentable day, most woeful day
That ever ever I did yet behold!
O day! O day! O day! O hateful day!
Never was seen so black a day as this.
O woeful day! O woeful day!

The life is gone from her lips. Death has come to her like an early frost. It lies upon the sweetest flower in all the field.

NURSE: Oh, sorrowful day!

LADY CAP: Oh, what a time of grief!

LORD CAP: Death has taken her to make me wail. Death has tied up my tongue and will not let me speak.

(Enter FRIAR LAURENCE and COUNT PARIS with MUSICIANS.)

FRIAR: Come, come, is the bride ready to go to church?

LORD CAP: She is ready to go but she will never return. Paris, my son, Death has taken your bride the night before your wedding day. He has slept with her and stolen her virginity. Death is my son-in-law. Death is my heir. He has married my daughter. I will die and leave him everything. Life—my worldly belongings—it all belongs to death.

PARIS: I have thought so long about the morning of my marriage to Juliet. Can I believe my eyes? Is this really happening?

LADY CAP: Cursed, unhappy, wretched, hateful day! This is the most miserable hour that time has ever seen. But one, poor one, one poor and loving child—she was my one joy and comfort, and cruel Death has snatched her from my sight!

NURSE: Oh! Such a grief-filled day! This is the worst, the most grievous day, that I have ever beheld in my life. Oh day! Oh day! Oh hateful day! There has never been a day as black as this. Oh grievous day! Oh grievous day!

Par. Beguiled, divorced, wronged, spited, slain!
Most detestable Death, by thee beguiled,
By cruel cruel thee quite overthrown!
O love! O life! not life, but love in death!
Cap. Despised, distressed, hated, martyred, killed!
Uncomfortable time, why camest thou now
To murder, murder our solemnity?
O child! O child! my soul, and not my child!
Dead art thou, dead! alack, my child is dead,
And with my child my joys are buried!
Friar. Peace, ho, for shame! Confusions's cure lives not
In these confusions. Heaven and yourself
Had part in this fair maid! now heaven hath all,
And all the better is it for the maid.
Your part in her you could not keep from death,
But heaven keeps his part in eternal life.
The most you sought was her promotion,
For 'twas your heaven she should be advanced;
And weep ye now, seeing she is advanced;
Above the clouds, as high as heaven itself?
O, in this love, you love your child so ill
That you run mad, seeing that she is well.
She's not well married that lives married long.
But she's best married that dies married young.
Dry up your tears and stick your rosemary
On this fair corse, and, as the custom is,
In all her best array bear her to church;
For though fond nature bids us all lament,
Yet nature's tears are reason's merriment.
Cap. All things that we ordained festival
Turn from their office to black funeral—
Our instruments to melancholy bells,
Our wedding cheer to a sad burial feast;
Our solemn hymns to sullen dirges change;

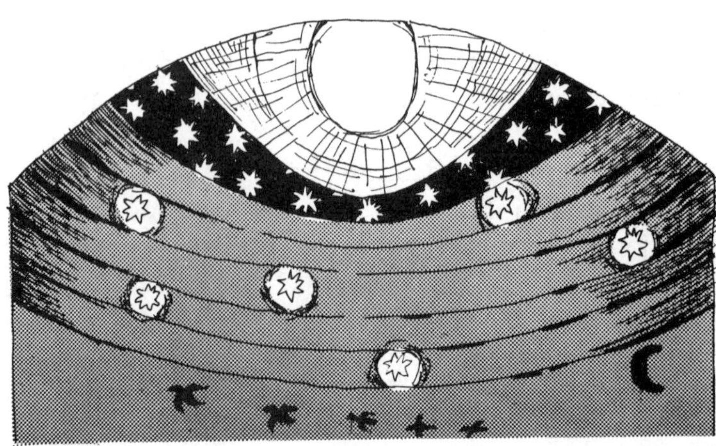

ACT IV, Scene 5

PARIS: I have been deprived, divorced, wronged, killed. Hateful Death, you have cheated me, and cruelly overthrown me. Oh love! Oh life! I have not been robbed of my life, but I have been robbed of love by Death.

LORD CAP: Oh Time! You are despised, distressed, hated, martyred, and killed! Why did you come to us now to destroy our happiness? Oh, my child! My soul! No longer my child! You are dead. My child is dead and with my child my joys are buried!

FRIAR: Please, let's pause a moment and reflect on what has happened. Try to understand that when Juliet was alive, you shared her with heaven. Now heaven has claimed her completely and she is better off. She is in a place of eternal life and has greater rewards than you could ever give her. The most you could give her was the advantage of a good marriage, but this good marriage was for your pleasure. Now she is raised above the clouds in heaven itself, so do not weep. Your love is selfish if it upsets you that she is happy in heaven. The woman who dies married young is better off than one who survives a long-lasting marriage and watches it decline. Dry your tears. Put rosemary around her body for eternal remembrance and carry her to church in her wedding gown. For though it is natural to lament, she has gone to a better place which is truly a reason to rejoice.

LORD CAP: All those things we had prepared for a happy celebration will be used for a different purpose. We turn from a wedding to a funeral. We change the happy music to the sound of melancholy bells and use our wedding food for a sad burial feast. And the solemn hymns of marriage change to mournful dirges.

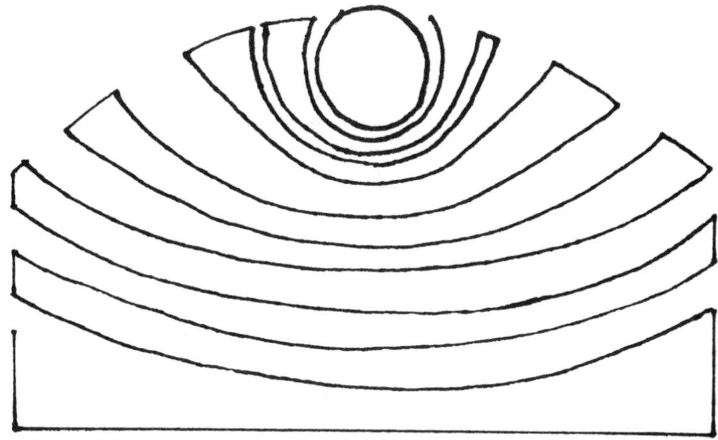

Our bridal flowers serve for a buried corse;
And all things change them to the contrary.
Friar. Sir, go you in; and, madam, go with him;
And go, Sir Paris. Every one prepare
To follow this fair corse unto her grave.
The heavens do lower upon you for some ill;
Move them no more by crossing their high will.
They all but the Nurse [*and Musicians*] *go forth, casting rosemary on her and shutting the curtains.*
1. Mus. Faith, we may put up our pipes and be gone.
Nurse. Honest good fellows, ah, put up, put up!
For well you know this is a pitiful case. [*Exit.*]
1. Mus. Ay, by my troth, the case may be amended.

Enter *Peter.*

Pet. Musicians, O, musicians, "Heart's Ease, Heart's Ease"!
O, an you will have me live, play "Heart's Ease."
1. Mus. Why "Heart's Ease"?
Pet. O, musicians, because my heart itself plays "My heart is full of woe." O, play me some merry dump to comfort me.
1. Mus. Not a dump we! 'Tis no time to play now.
Pet. You will not then?
1. Mus. No.
Pet. I will then give it you soundly.
1. Mus. What will you give us?
Pet. No money, on my faith, but the gleek. I will give you the minstrel.
1. Mus. Then will I give you the serving-creature.
Pet. Then will I lay the serving-creature's dagger on your pate. I will carry no crotchets. I'll re you, I'll fa you. Do you note me?

Our bridal flowers will be used for the burial; all things will be used not as they were intended.

FRIAR: Sir, please go in, and madam, go with him. Go, Sir Paris. Everyone prepare to follow this fair corpse to her grave. The heavens may be frowning upon you for your sins so do not anger them any further. (Exit LORD CAPULET, LADY CAPULET, PARIS, and FRIAR. NURSE puts rosemary on JULIET and shuts the curtains.)

MUS 1: Well, we can put away our instruments and leave.

NURSE: Yes, good fellows, put them away, put them away! Because, as you know, this is a pitiful event. (Exit NURSE.)

MUS 1: We'll put them in our cases and surely this could be a better case than we have here. (Enter PETER.)

PETER: Musicians, musicians, will you play that popular song for me called "Heart's Ease"? If you want to bolster my spirits, play "Heart's Ease."

MUS 1: Why "Heart's Ease"?

PETER: Oh, musicians, I need to hear it because my heart is full of sorrow. Play me some melancholy song which will give me comfort.

MUS 1: Not now. Not a mournful tune now.

PETER: You won't play for me, then?

MUS 1: No.

PETER: I will really let you have it if you don't do as I ask.

MUS 1: What will you give us?

PETER: I won't give you any money, but I will jeer at you and insult you and call you names.

MUS 1: Then I will give it right back to you, you dumb servant.

PETER: Then I will cut your face with my dagger. I will not put up with you. I'll have you dancing up and down the scale. Are you paying attention to what I'm saying?

1. Mus. An you re us and fa us, you note us.

2. Mus. Pray you put up your dagger, and put out your wit.

Pet. Then have at you with my wit! I will dry-beat you with an iron wit, and put up my iron dagger. Answer me like men.

"When griping grief the heart doth wound,
And doleful dumps the mind oppress,
Then music with her silver sound"—

Why "silver sound"? Why "music with her silver sound"? What say you, Simon Catling?

1. Mus. Marry, sir, because silver hath a sweet sound.

Pet. Pretty! What say you, Hugh Rebeck?

2. Mus. I say "silver sound" because musicians sound for silver.

Pet. Pretty too! What say you, James Soundpost?

3. Mus. Faith, I know now what to say.

Pet. O, I cry you mercy! you are the singer. I will say for you. It is "music with her silver sound" because musicians have no gold for sounding.

"Then music with her silver sound
With speedy help doth lend redress." *Exit.*

1. Mus. What a pestilent knave is this same!

2. Mus. Hang him, Jack! Come, we'll in here, tarry for the mourners, and stay dinner.

Exeunt.

ACT IV, Scene 5

MUS 1: So you think you are going to have us dancing up and down the musical scales? Note what I am saying.

MUS 2: Why don't you put away your dagger and show us your sense of humor instead?

PETER: All right, then, I will let you have it with my sharp wit, and I will put away my sharp dagger. We'll see who has brains! Who can answer this?:
"When griping grief wounds the heart
And doleful sorrows oppress the mind
Then music with her silver sound—"
Why does the poem say "silver sound"? "Music with her silver sound"? Well? What do you say, Simon Lute String?

MUS 1: Well, sir, because silver has a sweet sound.

PETER: Not bad! What do you say, Hugh Fiddle?

MUS 2: I say that "silver sound" means that musicians play their music for silver coins.

PETER: That's not bad either! What do you say, James Soundpost?

MUS 3: Dear me. I don't know what to say.

PETER: Oh, I beg your pardon. You are the singer. For you, I will say it is "music with her silver sound" because musicians get no *gold* for playing.
"Then music with her silver sound
With speedy help will lend relief."

(PETER leaves.)

MUS 1: What a pain in the neck he is!

MUS 2: Forget him, Jack! Let's stay here awhile. When the mourners return we can get a free dinner.

(They leave.)

[ACT V]

[Scene I. A street in Mantua.]

Enter *Romeo.*

Rom. If I may trust the flattering truth of sleep,
My dreams presage some joyful news at hand.
My bosom's lord sits lightly in his throne,
And all this day an unaccustomed spirit
Lifts me above the ground with cheerful thoughts.
I dreamt my lady came and found me dead
(Strange dream that gives a dead man leave to think!)
And breathed such life with kisses in my lips
That I revived and was an emperor.
Ah me! how sweet is love itself possessed,
When but love's shadows are so rich in joy!

Enter *Romeo's Man Balthasar,* booted.

News from Verona! How now, Balthasar?
Dost thou not bring me letters from the friar?
How doth my lady? Is my father well?
How fares my Juliet? That I ask again,
For nothing can be ill if she be well.
Bal. Then she is well, and nothing can be ill.
Her body sleeps in Capel's monument,
And her immortal part with angels lives.
I saw her laid low in her kindred's vault
And presently took post to tell it you.

ACT V

(Scene 1: A street in Mantua.)

(Enter ROMEO.)

ROMEO: If dreams can be trusted, then I will hear good news very soon. I feel wonderful and in a cheery mood today. Last night as I slept I dreamed that Juliet found me lying dead—how strange that a dead man could think!—and she was able to revive me so well with her kisses that I became an emperor. Love is sweet in and of itself. Even its darker sides are so rich in joy.

(Enter ROMEO'S man BALTHASAR in riding boots.)

Here comes Balthasar, which means he brings news from Verona. Tell me, Balthasar, do you have any letters from Friar Laurence? How is Juliet? Is my father all right? How is Juliet? I repeat myself purposely because nothing is wrong if she is well.

BALTH: Then she is well, and nothing is wrong. Her body lies in the Capulet's tomb and her soul is now with the angels. I saw her put into the family's tomb and quickly rode here to tell you.

O, pardon me for bringing these ill news,
Since you did leave it for my office, sir.
Rom. Is it e'en so? Then I defy you, stars!
Thou knowst my lodging. Get me ink and paper
And hire posthorses. I will hence tonight.
Bal. I do beseech you, sir, have patience.
Your looks are pale and wild and do import
Some misadventure.
Rom. Tush, thou art deceived.
Leave me and do the thing I bid thee do.
Hast thou no letters to me from the friar?
Bal. No, my good lord.
Rom. No matter. Get thee gone
And hire those horses. I'll be with thee straight.
Exit [*Balthasar*].
Well, Juliet, I will lie with thee tonight.
Let's see for means. O mischief, thou art swift
To enter in the thoughts of desperate men!
I do remember an apothecary,
And hereabouts he dwells, which late I noted
In tattered weeds, with overwhelming brows,
Culling of simples. Meager were his looks,
Sharp misery had worn him to the bones;
And in his needy shop a tortoise hung,
An alligator stuffed, and other skins
Of ill-shaped fishes; and about his shelves
A beggarly account of empty boxes,
Green earthen pots, bladders, and musty seeds,
Remnants of packthread, and old cakes of roses
Were thinly scattered, to make up a show.
Noting this penury, to myself I said,
"An if a man did need a poison now
Whose sale is present death in Mantua,
Here lives a caitiff wretch would sell it him."

I hope you will forgive me for bringing you such bad news, but you gave me that responsibility, sir.

ROMEO: Is this true? Then I defy you, stars! I will no longer follow the course that fate has plotted for me. You know where I am staying here in Mantua. Go to my lodgings and bring me paper and pen. And let's rent some horses—those swift ones used to carry mail. I will leave for Verona tonight.

BALTH: I beg you, Romeo, be patient. You look pale and wild, as if you might do something dangerous.

ROMEO: Don't worry. Your perception of me is not true. Do as I ask—get me pen and paper and arrange for those horses. Do you have a letter for me from Friar Laurence?

BALTH: No, I don't, good sir.

ROMEO: It doesn't make any difference now. Go on, and get the horses. I'll be with you soon.

(Exit BALTHASAR.)

Well, Juliet, I will lie by your side tonight. (He walks.) Hmmm, how will this plan be accomplished? When a man plans something devious, his wits are sharpened. Ideas come quickly to desperate men. I do remember a shabbily dressed druggist with bushy eyebrows who lives nearby and knows about the power of certain plants. He didn't look like much—in fact, he was bone thin. In his poor and unkempt shop he displayed a hanging tortoise, a stuffed alligator, animal skins, strange fish; on the shelves were a number of empty boxes, green earthen pots, sacks, musty seeds, wrapping twine, and small bunches of rose petals. Noting his poverty, I said to myself, "If someone were to need some poison, although the punishment for selling it is death, this miserable creature would probably sell it to him."

O, this same thought did but forerun my need,
And this same needy man must sell it me.
As I remember, this should be the house.
Being holiday, the beggar's shop is shut.
What, ho! apothecary!

Enter *Apothecary.*

Apoth. Who calls so loud?
Rom. Come hither, man. I see that thou art poor.
Hold, there is forty ducats. Let me have
A dram of poison, such soon-speeding gear
As will disperse itself through all the veins
That the life-weary taker may fall dead,
And that the trunk may be discharged of breath
As violently as hasty powder fired
Doth hurry from the fatal cannon's womb.
Apoth. Such mortal drugs I have; but Mantua's law
Is death to any he that utters them.
Rom. Art thou so bare and full of wretchedness
And fearest to die? Famine is in thy cheeks,
Need and oppression starveth in thine eyes,
Contempt and beggary hangs upon thy back;
The world is not thy friend, nor the world's law;
The world affords no law to make thee rich;
Then be not poor, but break it and take this.
Apoth. My poverty but not my will consents.
Rom. I pay thy poverty and not thy will.
Apoth. Put this in any liquid thing you will
And drink it off, and if you had the strength
Of twenty men, it would dispatch you straight.
Rom. There is thy gold—worse poison to men's souls,
Doing more murder in this loathsome world,
Than these poor compounds that thou mayst not sell.

ACT V, Scene 1

This is what I thought before I even needed it, and I know this same penniless man will sell it to me. This is probably his house, but his store is closed because of the holiday. (He calls.) Hey there, druggist!

(Enter DRUGGIST.)

DRUGGIST: Who calls so loudly out there?

ROMEO: Come here, sir. I know you are poor. Here are forty gold coins. Let me have a dram of fast-acting poison which will course through all the veins so quickly that the life-weary taker will fall dead; a poison that will cause the breath to leave the body as fast as gunpowder fired from a cannon.

DRUGGIST: I carry that kind of poison, but Mantua's law calls for executing anyone who sells it.

ROMEO: Are you so scared to die? Take a look at yourself now! Your cheeks are sunken from hunger and your eyes starve from need and oppression. Your poverty and anger at the world bends your back with their burdens. The world has not treated you very well and neither has its laws. There is no law to make you rich, but you need not be poor. Go ahead and break the law. Take this money.

DRUGGIST: I want to take the money because I need it so badly, but I would still be doing it against my will.

ROMEO: Then I shall pay your poverty and not your will.

DRUGGIST: Here is the deadly poison. Mix this with any liquid and drink it. Even if you had the strength of twenty men, the poison would still kill you instantly.

ROMEO: There is your money which does more harm to men's souls in this loathsome world than the poison you are forbidden to sell.

I sell thee poison; thou hast sold me none.
Farewell. Buy food and get thyself in flesh.
Come, cordial and not poison, go with me
To Juliet's grave; for there must I use thee.

Exeunt.

[Scene II. *Verona.* Friar Laurence's cell.]

Enter *Friar John* to *Friar Laurence.*

John. Holy Franciscan friar, brother, ho!

Enter *Friar Laurence.*

Laur. This same should be the voice of Friar John.
Welcome from Mantua. What says Romeo?
Or, if his mind be writ, give me his letter.
John. Going to find a barefoot brother out,
One of our order to associate me,
Here in this city visiting the sick,
And finding him, the searchers of the town,
Suspecting that we both were in a house
Where the infectious pestilence did reign,
Sealed up the doors, and would not let us forth,
So that my speed to Mantua there was stayed.
Laur. Who bare my letter, then, to Romeo?
John. I could not send it—here it is again—
Nor get a messenger to bring it thee,
So fearful were they of infection.
Laur. Unhappy fortune! By my brotherhood,
The letter was not nice, but full of charge,
Of dear import; and the neglecting it
May do much danger. Friar John, go hence,

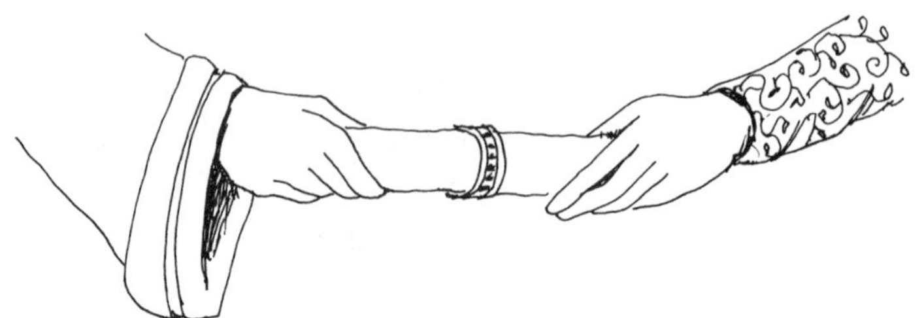

I'm giving you the real poison: money. What you have given me isn't bad at all. Farewell. Buy yourself some food and put some meat on your bones. (He speaks to the bottle of poison.) Come with me. You are like a liqueur to me and not a poison. Come with me to Juliet's grave, where I will put you to good use.

(Exit ROMEO.)

ACT V

(Scene 2: FRIAR LAURENCE'S cell in Verona.)

(Enter FRIAR JOHN.)

FRIAR J: Holy Friar Laurence! Brother, wait!

(Enter FRIAR LAURENCE.)

FRIAR L: Is that your voice, Friar John? Welcome back from Mantua. What did Romeo say in response to my letter? Or if he wrote a letter, please give it to me.

FRIAR J: Before I could see Romeo, I first had to find another Franciscan brother here in Verona who was visiting the sick. But the town's health officials suspected that we had both been in a house where they had the plague. Therefore, they sealed up the doors of the house and would not let us out at all. I never got to Mantua.

FRIAR L: Then who carried my letter to Romeo?

FRIAR J: Nobody—I still have it here. In fact, I could not even find a messenger to bring it back to you because there was such fear of infection.

FRIAR L: Oh, this is terrible! This was not a trivial note; it was a letter of great importance. Not delivering it may prove to be very dangerous. Friar John,

Get me an iron crow and bring it straight
Unto my cell.
John. Brother, I'll go and bring it thee. *Exit.*
Laur. Now must I to the monument alone.
Within this three hours will fair Juliet wake.
She will beshrew me much that Romeo
Hath had no notice of these accidents;
But I will write again to Mantua,
And keep her at my cell till Romeo come—
Poor living corse, closed in a dead man's tomb!
Exit.

[Scene III. A churchyard with the Capulets' tomb.]

Enter *Paris* and his *Page* with flowers and [a torch].

Par. Give me thy torch, boy. Hence, and stand aloof.
Yet put it out, for I would not be seen.
Under yond yew tree lay thee all along,
Holding thine ear close to the hollow ground.
So shall no foot upon the churchyard tread
(Being loose, unfirm, with digging up of graves)
But thou shalt hear it. Whistle then to me,
As signal that thou hearst something approach.
Give me those flowers. Do as I bid thee, go.
Page. [*Aside*] I am almost afraid to stand alone
Here in the churchyard; yet I will adventure.
[*Withdraws.*]
Par. Sweet flower, with flowers thy bridal bed I strew
He strews the tomb with flowers.
(O woe! thy canopy is dust and stones)
Which with sweet water nightly I will dew;
Or, wanting that, with tears distilled by moans.

would you please find a crowbar and bring it straight to my cell.

FRIAR J: Of course, Friar Laurence. I will bring it to you. (FRIAR JOHN leaves.)

FRIAR L: Now I must go to the Capulet's tomb. Juliet is supposed to wake up within three hours and she will blame me severely if Romeo was not told of our plan. But I will send another letter to Romeo in Mantua and keep Juliet at my cell until he comes for her. Poor Juliet, alive, but locked up in a dead man's tomb. (FRIAR LAURENCE leaves.)

ACT V

(Scene 3: The CAPULETS' tomb in a churchyard.)

(Enter PARIS and his PAGE with flowers and a torch.)

PARIS: Give me your torch, boy, and stand aside. No, put it out, because I do not want to be seen. Stretch out by that yew tree and hold your ear to the ground. If you hear anyone enter the churchyard, whistle that someone is approaching. The earth carries the sounds through freshly dug graves. Give me the flowers and do as I ask. Go.

PAGE: (Aside.) I am almost afraid to stay here alone in the churchyard—but I will take the risk. (PAGE withdraws.)

PARIS: Sweet maiden, Juliet, I will cover your bridal bed with flowers. (He covers the tomb with flowers.) Oh my heart is breaking. Your canopy here is dust and stones and so I will cover you with perfume every night as if it were the gentle dew. Or if I do not have that fragrant water I will cover you with mournful tears and moans.

The obsequies that I for thee will keep
Nightly shall be to strew thy grave and weep.

Whistle Boy.

The boy gives warning something doth approach.
What cursed foot wanders this way tonight
To cross my obsequies and true love's rite?
What, with a torch? Muffle me, night, awhile.

[*Withdraws.*]

Enter *Romeo,* and *Balthasar* with a torch, a mattock, and a crow of iron.

Rom. Give me that mattock and the wrenching iron.
Hold, take this letter. Early in the morning
See thou deliver it to my lord and father.
Give me the light. Upon thy life I charge thee,
Whate'er thou hearest or seest, stand all aloof
And do not interrupt me in my course.
Why I descend into this bed of death
Is partly to behold my lady's face,
But chiefly to take thence from her dead finger
A precious ring—a ring that I must use
In dear employment. Therefore hence, be gone.
But if thou, jealous, dost return to pry
In what I farther shall intend to do,
By heaven, I will tear thee joint by joint
And strew this hungry churchyard with thy limbs.
The time and my intents are savage-wild,
More fierce and more inexorable far
Than empty tigers or the roaring sea.
Bal. I will be gone, sir, and not trouble you.
Rom. So shalt thou show me friendship. Take thou that.
Live, and be prosperous; and farewell, good fellow.
Bal. [*Aside.*] For all this same, I'll hide me hereabout.
His looks I fear, and his intents I doubt. [*Withdraws.*]

I will observe the funeral rites for you and will come to you every night to scatter flowers on your grave and weep.

(Paris's PAGE whistles.)

I hear the boy whistle. Someone must be coming. Who on earth would be coming here tonight to interrupt my devotions to Juliet and my private expression of true love? Whoever it is has a light. Hide me, O night, hide me for a while.

(PARIS withdraws.)

(Enter ROMEO and BALTHASAR with a torch, a shovel, and a crowbar.)

ROMEO: Give me that shovel and the crowbar. Here, take this letter and be sure to deliver it to my father early in the morning. Give me the torch. I want you to swear on your life that whatever you hear or see, you will keep away and not interrupt what I am about to do. I am going into this tomb, this bed of death, to see my Juliet's face; but mostly to take a precious ring from her dead finger—a ring that is important to my plan. So leave here now. Let me warn you, however, that if you are suspicious or curious and you return to pry, I promise you, by heaven, that I will tear you limb from limb and scatter your remains across the churchyard. Tonight, my intentions are savage and wild—more fierce and driven than a wild tiger or the roaring seas.

BALTH: I am going, sir, and I will not trouble you.

ROMEO: If you consider yourself my friend, then you will show me your loyalty by leaving. Here, take this money. And I wish you luck. Live and be prosperous. And now, farewell, good fellow.

BALTH: (Aside.) No matter what I have promised, I am not going to leave. I will hide somewhere near. I do not like the way Romeo looks, and I am suspicious of his intentions. (BALTHASAR withdraws.)

Rom. Thou detestable maw, thou womb of death,
Gorged with the dearest morsel of the earth,
Thus I enforce thy rotten jaws to open,
And in despite I'll cram thee with more food.
Romeo opens the tomb.

Par. This is that banisht haughty Montague
That murdered my love's cousin—with which grief
It is supposed the fair creature died—
And here is come to do some villainous shame
To the dead bodies. I will apprehend him.
Stop thy unhallowed toil, vile Montague!
Can vengeance be pursued further than death?
Condemned villain, I do apprehend thee.
Obey, and go with me; for thou must die.

Rom. I must indeed; and therefore came I hither.
Good gentle youth, tempt not a desp'rate man.
Fly hence and leave me. Think upon these gone;
Let them affright thee. I beseech thee, youth,
Put not another sin upon my head
By urging me to fury. O, be gone!
By heaven, I love thee better than myself,
For I come hither armed against myself.
Stay not, be gone. Live, and hereafter say
A madman's mercy bid thee run away.

Par. I do defy thy conjuration
And apprehend thee for a felon here.

Rom. Wilt thou provoke me? Then have at thee, boy!
They fight.

Page. O Lord, they fight! I will go call the watch.
[*Exit.*]

Par. O, I am slain! [*Falls.*] If thou be merciful,
Open the tomb, lay me with Juliet. [*Dies.*]

Rom. In faith, I will. Let me peruse this face.
Mercutio's kinsman, noble County Paris!

ACT V, Scene 3

ROMEO: You detestable tomb, your disgusting mouth has filled your belly with death and gorged yourself on Juliet, the dearest morsel on earth. So I will force your rotten jaws open and, in defiance of you, I will cram you with more food, and feed my dead body to your appetite. (ROMEO opens the tomb.)

PARIS: I see that the intruder is none other than the banished, arrogant Romeo Montague who murdered Juliet's cousin and caused her the grief that led to her death. Now here he is again to do some indecent act to the dead bodies. I will arrest him. (Approaches ROMEO.) Stop your unholy work, you vile Montague! Is it possible that you want revenge so badly that you pursue it even after your victims are dead? You are as good as dead, and I am taking you into custody. Remember what the Prince decreed should you return to Verona. You had better obey and go with me, because you must die.

ROMEO: I agree with you. I must die and that is precisely why I came here. Good, gentle young man, do not tempt a desperate man. Leave here as quickly as you can. Consider the dead who lie here. Let the thought of them frighten you, I beg you. Do not put another sin on my head by infuriating me. Please go! I swear by heaven that I have more regard for you than for myself. I come here to destroy myself. Don't stay, go and live out your life. One day you will be able to tell the story of a madman who begged you to run away to save yourself.

PARIS: I do not want to hear all your begging and pleading. I intend to take you into custody as the criminal you are.

ROMEO: It seems you are determined to provoke me. Then I am going after you, boy!

(They fight.)

PAGE: Lord, they are fighting! I will go call the guards. (Exit PAGE.)

PARIS: You have killed me! (He falls.) If you are merciful you will open the tomb and lay me to rest beside Juliet. (PARIS dies.)

ROMEO: Out of decency, I will honor this request, but first I must look at this man's face. He is Mercutio's relative, the noble Count Paris!

What said my man when my betossed soul
Did not attend him as we rode? I think
He told me Paris should have married Juliet.
Said he not so? or did I dream it so?
Or am I mad, hearing him talk of Juliet,
To think it was so? O, give me thy hand,
One writ with me in sour misfortune's book!
I'll bury thee in a triumphant grave.
A grave? O, no, a lantern, slaughtered youth,
For here lies Juliet, and her beauty makes
This vault a feasting presence full of light.
Death, lie thou there, by a dead man interred.
[*Lays Paris in the tomb.*]
How oft when men are at the point of death
Have they been merry! which their keepers call
A lightning before death. O, how may I
Call this a lightning? O my love! my wife!
Death, that hath sucked the honey of thy breath,
Hath had no power yet upon thy beauty.
Thou art not conquered. Beauty's ensign yet
Is crimson in thy lips and in thy cheeks,
And death's pale flag is not advanced there.
Tybalt, liest thou there in thy bloody sheet?
O, what more favor can I do to thee
Than with that hand that cut thy youth in twain
To sunder his that was thine enemy?
Forgive me, cousin! Ah, dear Juliet,
Why art thou yet so fair? Shall I believe
That unsubstantial Death is amorous,
And that the lean abhorred monster keeps
Thee here in dark to be his paramour?
For fear of that I still will stay with thee
And never from this palace of dim night
Depart again. Here, here will I remain

What did Balthasar tell me when I was too upset to listen as we returned to Verona? I think he told me that Paris was supposed to marry Juliet. I think that is what he said—or did I dream it? Or am I insane and only think I heard him talk of Juliet? Oh, let me take your hand, gentle Paris, the same hand which wrote with mine the story of my life in a book of sour misfortune! I will bury you, Paris, in a splendid grave. A grave? No, it will not be a grave. It will be a cathedral tower with stained glass windows, because Juliet lies here with you. Her beauty will make this tomb appear as if it were a royal reception room full of light. Lie here, dead Paris, brought by me, who is almost a dead man himself.

(Lays PARIS in the tomb.)

Often when men are at the point of death they have been happy. Their nurses call it an easing of life's burdens before death. How can I tell if this is happening to me, also? My love! My wife! Death has sucked the honey of your breath but has no power yet to destroy your beauty. You have not been conquered. All the signs of beauty are still present; there is crimson in your lips and in your cheeks. Death's pallor has not overtaken you. Tybalt! Is that you there in a bloody sheet? What more can I possibly do for you with these hands that cut your youth short than to kill myself, your enemy and murderer? Forgive me, Cousin Tybalt! Ah, dear Juliet, why do you still look so fair? Shall I believe that Death loves you and that this lean, despised monster keeps you here in the dark to be his lover? Because I am afraid of that,I will stay here with you and never again depart from this palace of dim night. I will remain here

With worms that are thy chambermaids. O, here
Will I set up my everlasting rest
And shake the yoke of inauspicious stars
From this world-wearied flesh. Eyes, look your last!
Arms, take your last embrace! and, lips, O you
The doors of breath, seal with a righteous kiss
A dateless bargain to engrossing death!
Come, bitter conduct; come, unsavory guide!
Thou desperate pilot, now at once run on
The dashing rocks thy seasick weary bark!
Here's to my love! [*Drinks.*] O true apothecary!
Thy drugs are quick. Thus with a kiss I die. *Falls.*

Enter Friar [*Laurence*], with lantern, crow, and spade.

Friar. Saint Francis be my speed! how oft tonight
Have my old feet stumbled at graves! Who's there?
Bal. Here's one, a friend, and one that knows you well.
Friar. Bliss be upon you! Tell me, good my friend,
What torch is yond that vainly lends his light
To grubs and eyeless skulls? As I discern,
It burneth in the Capels' monument.
Bal. It doth so, holy sir; and there's my master,
One that you love.
Friar. Who is it?
Bal. Romeo.
Friar. How long hath he been there?
Bal. Full half an hour.
Friar. Go with me to the vault.
Bal. I dare not, sir.
My master knows not but I am gone hence,
And fearfully did menace me with death
If I did stay to look on his intents.

with the worms that will be your chambermaids. I will set up my everlasting rest and shake the burden of these unlucky stars from my world-weary flesh. Eyes look your last! Arms, take your last embrace! And lips, the doors of breath, seal with a noble kiss my eternal bargain with death which takes everything for its own. Come, bitter poison. Come, my unsavory guide! Desperate pilot, now quickly dash my ship against the rocks and end my weary seasick journey. Here is a toast to my beloved! (He drinks the poison.) O, able chemist! Your drugs are quick. Now with a kiss I die.

(ROMEO kisses JULIET and falls.)

(Enter FRIAR LAURENCE, with lantern, crowbar, and shovel.)

FRIAR: I pray that Saint Francis will be my protector! My old feet have stumbled at graves so often tonight, it is surely a bad omen. Who is there?

BALTH: I am a friend, and I know you very well.

FRIAR: May you be happy and serene. Tell me, my good friend, what is that torch doing over there, casting a useless light for grubs and eyeless skulls? It seems to be burning in the Capulet's tomb.

BALTH: You are right, holy sir. It is burning in the Capulet's monument and over there is my master, whom you love.

FRIAR: Who is it?

BALTH: Romeo.

FRIAR: How long has he been there?

BALTH: For fully half an hour.

FRIAR: Go with me to the vault.

BALTH: I do not dare go with you, sir. My master does not know that I am still here. He thinks I left awhile ago and he threatened me with death if I stayed to watch what he was doing.

Friar. Stay then; I'll go alone. Fear comes upon me.
O, much I fear some ill unthrifty thing.
Bal. As I did sleep under this yew tree here,
I dreamt my master and another fought,
And that my master slew him.
Friar. Romeo!

Stoops and looks on the blood and weapons.

Alack, alack, what blood is this which stains
The stony entrance of this sepulcher?
What mean these masterless and gory swords
To lie discolored by this place of peace?

[*Enters the tomb.*]

Romeo! O, pale! Who else? What, Paris too?
And steeped in blood? Ah, what an unkind hour
Is guilty of this lamentable chance!
The lady stirs.

Juliet rises.

Jul. O comfortable friar! where is my lord?
I do remember well where I should be,
And there I am. Where is my Romeo?
Friar. I hear some noise. Lady, come from that nest
Of death, contagion, and unnatural sleep.
A greater power than we can contradict
Hath thwarted our intents. Come, come away.
Thy husband in thy bosom there lies dead;
And Paris too. Come, I'll dispose of thee
Among a sisterhood of holy nuns.
Stay not to question, for the watch is coming.
Come, go, good Juliet. I dare no longer stay.
Jul. Go, get thee hence, for I will not away.

Exit [*Friar*].

What's here? A cup, closed in my true love's hand?
Poison, I see, hath been his timeless end.
O churl! drunk all, and left no friendly drop

ACT V, Scene 3

FRIAR: Stay here then. I'll go alone. But I feel overcome with fear. I am afraid that some ill, unlucky thing has taken place.

BALTH: I fell asleep under this yew tree here and dreamed that my master and another man had a fight and that my master killed him.

FRIAR: Romeo! (He stoops and looks at the blood and weapons.) What is here? What is this blood that has stained the stones at the entrance to the vault? What is the meaning of these gory swords? What are they doing here lying discolored in this place of peace?

(He enters the tomb.)

Romeo! You are so pale! Who else is here! What? Is that Paris, too, steeped in blood? Oh, what an unkind hour is guilty of this tragic stroke of fate! Juliet is awakening!

(JULIET rises.)

JULIET: Dear Friar, it is so comforting to see you. Where is my lord Romeo? I remember well where I am supposed to be, and here I am. Where is my Romeo?

FRIAR: I hear some noise. Juliet, leave this nest of death and spreading sickness and unnatural sleep. A power greater than all of us has destroyed our plans. Come, come away. Your husband, who lies near you, is dead and Paris, too. Come, I will take you to a convent and leave you with a sisterhood of nuns. Please don't stay to argue because I hear the watchman coming. Come, good Juliet, leave with me. I dare not stay any longer.

JULIET: Go! Leave right now, for I will not leave this place.

(Exit FRIAR LAURENCE.)

What's here? It is a cup, closed in my true love's hand. Poison, I see, has taken his life. My dear Romeo, like a miser, you drank it all, leaving me nothing—not a friendly drop

To help me after? I will kiss thy lips.
Haply some poison yet doth hang on them
To make me die with a restorative. [*Kisses him.*]
Thy lips are warm!
Chief Watch. [*Within*] Lead, boy. Which way?
Jul. Yea, noise? Then I'll be brief. O happy dagger!
[*Snatches Romeo's dagger.*]
This is thy sheath; there rest, and let me die.
She stabs herself and falls.

Enter [Paris'] Boy and *Watch.*

Boy. This is the place. There, where the torch doth burn.
Chief Watch. The ground is bloody. Search about the churchyard.
Go, some of you; whoe'er you find attach.
[*Exeunt some of the Watch.*]
Pitiful sight! here lies the County slain;
And Juliet bleeding, warm, and newly dead,
Who here hath lain this two days buried.
Go, tell the Prince; run to the Capulets;
Raise up the Montagues; some others search.
[*Exeunt others of the Watch.*]
We see the ground whereon these woes do lie,
But the true ground of all these piteous woes
We cannot without circumstance descry.

Enter [some of the *Watch,*] with *Romeo's Man* [*Balthasar*].

2. Watch. Here's Romeo's man. We found him in the churchyard.

to help me after. I will kiss your lips. Happily, there will be some trace of poison there to help me die with a final rush of passion. (Kisses him.) Your lips are warm!

CHIEF WATCH: (Within.) Take us there, boy. Which way?

JULIET: I hear noise. Then I must hurry. O happy dagger! (Snatches Romeo's dagger.) My body will be your sheath. Let it rust there and let me die.

(She stabs herself and falls.)

(Enter PARIS'S PAGE and WATCHMEN.)

PAGE: This the place—over there where the torch is still burning.

CHIEF WATCH: The ground is bloody. Search around the churchyard. The rest of you men fan out. Arrest anyone you find in the area.

(Exit some of the WATCHMEN.)

What a pitiful sight! Count Paris lies here murdered and Juliet is bleeding but still warm—and has obviously just died. How can this be when she was buried in this tomb two days ago? Hurry out, boy. Go tell the Prince, run to the Capulets, waken the Montagues! The rest of you continue to search.

(Exit other WATCHMEN.)

We see the ground where these three pathetic bodies lie; but we can't understand the true ground, or basis, for this horrible grief until we get a full explanation of what this is all about!

(Enter some of the Watchmen with BALTHASAR.)

WATCH 2: Here's Romeo's servant, Balthasar. We found him in the churchyard.

Chief Watch. Hold him in safety till the Prince come hither.

Enter *Friar* [*Laurence*] and another *Watchman.*

3. Watch. Here is a friar that trembles, sighs, and weeps.
We took this mattock and this spade from him
As he was coming from this churchyard side.
Chief Watch. A great suspicion! Stay the friar too.

Enter the *Prince* [and *Attendants*].

Prince. What misadventure is so early up,
That calls our person from our morning rest?

Enter *Capulet* and his *Wife* [with others].

Cap. What should it be, that they so shriek abroad?
Wife. The people in the street cry "Romeo,"
Some "Juliet," and some "Paris"; and all run,
With open outcry, toward our monument.
Prince. What fear is this which startles in our ears?
Chief Watch. Sovereign, here lies the County Paris slain;
And Romeo dead; and Juliet, dead before,
Warm and new killed.
Prince. Search, seek, and know how this foul murder comes.
Chief Watch. Here is a friar, and slaughtered Romeo's man,
With instruments upon them fit to open
These dead men's tombs.
Cap. O heavens! O wife, look how our daughter bleeds!

ACT V, Scene 3

CHIEF WATCH: Hold him. Keep him safe until the Prince comes.

(Enter FRIAR LAURENCE and THIRD WATCHMAN.)

WATCH 3: Here's a friar who trembles, sighs, and weeps. We took this pickaxe and shovel from him as he was coming from the side of the churchyard.

CHIEF WATCH: That sounds very suspicious to me. You had better hold the friar, too.

(Enter PRINCE and his retinue.)

PRINCE: What awful things have happened here that make it necessary to disturb my sleep so early in the morning? What is it that requires my presence so urgently?

(Enter LORD and LADY CAPULET with others.)

LORD CAP: What is so wrong that people are shrieking in the streets?

LADY CAP: The people in the street are shouting "Romeo," some cry "Juliet," and some "Paris." All of them run—in open panic—toward our tomb.

PRINCE: What has happened that has the people so frightened?

CHIEF WATCH: Your Highness, here lies Count Paris who has been murdered, and Romeo is dead; and Juliet, thought to be dead before, is strangely warm and killed again.

PRINCE: Search all over and find out how this foul murder happened.

CHIEF WATCH: Here is a friar and Romeo's servant, Balthasar. They carry tools with them for opening dead men's tombs.

LORD CAP: O, heaven above! O, wife, look at how our daughter is bleeding!

This dagger hath mista'en, for, lo, his house
Is empty on the back of Montague,
And it missheathed in my daughter's bosom!
Wife. O me! this sight of death is as a bell
That warns my old age to a sepulcher.

Enter *Montague* [and others].

Prince. Come, Montague; for thou art early up
To see thy son and heir now early down.
Mon. Alas, my liege, my wife is dead tonight!
Grief of my son's exile hath stopped her breath.
What further woe conspires against mine age?
Prince. Look, and thou shalt see.
Mon. O thou untaught! what manners is in this,
To press before thy father to a grave?
Prince. Seal up the mouth of outrage for a while,
Till we can clear these ambiguities
And know their spring, their head, their true descent;
And then will I be general of your woes
And lead you even to death. Meantime forbear,
And let mischance be slave to patience.
Bring forth the parties of suspicion.
Friar. I am the greatest, able to do least,
Yet most suspected, as the time and place
Doth make against me, of this direful murder;
And here I stand, both to impeach and purge
Myself condemned and myself excused.
Prince. Then say at once what thou dost know in this.
Friar. I will be brief, for my short date of breath
Is not so long as is a tedious tale.
Romeo, there dead, was husband to that Juliet;
And she, there dead, that Romeo's faithful wife.
I married them; and their stol'n marriage day

The dagger has mistaken her heart for its proper sheath! Romeo's sheath is empty. It is his weapon in her bosom.

LADY CAP: This sight of death is like a bell that summons me in my old age to my grave.

(Enter MONTAGUE and others.)

PRINCE: Come, Montague. We've brought you here this morning to see your son and heir lying in an early grave.

LORD MONT: Alas, your majesty, my wife died tonight. The grief of my son's exile killed her. What further misery conspires against my old age?

PRINCE: Look and you will see for yourself what has happened here.

LORD MONT: Oh, my dear boy, haven't you learned the laws of nature? What manners are these? Don't you know that your father should go to his grave before his son?

PRINCE: Control these emotional outbursts for a while until we can clear up this mystery. We must try to understand how all this happened from beginning to end. Then, and only then, will I listen to your lamenting and lead you in your sorrowing. But if you are guilty, I will lead you to your punishment and death. In the meantime, be patient in the face of your misfortunes. Now bring the suspects forward.

FRIAR: I am the one who is most suspected since the circumstances of the time and place implicate me seriously in these hideous murders. And I stand here ready both to accuse and clear myself of wrongdoing. At the same time I condemn and excuse myself as well.

PRINCE: Then tell us at once what you know about the events that led up to this.

FRIAR: I will be brief because at my age there is not much time to tell a long and tedious tale. Romeo, whom you see dead, was Juliet's husband. And Juliet was Romeo's faithful wife. I married them and their secret wedding day

Was Tybalt's doomsday, whose untimely death
Banisht the new-made bridegroom from this city;
For whom, and not for Tybalt, Juliet pined.
You, to remove that siege of grief from her,
Betrothed and would have married her perforce
To County Paris. Then comes she to me
And with wild looks bid me devise some mean
To rid her from this second marriage,
Or in my cell there would she kill herself.
Then gave I her (so tutored by my art)
A sleeping potion; which so took effect
As I intended, for it wrought on her
The form of death. Meantime I writ to Romeo
That he should hither come as this dire night
To help to take her from her borrowed grave,
Being the time the potion's force should cease.
But he which bore my letter, Friar John,
Was stayed by accident, and yesternight
Returned my letter back. Then all alone
At the prefixed hour of her waking
Came I to take her from her kindred's vault;
Meaning to keep her closely at my cell
Till I conveniently could send to Romeo.
But when I came, some minute ere the time
Of her awaking, here untimely lay
The noble Paris and true Romeo dead.
She wakes; and I entreated her come forth
And bear this work of heaven with patience;
But then a noise did scare me from the tomb,
And she, too desperate, would not go with me,
But, as it seems, did violence on herself.
All this I know, and to the marriage
Her nurse is privy; and if aught in this
Miscarried by my fault, let my old life

was Tybalt's doomsday—the very same day that Romeo was banished from the city for killing Tybalt. Juliet cried for Romeo and not for Tybalt as you thought. And you, Lord and Lady Capulet, to lighten the burden of her grief, arranged her wedding to Count Paris. It was then that she came to me in desperation, pleading that I find a way to avoid this illegal second marriage. She threatened to kill herself in my cell if I could not help her with this dilemma. Because I know about the art of medicine and herbs, I gave her a sleeping potion which was effective as I had promised. It put her to sleep but made her appear dead—this deceived everyone completely. Meantime, I wrote to Romeo telling him to return to Verona on this night. I told him to be here when she awoke and to take her from this temporary grave when the potion wore off. But Friar John, who took the letter, was delayed because of sickness in the city and a quarantine which held him here. He returned the undelivered letter to me, and so I promptly rushed alone to this tomb at the appointed hour of her awakening. I came here to take her from her family vault. I meant to take her secretly to my cell until I could conveniently send her to Romeo. But when I came, a minute before the time of her awakening, I found the dead bodies of the noble Count Paris and devoted Romeo. When Juliet awakened, I pleaded with her to leave with me and endure these acts of heaven with patience. Then a noise from outside the tomb scared me; but Juliet, too desperate, would not go with me. It seems that it was she who did this ghastly violence to herself. I know all of this, and her nurse knows all about the secret marriage. For whatever has gone wrong which is my fault I am prepared to

Be sacrificed, some hour before his time,
Unto the rigor of severest law.
Prince. We still have known thee for a holy man.
Where's Romeo's man? What can he say in this?
Bal. I brought my master news of Juliet's death;
And then in post he came from Mantua
To this same place, to this same monument.
This letter he early bid me give his father,
And threatened me with death, going in the vault,
If I departed not and left him there.
Prince. Give me the letter. I will look on it.
Where is the County's page that raised the watch?
Sirrah, what made your master in this place?
Boy. He came with flowers to strew his lady's grave;
And bid me stand aloof, and so I did.
Anon comes one with light to ope the tomb;
And by-and-by my master drew on him;
And then I ran away to call the watch.
Prince. This letter doth make good the friar's words,
Their course of love, the tidings of her death;
And here he writes that he did buy a poison
Of a poor 'pothecary, and therewithal
Came to this vault to die and lie with Juliet.
Where be these enemies? Capulet, Montague,
See what a scourge is laid upon your hate,
That heaven finds means to kill your joys with love!
And I, for winking at your discords too,
Have lost a brace of kinsmen. All are punished.
Cap. O brother Montague, give me thy hand.
This is my daughter's jointure, for no more
Can I demand.
Mon. But I can give thee more;
For I will raise her statue in pure gold,
That whiles Verona by that name is known,

pay the price under the severest penalty of the law.

PRINCE: We have always known you to be a holy man. Where is Romeo's servant, Balthasar? What does he have to say about all of this?

BALTH: I brought my master news of Juliet's death and he left Mantua immediately. He came directly here to this same place, to the same monument. He gave me a letter to deliver to his father and threatened me with death if I did not depart immediately and leave him alone as he ordered. It was then that he went into the vault.

PRINCE: Give me the letter. I want to read it. Where is Count Paris's page, the boy who called the watchmen? Young man, what was your master doing in this place?

PAGE: He came with flowers to spread on his lady Juliet's grave. He told me to stay away from him and so I did until I saw someone come with a light to open the tomb. Soon my master, Count Paris, drew his sword and threatened the trespasser with harm. It was then that I ran away to call the guard.

PRINCE: This letter from Romeo to his father proves the Friar is telling the truth since he writes about the course of their love, and the news of Juliet's death. He states that he did indeed buy poison from a poor druggist and afterward came to this vault to die and lie with Juliet. Where are these two enemies Capulet and Montague? See what a scourge your hatred has created! Heaven has found a way to kill your children because they loved one another. And I, too, have been guilty, for I closed my eyes to the real danger of your feud. I have lost two of my relatives—Mercutio and Paris. I fear we have all been punished, all of us.

LORD CAP: Brother Montague, give me your hand as I give you mine. This is my daughter's dowry, for I cannot give any more but this to you.

LORD MONT: But I can give you more, Lord Capulet. I will build a statue to Juliet of pure gold. And for as long as Verona is known by that name,

There shall no figure at such rate be set
As that of true and faithful Juliet.
Cap. As rich shall Romeo's by his lady's lie—
Poor sacrifices of our enmity!
Prince. A glooming peace this morning with it brings.
The sun for sorrow will not show his head.
Go hence, to have more talk of these sad things;
Some shall be pardoned, and some punished;
For never was a story of more woe
Than this of Juliet and her Romeo.

Exeunt omnes.

there will be no monument so highly valued as that of true and faithful Juliet.

LORD CAP: I, too, shall erect a statue of Romeo, equally as valuable, to stand by his lady's side. These are indeed poor sacrifices to make amends.

PRINCE: This morning brings a gloomy peace. Even the sun will not show his head for the sorrow it feels. Go now, both of you, and talk more of these sad things. Some people shall be pardoned and some shall be punished; because there never has been a story of more woe than this of Juliet and her Romeo.

(Everyone exits.)

WRITING, DISCUSSION, IMPROVISATION

These activities are meant to be used for writing, discussion, and improvisational drama. Because each class is unique and should have activities tailor-made for them, we leave it to the discretion of the teacher to adapt these suggestions to the needs of the students in order to best bring the material to life.

ACT I

Democratic Due Process

1. (Scene 1) It is apparent that Prince Escalus has the power to impose laws and issue decrees whenever he chooses. Everyone's life is in his hands. In this country, however, we believe in due process of law which, among other things, prevents the President from usurping the powers of the judicial and legislative branches of the government. What are the advantages and disadvantages of our system of government? Improvise a "Kangaroo court" where a mob of students decides to put the principal on trial for imposing an objectionable rule.

Friendship

2. (Scene 1) When Romeo's friends describe him as the play opens, they are concerned about him because of his self-imposed solitude. Both Mercutio and Benvolio try hard to lighten their friend's depression and encourage him to be social again. What care and consideration should one expect from friends?

Getting Involved

3. (Scene 1) When Benvolio and Tybalt see the servants fighting, how do they react? Why are people often reluctant to get involved in someone else's unpleasant affairs? Improvise a hostile street encounter and have witnesses react in different ways to the argument. People may want to mediate, take sides, provoke, ignore, or act immobilized because of fear.

Attitudes Toward Social Class

4. (Scene 2) Capulet's servant could not read the party guest list without Romeo's and Benvolio's help. What does their teasing of that illiterate servant suggest about the mistreatment of less educated people? What are the attitudes today toward different social classes, for example, the unemployed, the blue-collar, pink-collar, or professional people? What may be the consequences of such attitudes?

Ideal Mates

5. (Scene 3) Lord Capulet knows that his thirteen-year-old daughter, Juliet, will soon need a husband and feels that Paris, a wealthy and young "man of wax" (a man of outward perfection), will be a fine suitor. Considering the importance of marriage, what qualities would you look for in a mate? How do you think your ideals will change with your age? Remember, Juliet is thirteen years old and Romeo only sixteen.

Adult and Child Bonding

6. (Scene 3) The Nurse is undoubtedly very close to Juliet and loves her like a mother. How is it possible to love a child if you are not its biological parent? What are some examples of this kind of human bonding?

Power of Imagery

7. (Scene 4) Mercutio delivers the famous Queen Mab speech, a lengthy fantasy of forty-two lines, about the fairies' midwife. He describes Mab's miniature world of spider webs, nutshells, moonbeams, and little creatures riding through lovers' brains. This monologue also includes in-

ACT I (cont'd.)

sight into human emotions and an attitude of self-deprecation on Mercutio's part. Review this speech and write down those descriptive details that reveal either Queen Mab's uncommon size or her extraordinary power over people.

Party Crashing 8. (Scene 5) Romeo, Mercutio, and Benvolio crash the Capulet party. Why do people crash parties? What kinds of unexpected things could happen at a party when the host or hostess has uninvited and unwanted guests?

Group Dynamics 9. (Scene 5) When people get together at a party, certain aspects of their personalities become more apparent. What insights did you gain into the play's characters because of their interaction with one another at the Capulet ball? How have you seen your friends act differently in different settings? How do people act as catalysts on one another?

True Love 10. (Scene 5) After seeing Juliet for the first time, Romeo says, "Did my heart love till now?" Remember that he thought, only minutes before, that he was madly in love with Rosaline. How is Romeo's behavior different after meeting Juliet? What are the differences between infatuation and love? What is your opinion of "love at first sight"?

Party Planning 11. Plan an appropriate party for one of the characters in the play. Include the guest list, menu, entertainment, and the purpose of the party. How many people will be invited and who will they be? What kind of party are you planning? Design an invitation which includes an R.S.V.P. Plan a menu which complements the occasion.

Element of Chance 12. (Scene 5) Improvise and act out a scene in which Romeo seriously considers all the young women present at the Capulet party and expresses absolutely no interest in Juliet at all. What then would or would not have happened in the development of the plot?

ACT II

Practical vs. Romantic 1. (Scene 2) The balcony scene is a romantic episode in which Romeo and Juliet discover their passion for one another. Improvise a balcony scene in which Juliet, recognizing the danger of their love affair, decides to listen to her head and not her heart and rejects young Romeo vehemently.

Words and Connotations 2. (Scene 2) Juliet laments, "That which we call a rose by any other name would smell as sweet." What does this quotation mean to you? Although

ACT II (cont'd.)

Juliet is saying that the label does not matter, consider the power of language and the images that words do evoke. Language moves us, influences us, makes us laugh and cry, inspires and enrages us, expresses us. It is the currency of our lives. To examine this proposition more concretely, here is a vivid example of the power of words and the shocking response that they can arouse: if we called a rose a *blackhead,* how would it seem then to present a bouquet of twelve long-stemmed blackheads to your favorite person? Find and list additional words and phrases that have a positive or negative effect on you.

Folk Medicine 3. (Scene 2) The practice of medicine during Romeo and Juliet's time involved magic and the use of plants and herbs, including those used in Friar Laurence's hypnotic potion for Juliet. What kinds of folk medicine are practiced among your friends and relatives that do not involve taking pills or chemicals?

Mentors 4. (Scene 3) Friar Laurence is an important friend and advisor to Romeo. Everyone needs to talk to someone at one time or another who can be an objective listener and help with the problem. Improvise a scene involving a person who speaks with a helpful and supportive counselor. Then improvise a scene in which the counselor is unsympathetic and simply does not understand the problem.

Adolescence 5. (Scene 4) Romeo and his friends are not so different from today's teenagers. For example, they love to have fun and be with their friends. Make a class list on the chalkboard indicating similarities and differences between Verona's and today's teenagers.

Prejudice 6. (Scene 4) *Prejudice* refers to an opinion formed without knowledge or examination of the facts. The Montagues and Capulets were prejudiced against one another and hated each other on sight. As a result, many people were ultimately hurt by such destructive hatred. Where in today's world do we see prejudice at work?

Famous Lovers 7. (Scene 4) In 1327 Petrarch, a great Italian poet wrote beautiful love sonnets in honor of his beloved Laura. His verse won great acclaim for its delicate and melodious quality. He became the model of the courtly lover, who postured and suffered from unrequited love. Find the strange and bizarre tales of other famous lovers which made their stories survive the history of centuries: Thisbe and Pyramus, Antony and Cleopatra, Helen and Paris.

ACT II (cont'd.)

Colorful Characterization

8. (Scene 5) The Nurse is an important figure in Juliet's life. Write a brief description of this colorful old woman. Include at least four adjectives, starting with *garrulous*, which vividly capture her personality. Make sure you cite incidents from the play which support your choice of adjectives.

Marriage that Endures

9. (Scene 6) When Friar Laurence marries Romeo and Juliet in his cell, he counsels them, "Love moderately. Long love doth so." Romeo and Juliet only knew each other a short time—less than a day! In fact, they had only been in each other's company for a few hours. Based upon their meager time together, do you believe that Romeo and Juliet could have had a long-lasting relationship? Can you imagine yourself marrying someone after knowing them for only several hours? Considering the high rate of divorce today, what do you think are the contributing factors to the failure of so many marriages? What do you think are the qualities of an enduring relationship? What holds a marriage together?

ACT III

Heroism or Foolishness

1. (Scene 1) Mercutio is so outraged by the insults which Tybalt heaps upon Romeo that Mercutio literally gives up his life to defend his friend's honor. Is it sensible to fight someone else's battles? Is this kind of self-sacrifice foolish or heroic?

Vigilante Actions

2. (Scene 1) When Tybalt kills Romeo's gallant friend Mercutio, Romeo takes his revenge and kills Tybalt. Not waiting for the justice of Verona's civil law to punish Tybalt, Romeo instead takes the law into his own hands.Do you believe there are any situations that justify such an act? What are the dangers of one or more people taking the law into their own hands? How could it affect you?

Heat and Temperament

3. (Scene 1) As Benvolio and Mercutio stand in the public square on a hot afternoon, Benvolio expresses concern that if they meet the Capulets, a brawl is inevitable because in the extreme heat " . . . is the mad blood stirring." It is a fact that extreme heat affects temperament. It can cause a change in mood of dramatic proportions. Tempers flare and the summer heat often provokes violence. After researching civil disturbances what correlation do you find between the summer months and violence?

Mixed Feelings

4. (Scene 2) When Juliet hears that her husband killed her cousin Tybalt, she is overcome with sadness and confusion. She cannot take sides

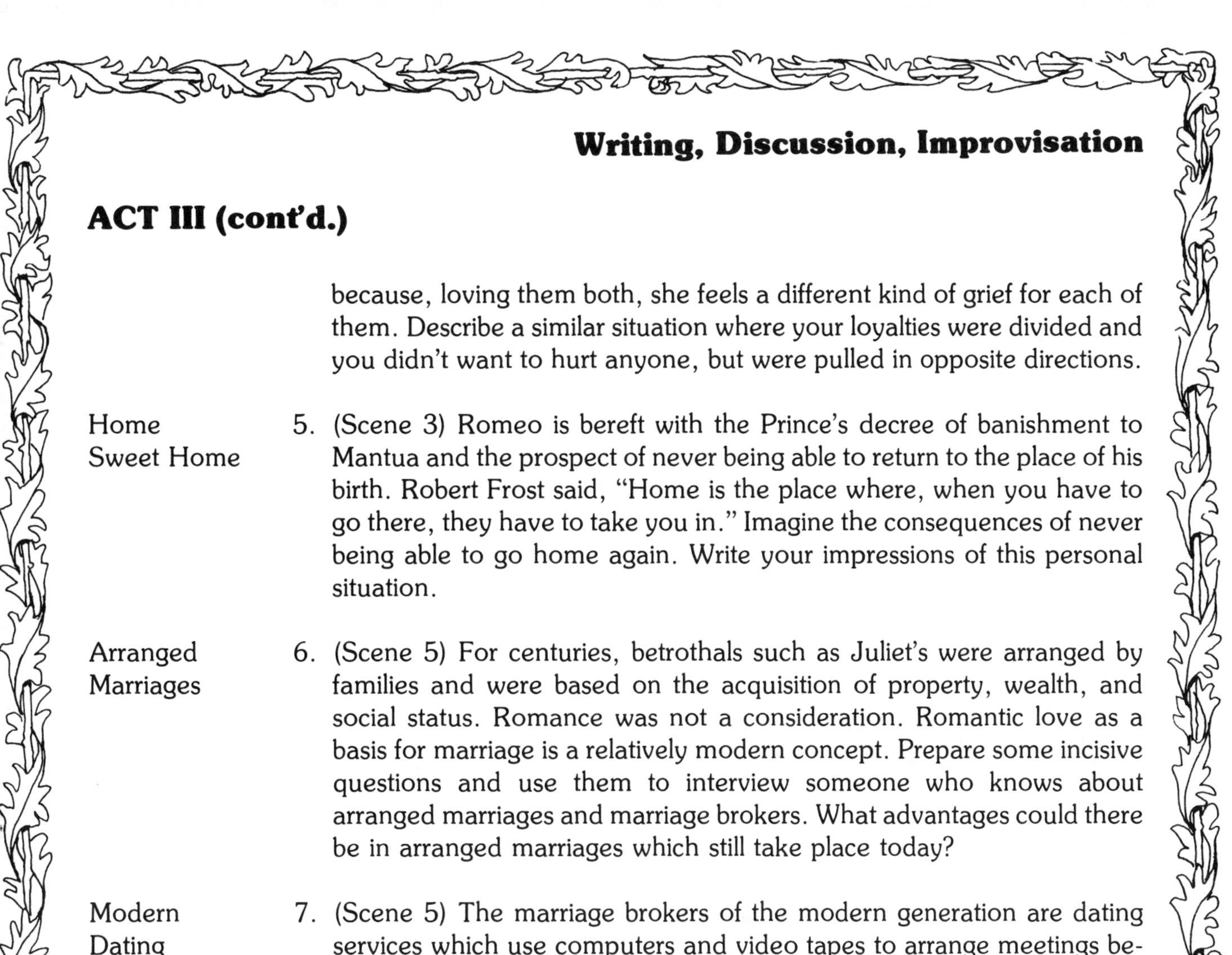

ACT III (cont'd.)

because, loving them both, she feels a different kind of grief for each of them. Describe a similar situation where your loyalties were divided and you didn't want to hurt anyone, but were pulled in opposite directions.

Home Sweet Home

5. (Scene 3) Romeo is bereft with the Prince's decree of banishment to Mantua and the prospect of never being able to return to the place of his birth. Robert Frost said, "Home is the place where, when you have to go there, they have to take you in." Imagine the consequences of never being able to go home again. Write your impressions of this personal situation.

Arranged Marriages

6. (Scene 5) For centuries, betrothals such as Juliet's were arranged by families and were based on the acquisition of property, wealth, and social status. Romance was not a consideration. Romantic love as a basis for marriage is a relatively modern concept. Prepare some incisive questions and use them to interview someone who knows about arranged marriages and marriage brokers. What advantages could there be in arranged marriages which still take place today?

Modern Dating Services

7. (Scene 5) The marriage brokers of the modern generation are dating services which use computers and video tapes to arrange meetings between interested men and women. Set up a scene in a dating service with a client and a consultant who is giving a sales pitch for the service. Have the consultant also interview the client thoroughly in order to collect the required data.

Ambiguous Communication

8. (Scene 5) Juliet and her mother discuss Juliet's marriage to Paris. They talk, too, about seeking revenge against Romeo. Juliet does not lie in this scene, but she does manipulate the language cleverly. She says exactly what she means, but sends out a totally different message because she deliberately phrases her thoughts ambiguously. Construct a three-column chart analyzing the double meanings in Juliet's lines. Quote the line, give her meaning, and then her mother's inference.

Creative Writing and Ballads

9. (Scene 5) When Romeo and Juliet say good-bye, after their only night together, their parting takes the form of an "aubade." This sad dawn-song takes place between lovers as they say their reluctant farewell in a special way. This allows them to debate whether dawn's early light is truly morning or the leftover rays of moonlight spilling on the landscape. One of the lovers contends that the song they hear is the morning lark's while the other lover argues that they hear the strains of the nightingale. The

ACT III (cont'd.)

aubade is always replete with intense love, torment at parting, and the need for the cloak of secrecy. Compare and contrast the language, style, mood, and endearments in Romeo and Juliet's love song with a modern ballad of your choice.

Generation Gap

10. (Scene 5) Lord and Lady Capulet proceeded with wedding plans and their commitment to Paris in all innocence since they did not know that Juliet was already married. Juliet could have prevented the tragedy and grief which ensued. Why didn't she sit down with her father, admit that she was already married, and try to talk out the problem? Select a person to role-play Lord Capulet and another person to role-play Juliet. Construct a similar situation with dialogue in a modern frame of reference.

Risks of Revealing Oneself

11. (Scene 5) The Nurse, seeing the practical side, encourages Juliet to forget her marriage vows to Romeo and marry Paris as her parents wish. Juliet, feeling abandoned, is disillusioned with her Nurse and vows never to share her secrets with the old woman ever again. When you reveal something personal about yourself to a friend, you are then vulnerable and unprotected in many ways. What are the changes that can occur in a personal relationship that could make you regret telling your secret to a friend?

Status of Women

12. The play would not have developed as it did were it not for the social mores and customs of historical Verona. The setting, then, is very important. How did the time and place of the story influence the age at which people married? Discuss the total dependence of a young woman on her father and husband in that society. What were her alternatives if she did not marry?

ACT IV

Mourning

1. (Scene 2) Juliet's father is concerned about her uncontrolled grief over Tybalt's death. It is generally acknowledged that people must go through stages of mourning for their own mental health. Elisabeth Kubler-Ross, in her book *On Death and Dying,* lists the five stages of mourning as *denial/isolation, anger, bargaining, depression,* and *acceptance with hope* persistent throughout. Some people also experience *guilt.* Act out one or more of these stages, articulating the thoughts that would be appropriate to that stage.

Coping

2. (Scene 3) When Juliet decides to take the potion, what worries torment

ACT IV (cont'd.)

her? Is Friar Laurence's plan the best she can implement? Do you believe that Juliet is being strong or weak, courageous or immature? We know that people cope with anxiety in a variety of ways: some people laugh out of control, others deny the situation, some overeat, some try to shift blame onto others. Suppose the teacher accused an innocent student of cheating on a test in front of the entire class. Select one person to role-play the teacher and several people to role-play the student involved, using different coping styles that could develop from this upsetting situation.

Deception

3. (Scene 3) In the play some characters are compelled to deceive others. In Scene 3, Juliet deceives everyone by going through the charade of preparing for a wedding that she knows full well will never take place. We have all had the experience of telling a lie or practicing a deception that grows more and more complex. Sir Walter Scott in *Lochinvar,* said "Oh, what a tangled web we weave when first we practice to deceive." Can you name a few things that happened in the play because of the lovers' deception? Modern situation comedies and soap operas often base their plot lines on deceptions such as mistaken identity or guarded secrets. Take a close look at such television programs and write down the deception and the complications that spin the "tangled web."

Death Rites

4. (Scene 5) Friar Laurence comforts the bereaved Capulet family, assuring them that Juliet is happy in heaven and will be cared for eternally. You will recall that Juliet and her ancestors were interred in a family vault; they were not buried, but were placed in shrouds on catafalques, or stone slabs. All peoples and religions have beliefs about the body and soul after death. What are some of these beliefs from both ancient and modern cultures which are strikingly different from yours? What are your views of the afterlife? React to Friar Laurence's philosophy about heaven. Investigate the death customs and rites of other societies.

Emergencies

5. (Scene 5) In Scene 5 the Nurse pulls back the curtains and is horrified to find Juliet "dead." In our lifetime we will all experience emergencies. In our quieter moments, when we should think it through, we rarely consider what necessary steps must be taken when we find ourselves in an intensely stressful situation. Depending upon the emergency, whom would you call, what information would you need to impart, and what should be done until help arrives? If, as Juliet's sister or brother today, you were faced with the emergency of that fateful morning, what exactly would you do?

ACT IV (cont'd.)

Power of Music

6. (Scene 5) In Shakespeare's time, as in ours, music was a significant part of life. For example, in Scene 5, Peter requests the musicians to play a popular song entitled "Heart's Ease" to console him. Music pervades our modern environment. From the supermarket where we shop to the dentist's office where we wait nervously, music, like language, has the power to soothe, comfort, and to inspire us. How has music been used to affect people and their dispositions throughout history? Think of settings where music is used as an influence: church, pep rallies, holiday parades, political conventions, or a baby's nursery. Bring in a record which is guaranteed to bring about a mood change in the class.

Humor

7. (Scene 5) In television or the movies, scenes and moods switch quickly from dark to light because of the freedom afforded by the technology of the medium. On the stage and in Shakespeare's theatre, this technique is not possible. How does Shakespeare relieve the tension in Scene 5, after the funeral when the musicians and Peter engage in a battle of wits? What was your reaction to humor at this point in the play? What was Shakespeare trying to effect? Humor takes many forms, and the response is equally diverse. Think about the things and people which make you laugh. Can you then analyze the things that tickle your funny bone.

Rituals

8. (Scene 5) Because he thinks Juliet is dead, her father tells the members of the household that all the preparations for her festive wedding ironically will be used instead for her funeral. The similarities in their observance are strangely parallel—flowers are displayed, food and drink are served, guests are invited and music is played. Rituals—special times, events, or happenings, always observed in the same way—have governed the lives of people since the beginning of humankind. Some common rituals are birthdays, weddings, and funerals as well as holidays and anniversaries. List the rituals your family practices throughout the year. Which have the most meaning for you?

Character Descriptions

9. Sometimes in reading we encounter unfamiliar names. It can be difficult to identify a cast of characters, especially when the names are unlike those we are accustomed to hearing. A good learning strategy involves using a *mnemonic aid* which helps associate unfamiliar names, words, and concepts with those which are familiar. In order to remember the people in *Romeo and Juliet,* try to match a character with a word or phrase which begins with the first letter of his name and sums up his personality. For example, Tybalt might be remembered as "a troublemaker."

ACT IV (cont'd.)

Character Insights

10. Many of the characters in the play are pivotal though we do not hear from them often. Each in his own way is critically involved in the lives of Romeo and Juliet. To learn more about them, call a Verona "news conference" and have the reporters ask questions of these minor characters. Interview Mercutio, Benvolio, the Nurse, Friar Laurence, Paris, and Prince Escalus. What opinions do they hold about the feud and the romance. Be sure to ask meaningful questions which may give the characters some discomfort and perhaps make them defensive.

Importance of Detail

11. Everything that happens in a well-written story occurs in a logical order and is caused by a previous episode. Every incident in the story is crucial to the others. To change or omit an event in a well-written story would drastically alter, if not destroy, the outcome and the overall effect. Using this information, assume Lord Capulet did not move the wedding up to Wednesday, but held it on Thursday as planned. What events would never have occurred? What else might have occurred because of this great shift in the plot line?

Changing the Outcome

12. Using the information in the above question, speculate on a similar shift in events if Friar Laurence had not been an expert on herbs and folk medicine.

ACT V

Fate vs. Control

1. (Scene 1) When Romeo hears of Juliet's death, in his anguish he decides that he will take control of his life. He turns to the night sky and shouts, "Then I defy you stars!" Does he really defy the stars or is that moment, too, another phase of his life governed by Fate? Some say people live by chance and die by chance; others believe we live by choice and die by choice. How much control *do* people have over their lives?

Situational Ethics

2. (Scene 1) In this scene Romeo encounters an impoverished druggist. He coerces the man to commit the crime of selling poison, a transaction that would likely not have otherwise occurred if the druggist had not been so poor. Improvise a courtroom scene in which the druggist is on trial for selling poison to Romeo. What strategies would the druggist's attorney(s) use to defend him? What are "extenuating circumstances," and need we be concerned about them during this trial? What is the definition of *situational ethics*, and how do they apply to this trial?

Violence, the Law and Religion

3. (Scene 3) It is against the law to take anyone's life, including your own. It also violates religious doctrine. By the time Act V ends, the audience has watched three young men die at the point of a sword; they have

ACT V (cont'd.)

witnessed the suicides of two more young people; and they have heard of Lady Montague's death, caused by grief over Romeo's banishment. All of this takes place against a background of grandeur and nobility. However, there is a motif of enormous violence which demands scrutiny. In what ways does this carnage violate both civil and religious laws? A romantic aura always surrounds the lovers, despite the fact that Romeo murdered two men before he and Juliet died for love. How are they answerable to religious doctrine for their actions?

Feuds and Grudges

4. Throughout *Romeo and Juliet* there seems to be no memory of the beginnings of the Montague/Capulet feud. Nowhere do we ever discover the reasons for this enmity. A *feud* is defined as "formalized private warfare, especially between family groups." The most famous feud was between the Hatfields and the McCoys in the mountains of nineteenth-century North Carolina and Kentucky. Have you ever held a grudge against a person for so long a time that you forgot the cause of your bad feelings? Explain.

Character Insight

5. In a play, the audience knows what is going on because of the dialogue. We are not often privy to the characters' motives or private reactions as we are when we read a story. Assume the identity of one of the characters you find to be most interesting. Write a diary entry for that character, exposing his/her innermost thoughts about a particularly dramatic episode. This entry should express a dimension of the character not fully revealed on stage.

Daily Life in Verona

6. Familiarity with this play reveals details about the summertime in Verona. Looking back at the play you will discover details about weather, social life, church-goings, governance, and many other newsworthy aspects of daily living in the city. Use the information you have gathered to present a television news broadcast in historical Verona on any given day of the play, complete with local and national news, the weather, entertainment, sports, and people in the news.

Letter Writing—A Unique Expression

7. Personal expression is found in correspondence, face-to-face dialogue, and telephone conversation. Letter writing, however, differs markedly from the other two forms. When we write a letter, we can organize our thoughts carefully. We may pause, think things through, compose, and refine what we have written for the effect we want to achieve. There are other qualities unique to letter writing. We are free from interruption by

ACT V (cont'd.)

the recipient and are not diverted from our agenda. Instead we have our say in a free flow of expression. Letter writing may be an unburdening of emotion and is a commitment to permanence. Finally, a letter can be reread, examined, savored, and treasured. If you were Prince Escalus writing to your brother in another province, you might begin your first paragraph with, "You will never believe the recent problems I have had here in Verona!" As alternatives, you may choose to write a personal letter from Lady Capulet to her sister, or a letter of condolence to Lord Montague, or a letter from the imprisoned druggist to his wife and children.

Effects of the Plague

8. Friar John agreed to travel to Mantua carrying Friar Laurence's message regarding the complicated plan of Juliet's "death." The letter, however, never reached Romeo because John's mission was thwarted. Detained along the way and denied freedom of passage to Mantua he was placed in detention in a house under quarantine. The populace knew little of the causes of the plague but did understand that if strict isolation were imposed on those who were infected, it could prevent the spread of the disease. The effect of the plague is thought to have changed the face of history as radically as it changed the lives of Romeo and Juliet. Research the devastation of the plague in books such as *The Blood Death: A Chronicle of the Plague* by C.H. Clarke; *The Black Death* by Philip Ziegler; and *The Plague in Shakespeare's London* by F.P. Wilson.

Problems of Authority

9. It is comfortable to be an advocate of one point of view and make an enemy of those who oppose us. From an anti-establishment point of view, those in authority are always the enemy. Rarely do we have the opportunity to put ourselves into the position of our adversaries. What are the problems and dilemmas of the "other side"? Improvise an official meeting between the Prince and the city council. Force yourself into Escalus' shoes and bring understanding and empathy to his role as he proposes measures to control violence in the streets.

Suicide

10. A skillful writer often gives the audience clues about an event that will occur later in the story. Major events usually do not happen unexpectedly, or without warning, in a well-written tale; the suicides of Romeo and Juliet are no exception. By reviewing the play, a careful reader will see that, beginning with Act III, there are numerous lines spoken by the characters which repeatedly express their willingness to die for love, for honor, for friendship. This contempt for life expresses itself in modern times when we consider the staggering statistics on teenage suicide. What are the reasons for this alarming phenomenon? What do you regard as a solution to this problem?

ACT V (cont'd.)

Parent-Child Conflict

11. Lady Capulet is not unlike many mothers who want the very best for their children. Often parents do not agree with their sons and daughters about what is best. Juliet's mother truly believes that Count Paris can make her daughter's future secure since he is an aristocrat who has status, power, and money. Improvise a scene in which a modern mother and her daughter are having a heated difference of opinion about her daughter's fiance and his reputation.

Innocent Bystander

12. A heart-wrenching turn of events which affected Count Paris is known to us as the *fate of the innocent bystander*. We are all moved by Paris's pathetic death because he has been scarcely more than a shadow figure as he stand at the sidelines of the drama. We know from the daily newspapers that any one of us, as well, could meet an untimely death because we were in the wrong place at the wrong time. Clearly, life hangs on a thread for all of us. However, the characters in this play were created by Shakespeare who alone could decide their fate. Why then did he choose to destroy Paris? What dramatic purpose was served by sacrificing this kind and innocent young man and having him murdered by the sword?

Casting the Characters

13. *Romeo and Juliet* is rich in characterization and dramatic action. Assume that you are a casting director hired for the critical and skillful job of selecting the perfect actors to make these characters come alive. Your movie is about to go into production and your budget allows you to select any personalities from stage, screen, or television. Careful casting can make the venture the smash of the century or a financial flop. Who will be your choice for each role?

In Praise of Shakespeare

14. Let us put aside the scrutiny and discussion of Shakespeare, and take the time to marvel at the essence and the luminosity of his lyric expression. His poetry is beautiful for the grandeur of its language and the splendor of its emotion. It strikes to our hearts, thrills us on its own terms, and is its own reason for being. Find passages from *Romeo and Juliet* which you believe are especially powerful. Gather these lines expressing a variety of topics—among which are love, friendship, loyalty and fate. Begin your own personal booklet of quotations. Make the collection meaningful to you.

A SKETCH
SHAKESPEARE: HIS LIFE AND TIMES

1564 He was born on April 23 in Stratford-on-Avon.

1582 He married Anne Hathaway when he was eighteen years old.

1583 The Shakespeares had a daughter Susanna.

1584 The Shakespeares had twins—Hamnet, a boy, and Judith.

1586 Shakespeare left Stratford for London, at the age of twenty-two.

1594 He wrote *Romeo and Juliet* at the age of thirty, based upon Arthur Brooke's *The Tragicall Historye of Romeus and Juliet* (1562).

1609 Shakespeare published his *Sonnets.*

1616 He died at the age of fifty-two after having written fourteen comedies, eleven histories, and twelve tragedies—a total of thirty-seven plays.

1623 His complete works were published seven years after his death. This publication of the scripts was known as the *First Folio,* collected by two fellow actors John Heminge and Henry Condell.

Shakespeare's Life

William Shakespeare (April 23, 1564-1616) was born to a middle-class family in the market town of Stratford-on-Avon. His father, John, was a prosperous glovemaker who achieved status by taking part in civic affairs and later serving as the mayor of Stratford. William's mother, Mary Arden, was related to a family which was purported to enjoy some social position as well. Both his parents, it is noted, were illiterate.

William was the third of eight children and was educated in the Stratford Grammar School where, like all well-educated children, he became proficient in Latin and studied the ancients in their own language. There is no evidence that he was unlike any other child of the times, who endured the tedium of a joyless and strict education for nine hours every day. Nor was he "discovered" by any teacher who recognized in him the face of genius, though the school boasted a faculty, all of whom were graduates of Oxford University.

It was in 1582, at the age of eighteen, that William was married to Anne Hathaway, twenty-six, a daughter of one of the local farmers. Anne and William had three children—a daughter Susanna, followed by the twins Judith and Hamnet, his only son, who died as a child of eleven. Shortly thereafter, the meager history of Shakespeare's life indicates that he left his family in 1592 to live in London. The reasons for his departure are not clear.

A Sketch

Not much is known about Shakespeare's personal affairs, since in those days the life of a playwright was hardly deemed worthy of a careful chronicle, unlike the affairs of church and state that were committed to historical records. There is a vague period, therefore, in Shakespeare's life known as "the lost years," between the time of his marriage and his departure for the magic and excitement of London. It was in that teeming and vital city that he found work acting in a repertory theater company, a resident group of actors who played different roles in each production throughout the season. Eventually this company performed for Queen Elizabeth I, and there is evidence that the young Shakespeare enjoyed quick popularity as both an actor and playwright: by the year 1594, six of his plays were written and produced. His popularity flourished as a young man and continued throughout his mature years.

Originally Shakespeare's plays were not written to be read as literature—to be handed down in perpetuity. The plays were written as scripts and were consumable materials. Furthermore, it was not desirable to circulate these manuscripts because they might fall into the hands of other actors or producers in competitive companies. There were no protective copyrights or means of safeguarding plays. There was only the caution of competitive artists who understood the plays to be the source of their livelihood. It was, however, considered fair play for writers to use plots developed by other writers. Shakespeare, like many Elizabethan authors, borrowed widely from these sources and brought to these stories his own perspective and creativity.

Shakespeare performed and wrote for a group of actors called the Lord Chamberlain's Men in 1594. This was a very popular group which performed for royalty and most of the London theatergoers. There is evidence that around this time he became a shareholder in the Globe Theater. After Queen Elizabeth died and James I ascended the throne in 1603 the group, with Shakespeare as a shareholder, became known as the King's Men. They were distinguished by their private performances for the court and it was in this company that Shakespeare remained exclusively until his retirement.

In 1612, at age forty-eight, Shakespeare returned to Stratford, in partial retirement, dividing his time between a home in London and the town of his origin. Though less active, he basked in an aura of fame which has endured to the present—almost four hundred years later. Shakespeare was a poet and playwright who made not only monumental contributions to the world of language and literature, but significant contributions to the creative arts—music, dance, and art—as well. All fields of aesthetic endeavor were influenced by his genius and erudition.

One wonders how much more may have been produced by Shakespeare had he enjoyed the advantage of our modern life expectancy, for he died in 1616, at the relatively young age of fifty-two. He was buried inside Stratford's Holy Trinity Church where a statue of him stands as the only accurate likeness of the great poet whose talents were so diverse that in his lifetime he also achieved success as an actor, producer, and businessman.

Shakespeare's Times

It was the time of the English Renaissance—the late 1500's and early 1600's. Under the reign of Elizabeth I, London—the brilliant city—surged with a teeming population of 160,000 people. Travelers came from all over to partake of the culture which flourished in the rich metropolis. Music, art, literature, and theatre were offered to satisfy the appetite of literate and sophisticated people. The common people, too, yearned for diversion. Quite naturally, therefore, the gifted artists made their way to this mecca where there was a market for their talents.

When Shakespeare came on the scene, actors enjoyed hardly any status. Indeed, they were held in very low regard. They travelled in troupes and were considered to be nothing more than vagabonds engaged in a worthless pursuit. The support of Queen Elizabeth's court, however, ushered in an era of greater acceptance of actors and an appreciation for the entertainment they offered to an eager and enthusiastic city audience. It was then, during the emergence of more reputable players' groups, that Shakespeare became a member of the theatrical profession.

London, for all its exciting and dynamic qualities was, as well, a stink hole of considerable proportions awash with open gutters, raw sewage, and rotting garbage. This condition, present in major cities of the times, was noteworthy because of the repeated outbreak of the bubonic plague which made serious inroads into the vitality of the community from 1563 to 1603. There was an outbreak of the plague in London for two years in 1592 when theaters were ordered closed for the public welfare. It was during this hiatus that Shakespeare wrote much of his poetry, which was regarded as an authentic art form of the times.

There were many conditions which were hostile to the theater enterprise and which generated disfavor among royal and civic authorities. Theaters were a source of concern because of the danger of contagion, not only from the affluent patrons who sat in the galleries, but especially from the "groundlings" who stood in the dirt of the main floor, "glewed together in crowds." Civic and religious authorities were also afraid of antagonism, immorality, and profanity which might be encouraged and disseminated among the large numbers of citizens in attendance. On a different level, the royal authorities were afraid of subversion and propaganda in the actors' speeches, which might foment attitudes about foreign relations which were always in a state of tension.

Clearly, theatrical people and their patrons enjoyed an uneasy relationship with the authorities and so, in order to avoid abrasive encounters, theaters were located on the outskirts of the city in the slums, safely outside the jurisdiction of the county sheriff, the mayor, and the City council. These areas were called the "Liberties" which were actually a paradise for thieves, pickpockets, and scoundrels of every description. They were also a worry for employers whose workers would leave their jobs in the afternoon, lured by the diversions of the Liberties.

A Sketch

There were many public theaters in this Bankside district. The first theater to be constructed in 1576 was called, "The Theatre." The Globe Theatre, built in 1599 by Shakespeare and his associates, was one of the largest facilities with a capacity of two thousand patrons. The public theaters were similarly constructed in form and size, had no roofs, and were completely open to the weather. The few private theaters were heated, indoor structures. In 1600 the average weekly attendance for several theaters has been estimated at an amazing twenty thousand patrons a week! Theatergoing was the single most important entertainment available to the total population.

Inside the public theater were three galleries—each seating several classes of people—gentlemen, scholars, lawyers, clerks, and young students. The nobility were discreetly secluded and were in the minority, since theater attendance in Queen Elizabeth's time was not considered a fashionable or dignified form of entertainment.

The most entertaining historical information of this era comes from the Elizabethan audiences themselves. The performances took place in the afternoon to take advantage of daylight. The audience bought tickets just before showtime for the admission price of one penny, twopence (two pennies) or threepence. If a person was willing to pay a little more he could take a stool and sit up on the stage where, at closer proximity to the actors, he could badger the players, cheer them on, shout insults, and warn others of impending danger. This behavior was no different than that of the general audience who paid only a penny.

Those who paid a penny to stand on the ground constituted the largest number of patrons by far and were known as the "groundlings." They stood, crowded around on the dirt floor inside the theater, for as long as four hours before and during a performance. They were a disreputable and coarse lot who passed the time drinking beer and wine, eating, playing cards, and generally attending to whatever functions kept them happy and comfortable. Considering the stench of strong spirits and bad breath in an audience with as many as two thousand vulgarians assembled, it is easy to appreciate that they were also referred to as "penny stinkards," a term which most aptly captures the character of the robust patrons and the aura of Elizabethan popular theater.

Lest we romanticize about the sensitivity of the playgoer, it must be noted that these public theaters shared their popularity with other emporia nearby, where patrons paid to witness the cruel practice of bear-baiting and bull-baiting. These hideous entertainments required that a large animal, such as a bear, be tied to a post while it tried unsuccessfully to fend off the vicious attacks of other animals. When the poor creature was finally torn to pieces it was to the great satisfaction of the audience. The appetite of the theater crowd was equally ghoulish throughout play performances. Savage realism was achieved through ghastly ploys. For example, the "killing" of human actors had to be accompanied by the gushing of animal blood from a bag concealed under a costume. Shakespeare's use of blood and gore was a notable crowd pleaser.

A Sketch

The sequence of events surrounding the play was always predictable. As the play was about to begin, the sound of trumpets would herald the actor who delivered the prologue. He would appear on stage to summarize the drama for the audience. Then, at the end of each play, no matter how sad or somber, the stage would be filled with singers, acrobats, and tumblers for the grand finale.

The drama did not always appeal to everyone in the audience equally. Some members of the audience responded to the bloody fights, the heroic displays, the obscene remarks, and the fool's humor. Others, of a more sensitive nature, preferred the sophisticated and lyric turn of phrase, the convoluted puns, and the romantic episodes. Given the diverse social range, there was still something to please everyone. In thinking about Shakespeare's audience, two factors are of paramount importance: first, despite the mix of class and caste, the group was predominantly uneducated; secondly, it is grossly inaccurate to assume that Shakespeare's largest, most appreciative audience was drawn from the aristrocrats and the educated. It was with the common people that he achieved resounding success. For his livelihood and for the survival of theater as he knew it, Shakespeare, the consummate artist, played to them all!

BIBLIOGRAPHY

Alexander, Peter. *Studies in Shakespeare.* London: Oxford University Press, 1893.

Bartlett, John. *Concordance to Shakespeare.* New York: St. Martin's Press, 1963.

Bennett, Henry. *Shakespeare's Audience.* Philadelphia: R. West, 1977.

Bergeron, David M. *Shakespeare: A Study and Research Guide.* New York: St. Martin's Press, 1975.

Campbell, Oscar J., and Quinn, Edward G. *The Reader's Encyclopedia of Shakespeare.* New York: Crowell, 1966.

Chute, Marchette. *Stories from Shakespeare.* New York: New American Library, 1956.

Cullum, Albert. *Shake Hands with Shakespeare.* New York: Citation Press, 1968.

Ford, Boris. *The Age of Shakespeare.* Middlesex, England: Pelican Books Ltd., 1955.

Goddard, Harold C. *The Meaning of Shakespeare.* Chicago: University of Chicago Press, 1951.

Guthrie, Sir Tyrone. (ed.) *Shakespeare: Ten Great Plays.* New York: Golden Press, 1962.

Haines, Charles. *William Shakespeare and His Plays.* New York: Franklin Watts, Inc., 1968.

Harbage, Alfred. *Shakespeare: The Tragedies. A Collection of Critical Essays.* Englewood Cliffs, N.J.: Prentice Hall, Inc., 1964.

Harrison, G.B. (ed.) *Shakespeare: The Complete Works.* New York: Harcourt, Brace and World, Inc., 1968.

Highfill, Philip H. Jr. *Shakespeare's Craft: Eight Lectures.* Carbondale: Southern Illinois University Press, 1982.

Hillegass, Clifton K. *Cliff Notes on Shakespeare's ROMEO AND JULIET.* Lincoln, Nebraska: Cliff Notes, Inc., 1979.

Hodges, C. Walter. *Shakespeare's Theatre.* New York: Coward, McCann, Geoghegon, 1980.

Hosley, Richard. *Romeo and Juliet: An Outline Guide to the Play.* New York: Barnes and Noble, Inc., 1965.

Hosley, Richard. *Romeo and Juliet: The Yale Shakespeare.* New Haven: Yale University Press, 1917.

Jenkin, Leonard. *Monarch Notes and Study Guides, Shakespeare's ROMEO AND JULIET.* New York: Simon & Schuster, Inc., 1964.

Kokeritz, Helge. *Shakespeare's Pronunciation.* New Haven: Yale University Press, 1953.

Moulton, Charles W. *The Library of Literary Criticism.* New York: Moulton Publishing Co., 1959.

Onions, Charles T. *A Shakespeare Glossary.* Great Britain: Oxford University Press, 1911.

Priestley, J.B. *The Wonderful World of the Theatre.* London: Rathbone Books, Ltd., 1959.

The Riverside Shakespeare. Boston: Houghton Mifflin Co., 1974.

Rowse, Alfred L. *The Annotated Shakespeare.* New York: Clarkson N. Potter, Inc., 1978.

Quennell, Peter. *Quotations from Shakespeare.* Boston: Plays, Inc., 1971.

Schmidt, Alexander. *Shakespeare Lexicon.* New York: Benjamin Blom, Inc., 1968.

Stevenson, Barton. *The Standard Book of Shakespeare Quotations.* New York: Funk & Wagnalls, 1953.

Traversi, D.A. *An Approach to Shakespeare.* Garden City, New York: Doubleday, 1967.

Wright, Louis B., and LaMar, Virginia. *Romeo and Juliet.* New York: Folger Library General Reader's Shakespeare, Washington Square Press Inc., 1959.

Wright, Louis B. *Shakespeare for Everyman.* New York: Washington Square Press, Inc., 1964.

Wright, William A. (ed.) *The Complete Works of William Shakespeare.* Garden City, New York: Garden City Books, 1936.

~~tavern on the green~~ - 212-873-~~3111~~ ~~0147~~ 3200 -
Plaza Hotel - 212-546-~~5000~~
5485

Bloomies

CHINA
- Sophia
- Bloomies
- RalphLauren China

Waldorf Astoria 212-355-3000
Essex House 212 484-5141 (Matthew Anderson
212-484-5144

CASUAL
- Audun
- Villeroy + Bach
- Casual

(212) 546-5485 Larry Harvey -
~~Plaza~~ PLAZA Dec 14 - Booked -
Dec 15 - Sunday - available -
Baroque - Grandballroom
Dec 13 - Friday

STEMWARE
- Bedford - R. Lauren Stemware
- OR
- Bryant Stemware R. Lauren

Feb 14th - Friday night is available

~~Essex~~

FINIS

Tavern on the Green
Susan
212-873-4111
ext 214

Sat Dec 21st
Terrace Rm
Pavillion Tented
Rafters

~~...~~
250 people